D1758432

LF

XB00 000010 9910

The Luftwaffe's Blitz

Other Chris Goss titles available from Crécy Publishing

Luftwaffe Fighter-Bombers over Britain
The Tip and Run Campaign 1942-1943

The Luftwaffe Bombers' Battle of Britain
The inside story: July-October 1940

The Luftwaffe Fighters' Battle of Britain
The inside story July-October 1940

Bloody Biscay
The story of the Luftwaffe's only long range maritime fighter unit,
V *Gruppe*/*Kampfgeschwader* 40, and its adversaries 1942-1944

Brothers in Arms
An account of August-September 1940 through the deeds of
two opposing fighter units – 609 Squadron of the RAF and 1/JG53,
a Luftwaffe *Staffel* based in northern France

The Luftwaffe's Blitz

The inside story: November 1940-May 1941

Chris Goss

Crécy Publishing Limited

The Luftwaffe's Blitz
The inside story: November 1940-May 1941

Published in 2010 by Crécy Publishing Limited
All rights reserved

Christopher H. Goss is hereby identified as the author of this work in accordance with Section 77 of the Copyright, Designs and Patents Act 1988

A CIP record for this book is available from the British Library

ISBN 9 780859 791489

Printed in England by MPG Books Ltd

Crécy Publishing Limited
1a Ringway Trading Estate, Shadowmoss Road, Manchester M22 5LH
www.crecy.co.uk

Frontispiece: London

CONTENTS

Acknowledgements

Sadly, the vast majority of those German aircrew that I and others have contacted over the years, together with their RAF opponents, are no longer around and I hope that what I write, using their words, is a fitting tribute.

As usual, there are a number of friends, acquaintances, fellow historians and relatives who have been generous with their time and help so, in no particular order, I would like to thank:

Bill Norman, Hugh Trivett, Brian Bines, Simon Parry, John Foreman, Andy Saunders, (the late) Pat Burgess, Steve Hall, Sue Dickinson, Graham Day, Seb Cox, Alfred Price, Eddie Creek and Dave Hanson, and all the staff from the Air Historical Branch and the staff from Deutsches Dienststelle (WASt).

In particular, I would like to thank Ken Wakefield for his help, advice and generosity, and, as per normal, Bernd Rauchbach for his usual considerable 'behind the scenes' work

Again, if I have forgotten anyone, please accept my apologies!

Finally, as before, thanks to wife Sally and daughters Kat, Megs and Andra – I know it is another book and I have hogged the computer again but I hope you appreciate it, if not now but later!

Glossary and Abbreviations

AA	Anti-aircraft
Ac	Aircraft
AC	Aircraftman
AI	Airborne Interception (radar)
Angriff	Attack
ASI	Airspeed Indicator
Aufklärungsgruppe (Aufkl.Gr)	Reconnaissance Wing
B1E1	1kg incendiary bomb
Bandit	Hostile aircraft
Beobachter (BO)	Observer
Besatzung	Crew
Bordfunker (BF)	Radio operator
Bordmechaniker (BM)	Flight engineer
Bordschütz (BS)	Air gunner
Cat's Eye	Night patrol by day fighter
CO	Commanding Officer
Cpl	Corporal
Deutsches Kreuz in Gold	German Cross in Gold (award for bravery)
DFC	Distinguished Flying Cross
DFM	Distinguished Flying Medal
DSO	Distinguished Service Order
Do	Dornier
E/a	Enemy aircraft
Ehrenpokal	Honour Goblet
Einzelmeldung	Detailed report, such as detailing the activities of *Luftflotte 3*
Eiserne Kreuz (EK)	Iron Cross (in Class I or Class II)
Ergänzungs (Erg)	Training
Erprobungsgruppe (ErprGr)	Experimental Wing
Experten	Ace
Feindflug	Operational flight
Feldwebel (Fw)	Flight Sergeant
Flash Weapon	Turn on radar
Fg Off	Flying Officer
Flak	Anti-aircraft fire
Flam	Oil bomb
Flieger (Flg)	Aircraftman
Fliegerkorps	Air Corps

Flt Lt	Flight Lieutenant
Flt Sgt	Flight Sergeant
Flugbuch	Logbook
Flugzeugführer (F)	Pilot
Frontflugspange	Mission clasp – awarded for operational flights generally, in bronze, silver or gold
Führer	Leader
Führungsstab	*Luftwaffe* High Command Operations staff
FW	Focke-Wulf
GCI	Ground Controlled Interception
Gefreiter (Gefr)	Leading Aircraftman
Generalfeldmarschall	Air Chief Marshal
Generalleutnant	Air-Vice Marshal
Geschwader (Gesch)	Group (three *Gruppen*) commanded by a *Geschwader Kommodore (Gesch Komm)*
Gp	Group
Gp Capt	Group Captain
Gruppe (Gr)	Wing (three *Staffeln*) commanded by a *Gruppen Kommandeur (Gr Kdr)*
Hauptmann (Hptm)	Flight Lieutenant/Captain
HE	High explosive
He	Heinkel
Hrs	Hours
Ia	Operations Officer
IAS	Indicated Air Speed
IAZ	Inner Artillery Zone
IB	Incendiary bomb
Inj	Injured
Jagdbomber/Jabo	Fighter bomber
Jagdgeschwader (JG)	Fighter Group
Jericho	Screamer fitted to bombs
Ju	Junkers
Kampfgeschwader (KG)	Bomber Group
Kampfgruppe (KGr)	Bomber Wing or formation
Kette	Three aircraft tactical formation
Kg	Kilogram
Küstenfliegergruppe (KüFlGr)	Coastal Flying Wing
LAC	Leading Aircraftman
Lehrgeschwader (LG)	Operational Training Group/Technical Development Flying Group
Leutnant (Lt)	Pilot Officer/2nd Lieutenant

Leutnant zur See (LtzS)	Sub-Lieutenant (Naval rank)
Lotfe	Optical bombing sight
LZZ	Bomb fitted with a long-delay fuse
Luftflotte	Air Fleet
M	Missing
Major (Maj)	Squadron Leader/Lieutenant Commander
Mit Eichenlaub	With Oakleaves (see *Ritterkreuz*)
Me	Messerschmitt
MG	Machine gun
NCO	Non-commissioned officer
Nachtrichen Offizier (NO)	Officer responsible for communications
Oberbefehlshaber der Luftwaffe (ObdL)	Commander in Chief of the *Luftwaffe*
Oberfeldwebel (Ofw)	Warrant Officer/Master Sergeant
Obergefreiter (Ogefr)	Senior Aircraftman
Oberkommando der Luftwaffe (OKL)	*Luftwaffe* High Command
Oberleutnant (Oblt)	Flying Officer/1st Lieutenant
Oberleutnant zur See (Oblt zS)	Lieutenant (Naval rank)
Oberst	Group Captain/Colonel
Oberstleutnant (Obstlt)	Wing Commander/Lieutenant Colonel
OKL	*Oberkommando der Luftwaffe* – *Luftwaffe* High Command
Plt Off	Pilot Officer
POW	Prisoner of war
Regia Aeronautica	Italian Air Force
Reichsluftfahrt Ministerium (RLM)	Air Ministry
Reichsmarschall	Marshal of the Air Force
Ritterkreuz (RK)	Knights Cross
Ritterkreuz mit Eichenlaub	Knights Cross with Oakleaves
Rotte	Two-aircraft tactical formation
SC	*Sprengbombe Cylindrisch* – bomb with thin steel case
Schwarm	Four-aircraft tactical formation led by a *Schwarm Führer*
SD	*Sprengbombe Dickwandig* – bomb with medium case whose heavier steel caused a greater blast or fragmentation effect
Seelöwe	Sealion – code name for the invasion of Great Britain
Seenotdienst	Air-sea rescue
Seenotflugkommando	Air-Sea Rescue Detachment
Seenotstaffel	Air-Sea Rescue Squadron

Sgt	Sergeant
Sqn	Squadron
Sqn Ldr	Squadron Leader
Sonderführer (Sd Fhr)	Rank given to war reporters
Stab	Staff or Headquarters
Staffel	Squadron, commanded by a *Staffel Kapitän (St Kap)*
Stabsfeldwebel (Stfw)	Senior Warrant Officer
Störangriff	Nuisance attack
Stuka	Junkers 87
Sturzkampfgeschwader (StG)	Dive Bomber Group
Tiefangriff	Low-flying attack
Technischer Offizier (TO)	Technical Officer
Uninj	Uninjured
Unteroffizier (Uffz)	Sergeant
UXB	Unexploded bomb
W	Wounded
Werk Nummer (Wk Nr)	Serial number
Wg Cdr	Wing Commander
Zerstörergeschwader (ZG)	Heavy Fighter Group
+	Killed

Foreword

Gefr *Josef Schmauz (left). On the right is his pilot,* Uffz *Franz Paisdzor, who, with Josef, was shot down by Russian fighters on 29 June 1941. Only Josef and the* Bordfunker *survived.* (Schmauz)

All the members of my crew began their career in the *Luftwaffe* with night missions over England. Without any practical experience, we approached our task relatively relaxed. We had no firm idea as what to expect. Our first mission to Belfast in April 1941 did not change this as we continued with little contact with the enemy. However, the British defences demonstrated very quickly the meaning of the word danger. Frightened and shocked, we became eyewitnesses to the shooting down of a *Staffel* comrade; from this point on, fear was our constant companion. Now we associated each new mission with the hope that we would return home unharmed.

I am grateful to have survived the inferno. The suffering we inflicted by our missions and the war in general grieves me to this day. We were offenders and victims at the same time – a war does not produce winners, just losers.

(*Unteroffizier*) Josef 'Sepp' Schmauz
Beobachter, 6/*KG* 53 *'Legion Condor'*

April 2010

Preface

In part of his speech in Berlin on 4 September 1940, Adolf Hitler said the following:

It is a wonderful thing to see our nation at war, in its fully disciplined state. This is exactly what we are now experiencing at this time, as Mr Churchill is demonstrating to us the aerial night attacks which he has concocted. He is not doing this because these air raids might be particularly effective, but because his Air Force cannot fly over German territory in daylight. Whereas German aviators and German planes fly over English soil daily, there is hardly a single Englishman who comes across the North Sea in daytime.

They therefore come during the night – and as you know, release their bombs indiscriminately and without any plan on to residential areas, farmhouses and villages. Wherever they see a sign of light, a bomb is dropped on it. For three months past, I have not ordered any answer to be given, thinking that they would stop this nonsensical behaviour. Mr Churchill has taken this to be a sign of our weakness. You will understand that we shall now give a reply, night for night, and with increasing force.

And if the British Air Force drops two, three or four thousand kilos of bombs, then we will now drop 150,000, 180,000, 230,000, 300,000 or 400,000 kilos, or more, in one night. If they declare that they will attack our cities on a large scale, we will erase theirs! We will put a stop to the game of these night-pirates, as God is our witness. The hour will come when one or the other of us will crumble, and that one will not be National Socialist Germany. I have already carried through such a struggle once in my life, up to the final consequences, and this then led to the collapse of the enemy who is now still sitting there in England on Europe's last island.

Three days later, the *Luftwaffe*'s tactics in what became known as the Battle of Britain changed when London now became the target. What was soon to be known as the Blitz had begun.

Introduction

Following the publication of my books *The Luftwaffe Fighters' Battle of Britain* and *The Luftwaffe Bombers' Battle of Britain* (Crécy Publishing Ltd, 2000), I wanted to continue telling the stories of those German bomber crews whom I have contacted over the past thirty years, particularly those who flew in the Blitz from November 1940 to May 1941. With Britain still recovering from the Battle of France and the Battle of Britain, and the *Luftwaffe* still possessing a mighty bomber force, what exactly happened to the *Luftwaffe* bomber crews over the United Kingdom in the six months following the Battle of Britain and prior to the German invasion of the Soviet Union? Admittedly the seminal work *The Blitz Then and Now*, published in 1988, told much of the story, but I still feel that the German side needs to be told, and in this book I hope to do so using the words of those who were involved. Furthermore, despite numerical and technical superiority and being pitted against embryonic British night-fighting defences, the *Luftwaffe* failed, and I hope to show why this occurred.

Again, as with my previous books this one does not intend to be the comprehensive and definitive story of the *Luftwaffe*'s Blitz, but will hopefully give the reader an insight into the German bombing air war immediately after the Battle of Britain. Furthermore, it does not aim to glorify what occurred or to gloss over what those on the ground experienced (and in many cases paid for with their lives), but will hopefully explain what happened and why it failed.

Prologue

Like the RAF, it was expected that the *Luftwaffe*'s aerial bombardment would be conducted predominantly by day and, following the successful campaign in France and the Low Countries that ended on 22 June 1940, it was anticipated that German bombers could now operate easily over the United Kingdom from bases much closer to British shores. The first major attack against targets on the British mainland would be carried out during the night 18-19 June 1940 by Heinkel 111s from *KG 4*, then based at Merville and Lille-Roubaix in France. The reason for a night mission is given by one of the participants:

Oberleutnant Ulrich Jordan, Stab II/KG 4

Oblt Ulrich Jordan as a POW in Canada in 1943.

...On account of the skies over England being well guarded by day-fighters, we decided to attack by night – about twelve aircraft out of twenty-seven from our *Gruppe*; the remainder were under repair following an attack by Blenheims the day before or the crews lacked night experience...

The attack, a failure from the German viewpoint, taught both sides valuable lessons, lessons that were hard learned. Six Heinkel 111s were lost, nine aircrew killed and eleven taken prisoners of war (including *Oblt* Ulrich Jordan). RAF losses were not much better, with four aircraft lost in combat and five aircrew killed.

Throughout the Battle of Britain, the vast majority of German air attacks were still by day. For example, *Uffz* Robert Ciuraj of 4/*KG 51* flew nine bombing missions between 3 July 1940 and 26 October 1940, all of which were by day; his first night

Dunkirk as seen from a Ju 88 of 4/LG 1 at the end of May 1940.

An He 111 of Stab II/KG 4 *seen at the start of the Battle of France.*

attack was against London on 27 October 1940, after which all his missions (twenty-two in total before his *Geschwader* moved east at the end of March 1941) were by night. However, more specialist and experienced units such as the pathfinders of *KGr* 100 immediately switched from daylight attacks during the Norwegian Campaign to night attacks during the Battle of Britain. *Ofw* Paul Wiersbitzky and his crew flew their last daylight mission over Norway on 29 May 1940, after which they returned to Germany for further training. They moved to France on 9 August 1940, their first mission being on the 14th and their last, in the Battle of Britain, on 26 September, during which time they flew sixteen missions, all of which were by night against such targets as aircraft factories in Birmingham, Liverpool and Manchester and the docks at Birkenhead. However, most noticeable was the change in target after 7 September 1940 – from 8 September 1940 until they returned to Germany on 27 September to train new crews, the Wiersbitzky crew's target each time was London. Also, those pilots with blind/instrument flying experience, such as *Ofw* Ludwig Piller of *Stab* II/*KG* 51, were selected to fly night missions – from 29 June to 1 December 1940, when he was posted away, he flew seventeen night missions as opposed to just two day missions. Again, up to 18 September 1940 his targets were Plymouth, Southampton, Liverpool and Birkenhead, but from that date the target was London, ten times in a row, and only his last mission, on 19 November 1940, was against Birmingham.

He 111s of 6/KG 4 seen at Merville a few days before the attack of 18-19 June 1940.

Uffz *Robert Ciuraj, 4/KG 51.* (Ciuraj)

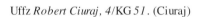

Ofw *Paul Wiersbitzky (second from left) and his crew of 2/KGr 100.*

An early Battle of Britain loss for KGr 100, *which is seen on the beach at Hourtin after crashing on returning from Birmingham on 15 August 1940.*

Why therefore did the target become London, and why even then was London being attacked by night? On the night of 5 September 1940, aircraft from *Luftflotte* 2 launched the first major night attack against London; two days later, the Blitz is acknowledged to have began when German bombers attacked London both by day and, using the fires from the earlier attack as a marker, by night. This was the start of the last phase of the Battle of Britain – a switch from military and industrial targets to now include commercial and civilian targets. Although it gave Fighter Command the break it needed, for those on the ground the opposite was the case. Interestingly, the *Flugbuch* of one pilot, *Oblt* Erwin Moll of 3/*KG* 76, states that the attack on London that day was a revenge attack; the RAF had bombed Berlin for the first time on the night of 25-26 August 1940 (in response to bombs having been dropped on London on the 24th), which had prompted Hitler's statement on 4 September 1940 that:

> ... if the British Air Force drops two, three or four thousand kilos of bombs, then we will now drop 150,000, 180,000, 230,000, 300,000 or 400,000 kilos, or more, in one night. If they declare that they will attack our cities on a large scale, we will erase theirs!

Eight days later what is now known as the climax of the Battle of Britain occurred when a series of massed attacks were launched against London. On 15 September 1940 the *Luftwaffe* flew in excess of 1,000 sorties for the loss of 56 bombers and fighters to furious RAF fighter defences. Although the bombers generally managed to reach London, damage was slight and it was clear that, having failed to achieve any of their primary aims, the *Luftwaffe*'s daylight bombing of London was not having the desired effect. As a result, Hitler postponed Operation *Seelöwe*, the planned invasion of Britain, and increasingly the bombing changed to attacks by night with London remaining, for the moment, the main target.

Do 17 Z of 4/KG 2 seen over the UK during the daylight phase of the Battle of Britain.

Do 17 Z of 5/KG 2 after having suffered an accident at Cambrai-Sud returning from London on 27 October 1940; its pilot was Lt Karl Von Manowarda (second from left).

Nevertheless, the Battle of Britain would still run until 31 October 1940 and the *Luftwaffe* did still try to attack London by day. The last major daylight attack occurred on 30 September 1940 and, again, it was broken up by RAF fighters. For some Germans it was still felt that the *Luftwaffe*'s tactic of targeting London was working, as one of that day's victims recalls:

Oberleutnant Fritz Oeser, 2/KG 77

Oblt *Oeser's Ju 88, 30 September 1940.*

According to our information, we were sure that the mission would be one of the last as we had been told that 'riots in London against the continuation of the war were at such a state that the Police and Army could not keep control any longer'. However, about 20 miles from London, the British fighters were diving into our formation, opening fire and continuing downwards. They managed to break up the formation. The result for me was one engine cooler out, oxygen bottle damaged, greenhouse front left side without Perspex, the rear upper machine gun out of action and the *Bordmechaniker* seriously wounded. I got an explosive bullet in the left shoulder and another caused a wide wound above my right eye...

The Battle of Britain from the point of view of the German bomber crews was all but over. October 1940 was very much an anti-climax and, with an increase in night operations and the onset of winter, only two daylight attacks of any note took place; now, the Blitz began in earnest.

1

'Nor did he break the morale'
November-December 1940

At the start of November 1940 a new plan of attack for the *Luftwaffe* was promulgated, stating:

1. London was to remain the main target with daylight attacks by escorted *jabos* and, when there was cloud cover, by single bombers. At night, attacks would be carried out by both *Luftflotte* 2 and 3.
2. Attacks on industrial areas of Coventry, Birmingham and Liverpool by smaller forces
3. Mining of the Thames, Bristol Channel, Mersey and Manchester Ship Canal by aircraft of X *Fliegerkorps*
4. Destruction of the Rolls Royce aero-engine factory at Hillington (Glasgow)
5. Damage to RAF fighters by fighter sweeps
6. Attacks, with fighter escort, on shipping convoys
7. Destruction of the British aircraft industry by *Luftflotte* 2 and 3
8. Attacks on RAF bases
9. Preparation for attacks on Coventry, Birmingham and Wolverhampton

The scene was set for the Blitz offensive.

The first day after the Battle of Britain ended saw *Luftwaffe* bombers ranging across England, the major focus being Portsmouth, which was the intended target for Messerschmitt 110 J*abos* of III/*ZG* 26. That night the main target was London, with a secondary target being Birmingham. For one pilot who had flown for much of the Battle of Britain, it would be the third and last time that he would be shot down:

The Luftwaffe *targeted the Rolls Royce works at Hillington (Glasgow) with a view to halting production of Merlin engines destined for Spitfire aircraft.*

Leutnant Hans-Adalbert Tüffers, 8/KG 55

Lt *Hans-Adalbert Tüffers at the controls of his He 111. To his right is* Ofw *Martin Reiser, who would be shot down and taken prisoner on 11 May 1941.* (via Trivett)

Flugzeugführer *and* Beobachter *in action.*

I joined *KG* 55 in the first days of July 1940. We were an instructor crew and had come from a reserve squadron. On 16 August 1940 we attacked Heathrow. After we had dropped our bombs on command from the lead plane, we were attacked by a lot of Hurricanes coming out of the sun and from behind. Suddenly, my port engine was on fire and I started losing speed and height. Over the radio we heard 'Let him go and stand by!', which was not a good feeling. I turned south and struggled to keep straight and height. The Hurricanes were turning around when suddenly a Messerschmitt 110 appeared overhead and indicated for me to go on. He stayed with me until the Channel and the pilot waved me goodbye. We managed to put out the fire and got as far as Villacoublay with one engine. Descending to land and putting down the gear, I was shown from the ground a big wheel disc with the letter 'R', which meant that I had lost the starboard wheel. I should pull the gear back up and made a crash-landing. I neared the ground very fast with the right engine running and with the right wing high, I touched the ground with the port wheel and tail wheel. The plane turned 60 degrees and stopped. I was lightly wounded over my right eye but *Uffz* Paul Brzoska was badly wounded.

Then on 15 September 1940 my plane was badly damaged by seven Spitfires after an attack on Portland harbour. Both engines stopped and I descended from 4,000 metres to land in the water nearly halfway between Portland and Cherbourg. After 2 hours in the water, *Uffz* Heinz Rothen and myself were rescued by the *Seenotdienst*. The rest of the crew were wounded and died in the sinking plane. My left arm had been wounded and I was operated on in the Cherbourg Marine Hospital. After ten days recuperation, I was back but changed from 9 *Staffel* to 8 *Staffel*.

I was finally shot down on 1 November 1940 during a night raid on the Victoria Docks in London. At 5,000 metres I was hit by heavy *Flak* in my port wing and lost nearly a metre of it. I throttled back the engines and push the stick forward to get the nose down; after some time I felt pressure on the stick and could pull the nose back. I could slowly add power to the engines and regain a normal flying position and turned to port towards the south to get out the range of the light *Flak*. After a short time, I was being reached by light *Flak* and lost the ability to steer the plane – we were only 1,200 metres high. After giving the order to bail out, it was very difficult for me to get out of the escape hatch above me. I was partly out and then hit my head on the radio antenna and lost consciousness. At dawn the next morning, I awoke to the sound of aircraft, lying in a cut cornfield. At 1100hrs I reached a cottage by crawling, where a nice couple helped me in and served me tea. After some time I was still thinking slowly and had an awful headache. I remarked that they didn't recognise my identity and told them I was a German pilot shot down over London last night. They didn't believe me so I told them they should call the Police. After that, the lady left the room and came back with a constable who brought me to the Hornchurch Hospital. I was badly injured in my legs, spine and head...

Just Tüffers and his *Beobachter* managed to escape the doomed Heinkel 111.

For the days that followed, the pattern of attacks were similar but the strength of the attackers varied; daylight attacks were still dictated by the weather. On 3 November 1940 a number of *Geschwadern*, specifically *KG* 3, *KG* 26, III/*KG* 51 and I/*KG* 54, used the cloud cover to attack such targets as Crouch End, Coventry, London, Banbury, Daventry, Rugby and Weymouth, but it did not stop Hurricanes from 46 Sqn intercepting a Dornier 17 of 8/*KG* 3 flown by 22-year-old Lt Wolfram Sonnenberg, which, badly crippled by the RAF fighters, unsuccessfully tried to crash-land on allotments at Bexley in Kent; one crewman was killed outright and the remaining three fatally injured.

5 Rumpfendkappe

Abb. 1: Rumpfwerkübersicht

1 Kanzelspitze
Abb. 2: Rumpfwerk, von oben gesehen

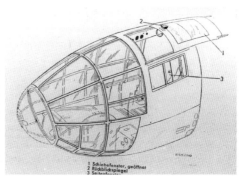

1 Schiebefenster, geöffnet
2 Rückblickspiegel
3 Seitenfenster

Contemporary manual sketches showing the emergency exits from the cockpit of an He 111.

A Do 17 Z of 8/KG 3, similar to that lost at Bexley on 3 November 1940. (via Cornwell)

London was again the focus of effort on the night of 4-5 November 1940, the attacks returning without loss, but the weather the following day allowed the German bombers to range across the UK, with limited success. The night of 5-6 November saw the *Regia Aeronautica* making its first major attack against mainland Britain, targeting the Ipswich/Harwich area for their bombs; the attack was ineffectual. The night also presented the RAF with a rare prize. German records for *KGr* 100 for that night are confused to say the least. The major attack was against London but no mention is made of participation by *KGr* 100 other than one of its number was forced to bomb the alternative target of Portland at 0120hrs with two high-explosive 250kg bombs and one incendiary 250kg bomb. However, using dead reckoning two aircraft bombed Birmingham at 2341hrs with three high-explosive 250 kg, one incendiary 250kg and sixteen HE 50kg bombs, while another two attacked Coventry at 2020hrs, dropping four HE 250kg and two incendiary 250kg bombs. No mention is made that an aircraft from 2/*KGr* 100 flown by *Fw* Hans Lehmann failed to return.

Breda 20s, the type used by the Regia Aeronautica *over the UK in the latter months of 1940.*

Apparently briefed to attack Birmingham, Lehmann was unable to utilise what was known as X *Gerät* equipment to locate the target and soon became lost; as dawn was breaking he was forced to ditch just off what they initially thought was the Brittany coast, but, not being familiar with the topography, they then believed they were off the coast of northern Spain. The reality was that they had ditched between Bridport and Eypesmouth in Dorset, and they were soon captured, albeit one of their number drowning while escaping from the floundering Heinkel.

He 111s of 2/KGr 100, showing the X Gerät *aerials on top of the fuselage.* (via Wakefield)

When the remains of the bomber were recovered, the X *Gerät* installation was discovered. The Germans had from the start of the war a precision Very High Frequency radio beam navigation and bombing system known as *Knickebein*. By using a powerful transmitter, an intersection of two narrow beams produced an accurate position fix. Positioning such an intersection over a target and utilising the standard Lorenz blind approach receiver allowed crews to bomb blindly with some degree of accuracy. The successor to *Knickebein* was X *Verfahren*, which was much more complex than its predecessor and required the installation of X *Gerät* on specific aircraft. It worked on the same principle as *Knickebein*, using a main approach beam, but this time three cross-beams that, together with a manual timer, checked the aircraft's speed over the ground, then provided automatic bomb release. Being next-generation, X *Verfahren* was more accurate than its predecessor and, contrary to popular belief, hard to jam or bend. *KGr* 100 was the unit dedicated to using X *Verfahren*, and this was the reason why *Ofw* Paul Wiersbitzky and his crew of 2/*KGr* 100 returned to Germany after the Norwegian Campaign – the *Flugbuch* of one of his crew notes bombing practice 'using X'. According to surviving German records, *KGr* 100 was using X *Verfahren* to some effect at the start of September 1940, but the first attack using it had actually been carried out by *KGr* 100 against Castle Bromwich on the night of 13 August 1940; it had therefore taken nearly three months for the RAF to get their hands on this German bombing aid, but subsequent attempts to counter it met with little real success. The RAF was aware of the existence of *Knickebein*, then, by mid-August 1940, X *Verfahren*, but despite what some have said since the war, it could to little to prevent the *Luftwaffe* from inflicting heavy damage and destruction on British cities night after night, as one German

Examples of fixed X Gerät *transmitters near Krefeld and Traunsee.* (via Wakefield)

Examples of fixed X Gerät *transmitters. The first picture shows one of the three transmitters at Calais in August 1940.* (via Wakefield)

The manual timer linked to X Gerät. (via Wakefield)

pilot recalls:

Unteroffizier Horst Götz, 1/KGr 100

I have no particular memories of individual operations. They were all quite routine, like running a bus service. The London *Flak* defences put on a great show – at night the exploding shells gave the place the appearance of bubbling pea soup; but very few of our aircraft were hit – I myself never collected so much as a shell fragment. On rare occasions one of my crew might catch sight of a

Destined for England: 250kg bombs ready to be loaded into He 111s of an unidentified unit in the winter of 1940-41.

British night-fighter but it seems they never saw us and we were never attacked. During our return flights the radio operator would often tune in his receiver to a music programme, to provide some relief from the monotony.

X *Verfahren* was not always necessary, as was shown on the night of 9-10 November 1940. German records show that the main attack was against London – *Luftflotte* 3 noted that *KG* 1, *KG* 77, I/*LG* 1, I/*KG* 51, II/*KG* 51, III/*KG* 51, I/*KG* 54 and II/*KG* 54 attacked London, while *KG* 77 attacked Hastings and *KGr*

Similarly camouflaged, an external bomb-load for an He 111 of KG 53.

606 attacked Liverpool, Birmingham, Bournemouth and Pembroke Dock without any assistance from *KGr* 100. Over the British mainland, three aircraft were lost – two to unknown circumstances and, yet again, one to anti-aircraft fire, as the German pilot well remembers:

Leutnant Max Probst, 2/KG 1

It was 9 November 1940. I had the task of attacking the London docks and took off just after nightfall with my crew, *Gefr* Giesinger, *Uffz* Krüger and *Fw* Gey. I was pilot and captain of an He 111 coded V4+IK, loaded with twenty 50kg bombs.

Because of the AA fire we climbed to a maximum altitude of 7,050 metres. I could only reach this enormous flying height with this load because this aircraft

Lt *Max Probst*. (via Saunders)

Lt *Max Probst (right) being interviewed after an earlier mission.* (via Saunders)

was almost as new. It was my 34th mission to England and everything went like clockwork.

Suddenly, it was just before we had reached London and only a few minutes before bomb-release, I found myself amidst exploding shells. In a fraction of a second the control column was knocked out of my hand. When I grabbed it again I did not feel the pressure of the rudder any more. The tail of the plane must have been hit or even shot off. Nearly at the same time shell fragments coming from the right side tore up the front part of the canopy, and hit my *Beobachter*, *Gefr* Giesinger, who sank down and must have been killed at once. The communication via throat microphone did not work any more so I turned round and shouted, 'Hit – shot down – bail out immediately!' But I could only hear the creaking of the aircraft, which was going down now out of control; perhaps it had already gone into a spin. I only remember that I tried to switch on the light to see what had happened to my comrade Giesinger. At the same time I pulled the throttle back and forth to regain some control. It did not work. Giesinger, who was lying next to me, did not move – I think I saw his smashed head with his brain coming out. Again I shouted, 'Get out – we are shot down!' No answer.

Then the centrifugal force of the spin pressed me against the upper part of the canopy. I do not know if I had sworn or prayed, but my second try was successful and I was able to open the slide window. I pushed it back and hung in my harness, my head in the air. But my senses were clear enough, so I opened the belt. I was thrown out at once, hitting my hand at the edge of the window opening and I also got a smack in my face caused by the rubber tube of the oxygen mask. For a few moments I felt like lying in a very soft bed – but I still was in my right mind and felt to see if my seat-parachute was still in place. Yes, it was there where it should be. I felt to my left shoulder and grasped the ripcord. Then I counted, twenty-one – twenty-two – until thirty, and pulled.

There was a hard jolt and a painful feeling between the legs when the belts tightened. I felt how I was swinging backwards and forwards. From time to time, hanging on my chute, I could see the nervous beams of the searchlights, nothing else. I felt that I got wet and knew I was in a cloud now. I think I prayed the Lord's Prayer, but also tried to calculate how long it would take to hit the ground. It must have lasted about a quarter of an hour.

At the very moment when I thought I could

(Right and next page) *The remains of Probst's Heinkel, together with its bomb-load.* (via Saunders)

see the ground I hit it. The impact was quite hard. I felt very weak, saw my parachute at my side, opened the lock and then the chute collapsed. I folded it up and hid it in a bush. Then, sitting on the grass next to the bush, I fished a packet of *Overstolz* cigarettes out of my pocket and lit one. Soon I heard some voices and saw the flashes of AA guns very close by. I stood up and for the moment I left this place without any plan or destination...

The remains of a Do 17 of 1/606, which crashed near Liskeard on the evening of 9 November 1940, killing Ofw *Walter Seifert and his crew.* (via Cornish Studies Library)

The initial threat – Flak *and searchlights*. (via Wakefield)

A Defiant of 264 Sqn showing its only armament.

A Blenheim of 29 Sqn.

A Beaufighter Mk 1 at Filton – this aircraft would survive until May 1943, when it was lost flying with 603 Sqn.

A Beaufighter crew walking to their night-fighter.

An unidentified pilot prepares for a flight by wearing dark glasses to help his night vision – not a carrot in sight!

Yet again, German losses were being inflicted by *Flak* as opposed to *nachtjäger*. The RAF's embryonic night-fighter force at the start of the Blitz was made up of six squadrons of Bristol Blenheims equipped with AI Mk III radar, and two squadrons of Boulton Paul Defiants with no radar. Occasionally, and when the situation dictated, Spitfire and Hurricanes were thrown into battle, but successes were few and far between and, when they were, it was a matter of luck that they found the German bombers and even greater luck if they shot it down.

Desperation forced the RAF to think of other ways to bring down German bombers. Obsolete Handley Page Harrow transport aircraft of 420 Flt (later 93 Sqn) were used to drop Long Aerial Mines into the German bomber stream. Each Harrow could carry around 120 of these mines, which were essentially a parachute, a 1lb bomb and 2,000 feet of piano wire. Dropped in front of the bomber stream, they would take about 10 minutes to drop through the flight path, the idea being that if a German aircraft hit the piano wire the shock would release the parachute carrying the bomb while a second parachute would open at the bottom of the wire, which would drag the bomb down onto the hapless bomber. However, luck certainly had to be with the pilot, as the Officer Commanding 420 Flt, Flt Lt Pat Burke, experienced on one of the first 'Mutton' sorties, as they were code named, on 26 October 1940:

> Mutton Patrol at 19,000 feet reached Worth Matravers at 2010hrs and received a vector 160 degrees Angels 18. After about 5 minutes, received order 'Port 90 degrees and fire'. Pressed release switch and after about 10 seconds there was an explosion in the rear of the aircraft. Three other explosions occurred at irregular intervals throughout the next half a minute. As aircraft still seemed airworthy, Flt Lt Burke requested homing vector from Worth Matravers and flew back slowly losing height and landed safely back at base at 2100hrs. Examination of the aircraft revealed (a) bullet holes in front fuselage (b) damage to main structure in centre portion of fuselage due to mines which, having been released but failed to fall clear, had exploded against the aircraft. No enemy casualties certain but of the two plots headed for Worth Matravers, only one was heard to go overhead.

Pat Burke's Harrow
showing the damage
caused by the mines.

The *Luftwaffe* still took the opportunity to attack by daylight when weather conditions were favourable. Two days after the *Regia Aeronautica*'s disastrous daylight attack on a convoy off Lowestoft, which cost them three fighters destroyed and countless damaged, and three bombers destroyed and several damaged, on 13 November 1940 a crew from 8/*LG* 1 tried unsuccessfully to attack an industrial target in the North of England in daylight using cloud cover as limited protection:

Feldwebel Erwin Zins, 8/LG 1

It was about midday when we took off from Chateaudun. Our target was the De Havilland airscrew factory at Lostock Hall near Manchester. This was the mission target for our crew and also for a second one of another unit, which we did not know. With the help of documents and air photographs we had prepared this attack thoroughly. The attack should take place in a weather situation favourable for us, which means cloud cover as far as the target area to escape fighter attacks. This was a so called 'Göring' mission. Our regular *Beobachter*, an old hand who was later killed over Malta, had been ill, so we were flying with a replacement.

The weather was good for our plan but only for two-thirds of the distance. Suddenly the cloud cover broke up and we were flying in a clear blue sky. We could have turned back, dropping our bombs over the secondary target London, which would have been the normal procedure. And, of course, we would have done this if our regular navigator, who was a prudent father of a family, had been on board.

Although every member of the crew had thought, as we noticed later, of turning back, we also wanted to complete the mission because we had already flown so far.

Then suddenly I saw fighters appearing behind us, which were coming nearer very quickly...

Flight Lieutenant William Leather, A Flight, 611 Sqn

Red Section was ordered to patrol Nottingham at 10,000 feet but when over Nottingham I was told to proceed towards Derby. When near Derby AA fire called my attention to one enemy ac about 5,000 above. Red Section then climbed to 15,000 and was then about 3 miles away from enemy aircraft. Enemy aircraft turned east then south and Red Section delivered a No 1 attack. Enemy aircraft dived to ground level and I carried out another attack when his port engine was hit. Enemy aircraft was last seen going south at about 20 feet. Return fire experienced in first attack but not second attack. Evasive tactics of enemy aircraft were a number of steep turns. Although I did not see the enemy aircraft crash, I was informed afterwards that it crashed near Didcot and prisoners were taken from it.

Erwin Zins continues:

...At once we dropped our two 1,000kg bombs, went into a dive and tried to escape from the fighters. Very soon they were on our tail and shot at us one after the other. Our own armament, machine guns firing 1,400 rounds per minute (a cartridge drum lasted just 4 seconds), did not impress them at all. It did not last long when the left engine was hit leaving a trail of oil in the air. The rudder did not work any more so we had to fly the aircraft with the help of both engines. The consequence was that we had to land if the damaged engine should break down. So we were flying low-level for a while. The fighters turned away – probably they had spent all their ammunition. Really, it is a very troubling feeling to look into the flashes of eight machine guns when you can answer with only one.

Just before our emergency landing we attacked an airfield with machine gun fire. I informed our unit via radio of what had happened and that we had to land if one engine should break down. And this happened soon. The engine stopped, the aircraft turned left and our pilot landed. When the kite touched the ground I was thrown out immediately. My only thought was to get away from the aircraft, which was still sliding after me. Then there was silence, apart from the humming of the generators. I called Willi but only Erwin could be seen in the cockpit. Blood was running down from a wound in his forehead. Then Wermuth also appeared, who also had been slightly wounded in the head. Only later I noticed a fragment/splinter in my left wrist.

Bossdorf was missing. We went all the way back to the point where the plane had first hit the ground, at least 40 metres, but could not find him. We assumed that he had fallen through the gunner's gondola during the crash-landing so that he had been buried by the plane. Our next thought was to destroy the aircraft. For this purpose there were special ignition devices on board, but probably they had been torn out of their mountings. We could not find them. We tried to start a fire by burning our maps, but even that did not work. The aircraft did not burn. So we destroyed all the other documents and soon after the first Englishmen appeared and came nearer showing a threatening manner, as we thought.

But before they could reach us a car arrived and stopped on the street next to the crash site. A woman and a man got out and, more or less, took us prisoner. They took us to the next police station, where we were treated really nicely. We had fried potatoes with fried eggs and were offered cigarettes. Some time later we were picked up, separated from each other and taken to an Army Camp.

For some weeks the RAF had been aware of an impending change in German tactics, and just over 24 hours after Erwin Zins had been taken prisoner the *Luftwaffe* commenced the tactic of major night attacks against specific targets or cities under the codename *Mondscheinserenade*, or 'Moonlight Serenade'. The night of 14 November 1940 saw the attack codenamed *Mondscheinesonate*, or 'Moonlight Sonata', with the suffix *Korn*. The *Luftwaffe* used a series of code names for target cities. For example, Birmingham was *Bild* (Picture), Slough was *Jahrmarkt* (Fair), and Newport in South Wales was *Nashorn* (Rhinoceros); the identity of *Korn* was not known by the RAF. However, the RAF knew that an attack was coming, and in the counter-plan named 'Cold Water' assumed that probable targets were London and the South East. Cold Water was an attempt to interfere with German radio navigation transmissions, which included known radio navigation transmitters in northern France as well as German airfields.

During the preceding week to ten days, two *Luftwaffe* units had been carrying out nocturnal attacks against one specific target. The X *Verfahren*-equipped *KGr* 100 had singled out Coventry at least three times, while III/*KG* 26 had targeted Coventry twice; both units had attacked the city on the night of 12-13 November as a possible dry run for a future attack. III/*KG* 26 was the unit recently equipped with a new navigation and bombing system called Y *Verfahren*. In simple terms, this used a single beam to provide track guidance together with a distance-measuring facility. The beam was produced by a *Wotan* II transmitter, which transmitted three directional signals per second, replacing the old dots and dashes with signals of equal duration with a dividing gap. A second ground station transmitter was used to measure the bombers' distance out along the beam by sending a modulated signal that triggered a transponder in the Heinkel 111 and sent a signal back. This allowed the ground station to measure the distance from the aircraft to the station and thus the distance to the target. When the aircraft's distance coincided with the target distance, instructions were sent for bombs to be released.

Fw Hans-Georg Blusch of 6/KG 51 was lucky to survive his encounter with 501 Sqn on the afternoon of 12 November 1940, crash-landing at Cap Blanc Nez. He would later be killed in an accident on 11 January 1941. (via Trivett).

A Do 17 of 1/KG 2, damaged over London, crash-landed at Vitry in the early hours of 14 November 1940.

By the afternoon of 14 November 1940 the RAF had ascertained the probable target that night, and that *Korn* was Coventry, but by that stage it was too late to bolster Coventry's defences, while any Cold Water countermeasures would prove helpless to prevent what was about to happen.

A Ju 88 of 4/KG 51 taking off for Coventry on 15 November 1940. (Ciuraj)

A Ju 88 from an unidentified unit heads for England.

He 111s of KGr 100 were the first bombers over Coventry that night.

Crews of III/KG 55 being briefed for a mission at Villacoublay in the winter of 1940.

For about 10 hours, 145 bombers from *Luftflotte* 2 and 304 bombers *Luftflotte* 3 dropped 503 tonnes of bombs together with nearly 32,000 incendiaries on Coventry, which had been identified as a city that was 'an important part of the English war industry'. Specific targets were stated as the Standard Motor Company, the Coventry Radiator & Press Work Co Ltd, Hill Street Gas Works, Alvis Ltd, Cornercraft Ltd, the British Piston Ring Company, and the Daimler Co Ltd. Damage and disruption were extensive, as the following wartime narrative shows:

> The raid on Coventry was the first example of a night attack of maximum intensity on a target of limited area.
>
> The raid began at 1920hrs on November 14 and continued without a break until 0615hrs next morning during which time it appears that there were some 600 incidents. Some 330 aircraft were engaged in the attack; had it not been for the RAF's aggressive action on enemy bases earlier in the evening, the number might well have been more than double.
>
> The attack opened by the dropping of IBs in the centre of the city where extensive fires were started in the area round the Cathedral. These fires lit up the target for the bombers who followed and concentrated their attack in an area of a few acres in the centre of the city. The active defences kept the attacking aircraft very high and the fire density of the AA barrage was greater that that put up on any one night by the London defences. Fighter aircraft were also active, some interceptions were made and several combats took place. No enemy aircraft came below the level of the balloon barrage which was in operation all night.
>
> Telephone communications failed at an early stage in the raid.
>
> By 0330hrs in the morning, 200 fires were reported; there was a serious lack of water, many of the hydrants were buried beneath debris and a number of fires were not being attended to. Police and fire reinforcements were drafted in and it was arranged to picket all roads round the city. Troops were applied for to assist in control and in the repair to damage.
>
> In addition to the shortage of water, gas supply was reported early in the morning as 'completely disorganised' and electricity services 'out of action'. Reinforcements of rescue and first aid parties and ambulances were sent from other groups within the region. The amount of wreckage in the streets made it difficult to deploy services. A large number of people had to be evacuated from their homes owing to unexploded parachute mines, of which there were eighteen.
>
> Soon after noon it was reported that there had been 525 incidents. By 1325hrs on the 15th the situation was reported as 'well in hand'. On the afternoon of 15/11/40 the Minister of Home Security and the Minister of Aircraft Production arrived in the City.
>
> Water shortage was still making fire-fighting difficult and debris blazed up from time to time during the afternoon. Water was relayed from the River Cherwell and barges with trailer pumps were in action on the canal. All fires were under control by the evening of 15/11/40.
>
> On the morning of 16/11/40 there were 1,130 troops in the city. Roads were extremely congested.

- By the middle of the morning only five fires were still burning. The visit of HM The King on this day made an astonishing difference to the spirit of the people. The situation had much improved. Some domestic water was available but pressure was still very low. All factory mains had been repaired, trunk main repairs were in hand and undamaged areas had their water supply.

The electricity situation was somewhat easier that that of the other services. Cable damage was comparatively slight, the main power station was not damaged and the supply of electricity to most factories could be undertaken. There was no supply of gas. There had been some 150-200 direct fractures. Fourteen unexploded mines and some 200 UXBs awaited disposal.

By 17/11/40 the situation had improved in a number of ways. Four fires were still smouldering but without glare. By the evening fourteen parachute mines had been satisfactorily dealt with and forty UXBs had been removed from Key Points.

During Sunday, owing to the damage to mains and contamination from sewers and gas, all water supplies were cut off. The gas situation was still unsatisfactory but electricity was available in the centre of the City and in several surrounding districts.

On 18/11/40 no gas was available by 1800hrs but electricity was 50% in production and the water position had also improved. Good progress was being made in the restoration of telephone services and several important factories had resumed work. All bus routes were working by Monday evening. On the night the Fire Brigade were called to seven outbreaks of old incidents but they were not serious and were soon under control.

The estimates of casualties were 380 killed and 800 seriously injured...

This narrative still tries to paint a somewhat positive picture. RAF night-fighters only reported one combat when Plt Off Lionel Kells of 29 Sqn claimed to have damaged an unidentified aircraft near Swaffham. In reality, no German aircraft were damaged and the only loss was a Dornier 17 of 6/*KG* 3 flown by *Oblt* Oswald Priess, which was shot down by *Flak* and crashed near Loughborough with the deaths of all of its crew. Furthermore, Cold Water countermeasures by Bomber and Coastal Command only occurred after the bombers had become airborne. Bombs were dropped at the bomber airfields of Rennes, Vannes, Lorient, Cherbourg, Orleans-Bricy, Villacoublay, Melun, Chartres and Chateaudun, but the only casualties were three aircraft lightly damaged and one badly damaged at Vannes (there is no mention of this in German records), and five *Luftwaffe* personnel killed and six wounded at Cherbourg – scant retribution for what the *Luftwaffe* had done to Coventry.

For *Lt* Karl Svata of 5/*KG* 53, this was his first operational flight. Even though he was not to know it, it would also be his penultimate as, the following night, during a follow-up attack on Coventry, his Heinkel 111 became iced up, then broke up in the air, and he and his *Beobachter*, *Fw* Alfred Achstalle, were the only two crew to successfully bail out. Understandably, their recollections of their first mission were vivid, even if they failed in their task, as the intelligence report shows:

...His first war flight was on the night of 14/15 November when six aircraft of 5/*KG* 53 started from Lille-Vendeville to bomb a waterworks to the west of Coventry.

(This page and opposite) *III/KG 55 He 111s sporting their distinctive night camouflage.*
(via Creek)

The *Staffel Kapitän* held a conference during the afternoon when he explained that the aircraft were to set off at 1-minute intervals. The leading aircraft was to carry a number of parachute flares in order to illuminate the target and the remainder were to carry four 250kg bombs and to follow on closely while the flares were still burning.

For this operation, *Knickebein* III was to be directed onto Coventry. A course card shows that *Knickebein* III was to be picked up in the Channel just north of Dieppe and from there they were to fly on the beam direct to Coventry.

The night was very misty from 3,000 feet upwards with a heavy cloud layer at 17,000 feet. The aircraft came in across the English coast at about 15,000 feet and, when south-west of London, they lost the beam and spent some time circling looking for it. While they were doing this, they encountered severe icing conditions. Ice began to form on the wings and made them lose height down to 13,000 feet. Eventually they were forced to scuttle the bombs and return home.

It is probable that, had they located their target, they would have turned eastwards and returned by way of the North Sea to a landfall near Dunkirk because another fragment of the Course Card gives the bearing and distance from Dunkirk to Vendeville.

The next day, when all the aircraft had returned, they learned that they had failed to find the Waterworks which was the main objective and instead had attacked the alternative target, an aircraft factory at Coventry...

There has always been controversy about the attack on Coventry being purely one to target the civilian population. Indeed, the mention that some of the bombs dropped were fitted with *Jericho* screamers, which would give the bombs the terrifying scream as they fell, could support this supposition. The British narrative goes further:

> The successful starting of fires in the centre of the city seemed to have a marked attraction for the enemy pilots and may well have caused the heavy and concentrated attacks which were subsequently made on an area already devastated and which would have been much more damaging if delivered on the industrial outskirts. If this bombardment was carried out according to plan, its object would seem to have been to paralyse the life of the City and destroy morale rather than to do the maximum damage to industry. In spite of the weight and seriousness of the attack, the enemy did not bring industry in Coventry to a standstill nor did he break the morale on which it so largely depends...

Surviving *Luftwaffe* documents do state that the aim was to disrupt industrial production as well has to hinder reconstruction and resumption of manufacturing in a city critical to military automotive production, by hitting the houses of its workers. Unpalatable as this might be, the bombing of Coventry was a clear example of Carl Von Clausewitz's Total War in that there was less and sometimes no differentiation between military and civilians, as both were actively involved directly and indirectly in the war effort. Sadly for Coventry, the official civilian death toll is now regarded at 568, with a further 862 injured.

The following night the major target was again London (with *Luftflotte* 2 targeting Coventry, although very few bombs landed on the city, even if the General Electricity Company's works was set on fire). Only one German aircraft was lost, a Dornier 17 of 9/*KG* 76 flown by *Lt* Bernhard Wagner, an apparently rare success to a night-fighter flown by Sgt Sidney Holloway of 25 Sqn, even though it was also claimed (and it would appear credited) to *Flak*, as the diary of Plt Off George Barclay of 249 Sqn shows:

> This evening some of us went to see a Do 17 that crashed owing to ack-ack last night – there was just a large crater, still smouldering, full of bits and pieces with bits and clods of earth strewn around for hundreds of yards. There were bits of German everywhere but so mangled that it wasn't as gruesome as one would have thought – the toes of one foot rather put me off, but in the failing light it didn't look human.

If there was any doubt as to who shot this aircraft down, three nights later would see the first confirmed kill to a night-fighter with airborne radar.

The primary target for the night of 19 November 1940 was Birmingham, and it would prove costly for the *Luftwaffe* for a number of reasons. First, the *Geschwader Kommodore* of *KG* 26, *Obstlt* Karl Freiherr von Wechmar, together with the *Kapitän* of the *Stabstaffel*, *Oblt* Karl-Georg Streng, were killed with the rest of their crew while taking off from Beauvais; a second bomber, this time from I/*KG* 26, also crashed near Beauvais. Over the United Kingdom two aircraft were lost, each of which was flown by *Ritterkreuzträger*. A Junkers 88 of 6/*KG* 30, flown by *Ofw* Willi Schultz, disappeared without trace, while a Heinkel 111 of 1/*KG* 26, flown by *Lt* Albert Von Schwerin, hit a balloon cable at Beckton Marshes and crashed, killing all the crew,

The other was Ofw *Willi Schultz of 6/*KG *30 (left), seen with* Ofw *Rupert Drachhauer, his* Bordfunker, *who was also lost with him.* (via Creek)

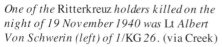

One of the Ritterkreuz *holders killed on the night of 19 November 1940 was* Lt *Albert Von Schwerin (left) of 1/*KG *26.* (via Creek)

which also included *Oblt* Hunno Phillips, *Kapitän* of 1/*KG* 26, and medical officer Dr Albert Leuchtenberg. Schultz and Von Schwerin had both been awarded the *Ritterkreuz* for operations over the North Sea and Norway, Schultz being credited with the sinking of HMS *Suffolk* on 17 April 1940 (though the cruiser was in fact just badly damaged). For *Oblt* Hans Klawe of 2/*KG* 55 and his crew, the night appeared doomed from the start, as the subsequent RAF intelligence report shows:

> The whole of I/*KG* 55 was to take part in the operation against Birmingham. For this operation, *Knickebein* III was set on to Birmingham and the aircraft were to pick up the beam north of London at about 13,000 feet.
>
> The G1+LK had an individual target, an aircraft factory to the north of Birmingham. They had two 250kg bombs in the chutes on one side of the fuselage and one 500kg bomb stowed externally on the opposite side. This bomb was painted black.
>
> They were to have taken off second or third of the *Gruppe* but, when taxiing to the far side of the aerodrome [Dreux] for the take-off run, the pilot and observer relaxed their attention and the aircraft overran the boundary lights, went off the grass into a ploughed filed and sank in up to the axles. The ground staff had to come along and manhandle the aircraft out, and as a result they had to start much later in the list.

They flew by ordinary navigation methods, picked up the beam satisfactorily and started to fly along it. After a time, the equi-signal zone became very variable, sometimes being heard at full strength and at others fading away so that it was almost inaudible. Finally it disappeared altogether and no matter how they tried they could not pick it up.

Soon after this, the electrical equipment went wrong; neither the compasses nor the artificial horizon functioned properly and the night was so dark that the pilot could not keep the aircraft on a level course. The wireless operator [*Uffz* Rudolf Zeitz], however, insists that his apparatus continued to function. The observer [*Fw* Wilhelm Gutekunst] suddenly found himself pressed against the side and concluded that they were side-slipping. He scuttled the bombs, but this did not improve the situation and eventually he and the wireless operator bailed out. The other two members of the crew were killed when the aircraft crashed...

Although the survivors did not mention it, the demise of their Heinkel 111 was due to *Flak*. However, a Junkers 88 of 3/*KG* 54, flown by *Uffz* Kaspar Sondermeister, was destined to be the first of many whose loss was due to a night-fighter equipped with airborne radar, something that was mentioned in the intelligence report on the crash:

On the night of 19/20 November between 10 and 14 aircraft from I/*KG* 54 started from Evreux to bomb the industrial area to the north of Birmingham. They had no more exact target than this.

Aircraft first flew by ordinary direction finding on to the beacon near Deauville then continued till they were in the Channel off Cherbourg where they were to transfer to the beacon at Cherbourg and fly to pick up *Knickebein* V to the west or south-west of London. However, before they had flown far across the Channel something went wrong with the direction-finding bearings and the pilot turned westwards and picked up *Knickebein* V over the Channel instead of over England. They flew then from this point to Birmingham at about 20,000 feet. During the journey they did not experience any AA fire but shortly after reaching Birmingham they were attacked, they say now, by two night-fighters...

At 2221hrs a Bristol Beaufighter of 604 Sqn, call sign Blazer 24, lifted off from Middle Wallop in Hampshire. The pilot of this night-fighter was the as yet unknown Flt Lt John Cunningham, and his radar operator was Sgt John Phillipson. Their dry and inconclusive combat relates what happened:

Flt Lt John 'Cat's Eyes' Cunningham, 604 Sqn.
(via Foreman)

Blazer 24 engaged a four-engined e/a type uncertain (FW Condor?) near Brize Norton at 18,000 feet at nearly same level and about 200 yds astern and at about same speed. E/a returned fire almost immediately and appeared to slow down suddenly and turn to starboard. This e/a had no navigation lights and was intercepted by aid of (a) Wallop control (b) searchlight concentration on cloud (c) AI operator (d) exhaust flames of e/a 1,000 feet above and (e) further instructions from AI operator. Result inconclusive. Our casualties nil prior to this interception. Blazer 24 sighted a smoke trail and 2 twin-engined e/a with navigation lights (believed formation of 3 twin-engined a/c: 6 red lights were fired in pairs).

Despite misidentifying their victim, they did not claim to have shot down the aircraft but, following interrogation of the two German survivors, the claim was amended to 'destroyed', and at the bottom of the combat report was penned 'Ac crashed near Wittering'.

The remains of the first AI-assisted kill, at Bracklesham Bay, West Sussex. (via Saunders)

Despite this initial success, and 604 claiming before the end of 1940 two Junkers 88 probably destroyed, a Heinkel 111 and two Junkers 88s damaged, there would only be one more confirmed AI-assisted kill before the year was out, while non-AI assisted fighters claimed two damaged and three destroyed, and, of those destroyed, only one can now be confirmed. For the time being *Flak* and accidents would remain the main causes of *Luftwaffe* attrition.

The remainder of 1940 saw very little change to the *Luftwaffe*'s plan of campaign, with many of the major cities and ports being attacked night after night. Of interest is that, as dawn was breaking on 29 November 1940, three Focke-Wulf 200 Condors, until now only seen being used for maritime reconnaissance and anti-shipping operations, put in an appearance over the Scottish mainland. The identity of the pilots of these four-engined bombers is not known, apart from the fact that all three came from I/*KG* 40 and it is believed that one of the pilots was *Lt* Otto Gose of 2 *Staffel*. One plane dropped two SC500, twelve SC 50 and sixty B1 E1 incendiaries to the north-west of Glasgow between 0720 and 0755hrs, another attacked Falkirk due to the cloud cover over Glasgow, dropping four SC250, twelve SC 50 and sixty incendiaries between 0710 and 0720hrs, while the final Condor encountered similar problems with the cloud and dropped its load of four SC250, twelve SC50 and sixty incendiaries to the south of Glasgow between 0620 and 0710hrs. What would have been of concern to the British was the time all three bombers were allowed to loiter over the target, then return, without having been engaged by any of the defences. This would appear to have been a one-off attack by I/*KG* 40, and the reason why it was carried out is not known.

*FW 200s of 3/*KG *40 seen at Bordeaux in early 1941.*

December 1940 saw the *Luftwaffe*'s offensive operations continuing unchanged, with major attacks against Southampton, Bristol, Birmingham, Portsmouth, Sheffield, Liverpool/Birkenhead and Manchester. London was attacked on numerous nights, the most memorable being the night of 29-30 December 1940, which resulted in a fire storm. Thankfully for Britain, typical December weather did interfere with operations on a number of nights, but from the German point of view *Luftwaffe* bomber losses were light. The heaviest occurred on the night of 8-9 December, when *Lt* Hans Guhre of 6/*KG* 77 and *Uffz* Max Jappsen of 6/*LG* 1 were shot down by *Flak* attacking London, and again on 11-12 December, when *Hptm* Heinrich Richard, the new *Staffel Kapitän* of 1/*KG* 26, went missing in an attack on Southampton and *Hptm* Hans-Joachim Dittler, *Staffel Kapitän* of 7/*KG* 26, went missing attacking Birmingham. All four were victims of *Flak*.

A surprise for KG 53: this Wellington of 99 Sqn became lost attacking Turin on the night of 4 December 1940. Flt Lt Frank Vivian and his crew were taken prisoner.

This is believed to be Wk Nr 3354 of 9/KG 55, which crashed on take-off from Villacoublay on 8 December 1940, killing Lt Walter Lehenbauer and his crew.

Oblt *Ulrich 'Harry' Hensolt of 8/KG 26 crashed on take-off from Poix on the night of 20 December 1940. He and three of his crew were injured and one killed; Hensolt himself would survive the war.*

Ofw *Josef Butz and his crew from 3/606 went missing attacking Liverpool on the night of 21 December 1940.*

However, the night of 22-23 December would see a number of combats between RAF night-fighters and German bombers. Flt Lt Pat Burke of 93 Sqn (formerly 420 Flt) was credited with the destruction of an enemy aircraft through the use of Long Aerial Mines, although there is no conclusive evidence that any German bomber was lost to the Harrow's mines. A crash of a German bomber was witnessed by German crews, who reported seeing an aircraft burning on the ground near Hastings at 1902hrs, even though they thought it was a victim of *Flak*. Plt Off James Benson and Plt Off Leonard Blain in a Defiant of 141 Sqn had in fact shot down a Heinkel 111 of 3/*KG* 55 flown by *Uffz* Bruno Zimmermann, which crashed at Etchingham at 1805hrs (UK time), the times and location being positive proof of the non-AI-assisted kill. Their report makes quite brutal reading:

Oblt Siegfried Fidorra (left) of 1/120 carried out an armed recce against an aluminium factory at Fort William in the early hours of 22 December 1940. He would be killed in an accident in 1942.

A war reporter's sketch makes a dramatic if not hard to believe impression of such an attack.

...My gunner directed his initial burst of fire on the lower gun turret and port engine and his last two bursts at the pilot and it must have been the rear gunner whom I saw fall away from the plane after the first burst...

...After the second and third bursts, I went round in front of him and flew forwards and backwards underneath him. He took no evasive action whatever, probably because of the complete surprise of the attack. I then saw smoke coming from both engines and flames from the fuselage...

The man whom they saw had bailed out was the *Beobachter*, *Ofw* Walter Richter; he was the only survivor. He later stated that he had a premonition and did not want to make this flight – how right he had been.

Another German aircraft was intercepted by an AI-equipped 604 Sqn Beaufighter flown by Sgt Peter Jackson with Sgt Arthur O'Leary, and a crew from I/*LG* 1, on their way back from Manchester, reported that at about 2100hrs they had been intercepted by a night-fighter that they had hit and set on fire, and that it had disappeared into cloud; in reality, that was almost true, as the Beaufighter crew later reported:

...Shortly after, a blip was received on the weapon [radar] and after following it up, an ac was seen at 17,000 feet with all navigation lights on. Sgt Jackson went within 30 yds to investigate machine and prepared to open fire. He identified it as a Ju 88 as the rear gunner from below the e/a opened fire, which pierced the bullet-proof windscreen, injuring the pilot. Sgt O'Leary was also wounded and told to bail out and was subsequently picked up. Sgt Jackson brought the machine back and landed it safely...

The following night would see the last German bomber loss in combat over the United Kingdom in 1940, even though the German crew were unaware that they had been intercepted by an AI-equipped night-fighter, again crewed by Flt Lt John Cunningham and Sgt John Phillipson of 604 Sqn:

AI Operators of 604 Sqn. Sgt O'Leary is on the extreme right, and Sgt Phillipson second from the left.

There was no need to use AI as it was not yet dark. The pilot was flying on a south-easterly course about 50 miles south of Lulworth at 15,000 feet when he saw an e/a about 1,500 feet above on his right. He circled round behind and followed the ac, which was identified as a Heinkel 111 on a course of 45 degrees and steadily climbed up to 19,000 feet for 10 minutes during which time the e/a altered course to 20 degrees. Flt Lt Cunningham, travelling at 160/170 ASI, came up behind and from 200/300 yds gave a short burst of approximately 4 seconds which hit the e/a amidships. The ac blew up, causing pieces and three parachute flares to fall out. No return fire was received. The weather was good above cloud with excellent visibility. Ac landed at base at 1906hrs. Approximate total rounds fired 80...

Feldwebel Georg Deininger, 3/KGr 100

...Our aircraft was hit by what we thought was a direct hit by a shell fired by what could only have been a *Flak* ship as we were still over the sea. The Heinkel 111's starboard engine failed immediately, the port engine lost power and I felt the flying controls lose their effectiveness. The nose of the aircraft was shattered, jagged holes were seen in the right wing and the radio was smashed

At the same time, fired erupted in the badly damaged fuselage and a few minutes later the second engine failed completely. I assessed that at this height I could probably glide back to the French coast if only I could maintain control of the aircraft, and with this aim I turned onto a reciprocal heading. Jettisoning the bombs, I managed to get the Heinkel 111 into a controlled glide. The *Beobachter* had been hit by a splinter above his right eye, the *Bordfunker* was also wounded and the *Bordmechaniker* had been hit in both legs by several small splinters. Fire had broken out in the bomb bay where canisters of incendiaries blazed furiously. Fortunately, as I jettisoned the bomb load, these fell away to the sea far below.

Deininger succeeded in making the French coast near Cherbourg and managed to carry out a dead-stick landing on top of some trees, which caused the bomber to break in two, ripping off the port wing in the process. Apart from his head connecting with the control column, there were no further injuries to the crew.

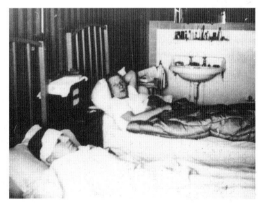

The Deininger crew after their meeting with John Cunningham's Beaufighter.

Deininger and his crew would spend the remainder of 1940 in hospital, still unaware that they had been a victim of a night-fighter. In just over six months time, Georg Deininger would be shot down by another night-fighter, another victim of an increasingly more effective RAF defence. The Blitz would continue for another five months, during which time many more lives would be lost both in the air and on the ground as Germany struggled to bring the British military and civilian population to its knees.

A early Christmas present: Rudolf Hess visits KG 55 at Villacoublay on 24 December 1940.

He 111s of 6/KG 53 head off on a mission during the winter of 1940-41.

2

The Calm before the Storm
January-February 1941

The year 1941 began with Europe in the grips of very cold weather. The first major attack occurred on the night of 2-3 January when Cardiff was targeted by *Luftflotte* 2 and 3. The attack was led by *KGr* 100, one of whose aircraft almost fell again to the up and coming ace, Flt Lt John Cunningham, as his combat report proves:

> ...Flt Lt Cunningham opened fire till the magazines were empty except one gun which stopped. An object was seen to fall away from the e/a. The first flashes were seen hitting the fuselage and presumably killed both rear gunners as there was no return fire. Shells were also seen hitting the port engine and lastly the port wing just outside the engine.
>
> The e/a carried on an even course for about half a minute after which it turned to port losing height and flying due south. The pilot turned inside e/a which appeared to be using no power from the engines. These were giving out vapour or white smoke. The e/a had begun to dive and continued diving more steeply until it went into cloud at about 10,000 feet at an angle of 50 degrees below horizontal. It was noticed from a side view of the e/a silhouetted against the sky that there were three large aerial masts evenly spaced along the top of rear half of fuselage...

He 111s of KGr *100, clearly showing the three masts spotted by John Cunningham.*

A Heinkel 111 of 2/*KGr* 100 returned to France having suffered combat damage; the gunner, *Uffz* Armin Heidemann, had been wounded by gunfire from John Cunningham's Beaufighter. Again, losses were light, with a Junkers 88 of 7/*KG* 1 being reported missing and a Dornier 17 of 8/*KG* 2 reported having been damaged in combat with a night-fighter (the identity of which cannot be ascertained as, apart from the 604 Sqn claim, no others were logged) and returned with two wounded crew. Damage to Cardiff was quite extensive, as a contemporary Air Ministry report noted:

> Bombs fell in most districts of the city, suburbs and nearby areas especially to the south-west towards Penarth and Barry, with no noticeable concentration.
>
> The damage is described as 'of a general nature'. Nine key points were affected, mostly indirectly through UXBs or loss of utility supplies. No serious damage was reported from the Docks. The buildings of the British Oxygen Co Ltd were completely demolished.
>
> The most important damage was done at the Gas Light and Coke Company's premises at Grangetown. No important damage was done to the water system.
>
> There was a good deal of delay and dislocation on the railways but damage was mainly temporary.
>
> Public buildings and service establishments suffered including Llandaff Cathedral and Llandaff Barracks.
>
> The casualties were 103 killed and 403 injured.'

This would prove to be the Welsh capital's heaviest attack of the war.

The nights that followed saw continued attacks against ports such as Swansea, Plymouth, Bristol and Avonmouth, with few if any German losses, a fact assisted by the poor weather, especially during the period 5-10 January. The poor weather did assist lone German bombers carrying out what was known as *Pirateinsätze* – lone attacks by experienced crews utilising poor weather and low-level flying as a form of defence. For example, on 8 January 1941 the miserable weather allowed *Lt* Karl Höflinger of 8/*KG* 77 to approach Coventry unseen. His target was the Standard Motors factory, and at 1454hrs it was reported that a lone raider had dropped bombs in the city but that no extensive damage had been done to property and that there had been no casualties. Höflinger reported having dropped three SC 500 bombs on the factory from an altitude of 100 metres, and the German propaganda machine hailed him and his crew, *Ofw* Karl Vogelhuber, *Ofw* Karl Odelga and *Fw* Karl Herfort, as heroes. Höflinger would be awarded the *Ritterkreuz* on 7 March 1941, but just over a month later he and his crew were shot down by *Flak* while attacking Portsmouth, and there were no survivors when his Junkers 88 plunged into the sea off the Nab Tower.

Do 17s and Ju 88s practising low-level flights – altitudes would be even lower on Pirateneinsätze.

RAF night-fighter victories were still sporadic during January 1941. For example, 604 Sqn claimed one probably destroyed and one damaged (Flt Lt John Cunningham in each case), but the non-radar-equipped Hurricane and Defiant squadrons claimed three destroyed, two damaged and two probably destroyed. Claims yet again were overly optimistic apart from the night of 15-16 January, when Plt Off Richard Stevens of 151 Sqn shot down a Dornier 17 of 4/*KG* 3 at Brentwood and a Heinkel 111 of 2/*KG* 53 off Canvey Island. However, such victories were rare, as one Polish fighter pilot reported the following night; the reality in this case was quite the opposite:

Flying Officer Jan Falkowski, 32 Sqn

Jan Falkowski (extreme left), seen as a Flight Lieutenant and Flight Commander with 315 Sqn in late 1941.

On the evening of 16 January 1941 I received orders to take off at 1900hrs and to patrol at 20,000 feet between Portsmouth and Hayling Island. It was a cold evening and extremely dark. I could see shell bursts over Portsmouth; a big raid was on and anti-aircraft fire was heavy. I could see the bombs exploding below and fires breaking out in various parts of Portsmouth.[1]

I was making my second circuit of my 'beat' when I saw a small light. It came from the exhaust of a two-engined bomber that had evidently dropped its bombs and was going back to the French coast.[2] It was a fast one and I only had a glimpse of it but I caught it and I shot it down. My first night kill! I watched gleefully as the German spun down in flames.

[1] Just one Junkers 88 from I/*KG* 51 is reported to have bombed Portsmouth on 16 January, but British records do not make mention of any attack on Portsmouth or Southampton that night.
[2] This would match with the aircraft involved in the attack on Avonmouth, the main effort that night.

I felt proud and happy that at last I had shot down a night bomber and I started my patrol again with renewed vigour, but that I hadn't escaped unscathed in the brief but sharp air battle became apparent almost immediately. The Hurricane started vibrating and the engine missing. My oil pressure was nil. The German gunner must have damaged the engine before I got the enemy bomber. I had to get back to base.

I was well over the Channel, on a bearing for Portsmouth with the engine getting rougher all the time and I was losing height. At 10,000 feet I realised that I wasn't going to make the coast. I had to bail out and the thought of the cold water below wasn't pleasant but there was nothing else for it. I cut the switch and the engine stopped and quickly I pulled back the canopy and tried to step out. I stuck halfway out of the plane!

My parachute had become entangled in the hood of the cabin and stuck there. I could neither go up nor go down. The plane was getting lower and lower but hadn't got into a spin. I recall how quiet it was. There was a smell of smoke from the engine.

I tried a desperate measure. I pulled the parachute ripcord. It worked. It opened and I was pulled right out of the aircraft, which then went down with a whistle. I didn't know how high I was but apparently was very low. I landed with a thump – it wasn't the Channel – and I felt a terrible pain in my left leg. I had struck ground and I hadn't been braced for the landing...

The remainder of January 1941 saw the Luftwaffe attacks following a similar pattern – attacks on major cities by night and attacks by lone aircraft against specific targets such as airfields by day. The last major attack by night was against Southampton on the night of 19-20 January and again saw a reduced number of aircraft attacking – just *KG* 1, *KG* 77 and III/*KG* 26 were involved from *Luftflotte* 3. The British report of the attack, which matches well with German records, stated:

An attack started at 1950hrs and continued spasmodically until 2230hrs. A few HE and IB were dropped and 14 fires were caused in dwelling house property. All fires were extinguished during the course of the raid. Two water mains were cut, opposite the north end of the Airport. Three houses were demolished and about 120 damaged and there were three casualties, one of which was fatal.

Despite the low numbers of aircraft participating, three were lost to anti-aircraft fire, two of which crashed on land. One of the latter came from the Y *Gerät*-equipped 9/*KG* 26, but the wreckage revealed little of use to the RAF. The other aircraft to crash on land was flown by the 29-year-old *Staffel Kapitän* of 2/*KG* 1, *Hptm* Gustav Friedrich Graf zu Castell-Castell; he came from a renowned aristocratic German family, and after the war they went to great lengths to find out exactly what had happened. In a letter dated 5 May 1955, the Vicar of Steyning wrote:

The plane came in from the sea laden with incendiary bombs but evidently the plane had been hit and the pilot knew they were losing height and that he would have to make a forced landing. He was just over our little town and was making valiant efforts to avoid landing on the town. He did so and he was a very brave man and showed all possible courage...

The remains of Hptm *Graf zu Castell-Castell's He 111.* (via Saunders and Parry)

Evidently hit by anti-aircraft fire, the Heinkel 111 caught fire, and as it approached Steyning it appeared that the pilot tried to avoid crashing on the town. However, as it approached Kings Barn Farm, Steyning, 'fire began to fall from it. In then turned north and masses of flame poured from it, coming lower and lower, it crashed.'

All five crew were killed, and were buried at Steyning three days later with full military honours, something insisted on by Major-General Sir Oliver Leese Baronet DSO CB CBE, the West Sussex Divisional Commander. *Gräfin* Vibecke zu Castell-Castell, Gustav Friedrich's mother, was told on 13 February 1941 that a *Hauptmann* and his crew had been killed 'near the coast', and it was assumed that this was her son. It was not until 29 November that it was confirmed that her son had been buried on 23 January at St Andrew's Churchyard at Steyning. After the war his body was returned to Germany to be buried alongside other members of this aristocratic family.

The weather for the remainder of the month was so poor that no further major attacks took place, the German modus operandi being attacks again factories, airfields and shipping by daylight. One unit particularly active was III/*KG* 30, a *Gruppe* that had been formed in mid-October 1940 from III/*KG* 4. On 26 January 8/*KG* 30 tried to attack shipping in the Thames Estuary, apparently lured by radio interceptions stating that a ship believed to be carrying aircraft had run aground on a sandbank. The aircraft took off at regular intervals from Schiphol in Holland, but the first Junkers 88 failed to return, having flown through the masts and rigging of the ship it was attacking. Later that day another two Junkers 88s of 8/*KG* 30 were lost on similar missions.

The following day saw the United Kingdom blanketed in low cloud, rain and associated poor visibility. However, this did not stop two aircraft from 9/*KG* 30 carrying out a *Pirateinsätz*.

The British Manufacturing & Research Company (BMARC), located at Springfield Road, Grantham in Lincolnshire, was well known to the *Luftwaffe*, who believed it to be the only company in the United Kingdom making Hispano Suiza aircraft cannon. Their intelligence was not far wrong – by 1943 BMARC manufactured 46% of the 20mm cannon, vital in the air war when it was found to be far more effective in air combat than the standard .303 machine gun.

Grantham first came under air attack on the night of 30 September 1940, which resulted in seven deaths and eighteen injured as well as damage to houses, a factory, gas, water and electricity mains. On 23 November *Lt* Kurt Dahlmann of 9/*KG* 30, who would later be a decorated bomber and fighter-bomber pilot with the *Ritterkreuz mit Eichenlaub*, reported to have carried out a devastating attack on the BMARC factory, the report reading:

Fight against English 'bottleneck industry'

Dawn attack on Hispano-Suiza motor cannon factory in Grantham. Glide attack – dropped four SC 250 and ten SC 50. Two, probably three SC 250 hit the main workshop, all other detonations in factory buildings and on the factory site. According to reports by agents, factory had been put out of operation for six weeks.

Remarks: Detonations observed by *Oblt* Elle's crew. Official recognition of the attack by *General der Flieger* Cöhler, commanding general of *IX.Fl.Korps*. Official recognition in *Frontnachrichtenblatt der Luftwaffe*.

Lt *Kurt Dahlmann, seen here as a* Hauptmann *in 1944.*

Strangely, no record of this attack was made from the British side. The next attack, by an unidentified unit, took place on the night of 9 January 1941, when sixteen houses were destroyed, fifty rendered uninhabitable and 250 damaged. Thirteen civilians were killed, with ten seriously and twenty slightly injured.

The next attack was in the early afternoon of 27 January 1941, when, in order to celebrate his 100th operational flight, the *Staffel Kapitän* of 9/*KG* 30, *Oblt* Friedrich-Karl Rinck, decided that the BMARC factory would make a fitting attack. He decided that this attack would be made in a brand-new Junkers 88 A-5, which had been delivered a few days before.

Oblt *Rinck (2nd from left) and his crew.* (Wissing)

Rinck's Ju 88. (Wissing)

Rinck was an experienced pilot who had already been shot down by Dutch fighters on 10 May 1940 and taken prisoner whilst attacking Schiphol airfield, the very airfield he was flying from this day. He decided to fly alongside another member of his *Staffel*, someone who had apparently attacked BMARC before, *Lt* Kurt Dahlmann. Dahlmann took off first, but his report reads:

> Planned lowest-level attack on Hispano-Suiza motor cannon factory in Grantham was not possible, although three attempts were made, because of the weather and much haze. Low-level attack with two SC 500, two SC 250 and ten SC 50 on alternative target, the ironworks Moulders and Pieters in Newark. Two SC 500 hit industrial railway lines, all the other detonations in factory plants.
>
> Remarks: Confirmed by photos taken of the works before and during the detonations.

Rinck, unaware that Dahlmann had failed to find his target, took off and headed west, making landfall just north of Great Yarmouth. The weather was terrible – 200 metres visibility with a low cloud base. Crossing the coast at 1,300 feet, they skirted Boston, then picked up the Sleaford-Grantham railway and soon spotted the factory with, to his surprise, a new factory building.

Unseen by the German crew, on the factory roof was a section of Home Guardsmen from the 3rd Kesteven (Grantham & Spittlegate) Battalion. Apparently, on 3 December 1940 they had engaged, damaged and driven off a German bomber that had been attempting to bomb the BMARC factory. The platoon commander was a Mr A. L. Dawrant, the Company Secretary, with Mr R. W. Ellacott, a clerk, Mr G. A. M. McNicoll, and accountant, and Mr R. H. T. Ridler, Chief Accountant. Seeing Rinck's bomber approaching, they opened fire. In the Junkers 88 Rinck was surprised that they were encountering light *Flak*. At 500 feet and in a leisurely fashion he dropped four SC 250 and ten SC 50 bombs, the gunner, *Uffz* Ferdinand Wissing, reporting that two hit the target and that one factory building was damaged. In all, the fourteen bombs landed in and around BMARC, killing twelve at the factory and another three in the local area, and wounding two seriously and four slightly. Four houses were badly damaged and thirty others damaged to varying degrees.

The welcome that awaited Rinck – the AA gun situated on the roof of the BMARC factory. (via Pinchbeck)

Uffz *Ferdinand Wissing*. (Wissing)

Damage to the factory. (via Pinchbeck)

As the Junkers 88 made good its escape, its pilot quickly realised that all was not right. The port engine was leaking oil and quickly began to vibrate and overheat, forcing Rinck to shut it down. They had taken numerous hits from machine gun and 20mm bullets and the port wing appeared to have suffered badly. At such a low level, they were unable to climb, and by the time they reached Boston they were below tree level, so the only option was to crash-land, which they did at Pilley's Lane on the outskirts of Boston. All four crew clambered out and, before being captured, succeeded in setting off an explosive charge that destroyed all but the wings and an engine. The crash-landing was quite exciting for the people of Boston:

The successful gunners pose beneath their trophy, the spinner from Rinck's Ju 88 in the BMARC canteen. (via Pinchbeck)

A crash-landed Ju 88 of III/KG 30.

Norman Melson

I was in my last year of school and the news went around. At leaving time, I think every boy in Boston was heading for Pilley's Lane a little more than a mile from my school. The weather was damp and grey and drizzly (I often wondered how they managed to find BMARC at Grantham in the overcast). The aircraft was in a ploughed field surrounded by RAF, Fire Service and Police. It didn't look too badly damaged despite the demolition charge.

The attack killed three Boston men – Reg Pearson, Edwin Hadwick and Robert Sissons – all of whom were motor mechanics and had been drafted in to work at BMARC. The 10-year-old daughter of Reg Pearson went to the same school as myself.

On the Saturday following the clearance of the wreckage, the land-owner gave a friend and myself permission to search for souvenirs. I found a large piece of cast alloy radio chassis complete with a few switches and tuning dials – the only piece now left is a small electric motor. I also have an inspection panel about 15 inches by 12 inches.

Shortly after the incident, a senior fire officer was charged and fined for 'acquiring' an aerial camera and a machine gun, ditto his assistant for a drum of ammunition...

It had been a costly two days for III/*KG* 30, but it had been a terrible day for Grantham. Sadly, it would not end there, as on the evening of 4 February 1941, just before his *Gruppe* headed off to the Mediterranean, *Lt* Kurt Dahlmann carried out yet another attack on the BMARC factory. His report read:

Glide attack on Hispano-Suiza motor cannon factory in Grantham, which had taken up production again after the last attack. Two SC 250 direct hits in large assembly shop. All the other detonations on factory site, the sighting-in range and its ammunition store. A lot of colourful explosions (sighting-in ammunition) and detonations followed. Extensive fire damage.

Remarks: Attack and its effects observed and confirmed by *Oblt* Elle's crew who had attacked the same target.

Yet again considerable damage was done to a factory, with five killed, five seriously wounded and twelve slightly. There was also extensive damage to residential property, where another three were killed and nine injured. This time one of the Home Guardsmen defending the factory, 18-year-old Philip English, was one of the fatalities.

The results of the attack by Oblt *Elle and* Lt *Dahlmann on 4 February 1941.* (via Pinchbeck)

The victor for much of February 1941 was the weather, giving the British and the *Luftwaffe* a brief respite. It also saw the *Luftwaffe* continuing modernisation of its bomber aircraft with many Dornier 17 units, such as *KG* 76, returning to Germany for conversion to the Junkers 88 as well as giving some crews rest from operations. The *Flugbuch* of *Oblt* Erwin Moll of 4/*KG* 76 clearly illustrates this. His first operational flight had been on 13 May 40 and by the end of the month he had flown nine sorties.

However, his tenth, which was against Dunkirk, saw his Dornier 17 being hit by a fighter, two of his crew killed and he and his remaining crewman wounded. He did not return to operational flying until late July 1940, flying his first mission of the Battle of Britain (a night attack on the Victoria Docks in London) on 5 August 1940. By the end of the Battle of Britain he had flown thirty-five missions. He and his *Gruppe* then returned to Germany and his first flight in a Junkers 88 was on 8 November, but he and his *Gruppe* did not return to the front line until 7 March 1941; his subsequent operational career would last just over a month more.

He 111 H-5 Wk Nr 3549 of 3/KG 53 suffered 15% damage by Flak over London 4 Feb 41 and landed at Vitry. It was later more severely damaged over Russia when on 28 August 1941 it crash-landed with a wounded gunner.

The Ju 88 from KG 51 was far superior to the Do 17.

The first half of the month saw sporadic attacks against industrial targets, docks and airfields. Mining of harbours was attempted by aircraft of IX *Fliegerkorps*, predominantly *Hptm* Klaus Nöske's I/*KG* 4 (less *Hptm* Hermann Kuhl's specialist mining *Staffel*, which had transferred to the Mediterranean at the end of December 1940) and *Hptm* Holm Schellmann's I/*KG* 28. The latter unit had been formed from *KGr* 126 in mid-December 1940 and its main aim was to deliver the 1,000kg *Luftmine* (parachute mine) either against land targets (where they were used as blast weapons) or at sea. As one pilot from 1/*KG* 28 recalls, they took their task seriously:

The Luftmine. (via Griehl)

Leutnant Wilhelm Neumann, 1/KG 28

Officers of I/KG 28 seen in January 1941. Lt Wilhelm Neumann is second from left. Hptm *Reinhold Gottschalk (killed on 31 January 1941) is in the background on the extreme right facing the camera. Lt Hans Arber (fourth from the left) would be killed over London on 14 June 1941, while Lt Otto Krüger (fifth from the left) would be shot down over London on 11 May 1941 and taken POW.*

The aircraft in which I was eventually shot down was an anti-aircraft balloon cutter. We used it for clearing the shipping lanes by cutting their steel cables, for example off the Isle of Man to the port of Liverpool. For this purpose, a sharp steel reinforcement was fitted to the leading edge of both wings...

I/*KG* 28 did not have a good start to its operational career, and by the start of March 1941 had lost three aircraft in accidents and three in combat. Casualties included the *Staffel Kapitän* of all three *Staffeln* – *Maj* Dr Roman Auernig (1 *Staffel*), *Hptm* Paul Claas (2 *Staffel*) and *Hptm* Reinhold Gottschalk (3 *Staffel*). Only Claas survived, and in fact survived the war However, no aircraft at all were lost by I/*KG* 28 in February 1941 due to the weather.

The night of 13-14 February saw a minor attack on London, when a new weapon was used. On the night of 21-22 December 1940 III/*KG* 26 had dropped a massive bomb on London – the new SC 2500, nicknamed 'Max'. Such bombs were dropped sporadically by III/*KG* 26 over the following months, probably due to their scarcity and a need for precision, but on the night of 14 February one was dropped by an unidentified crew. It landed close to its target, believed to be the De Havilland Factory in Edgware Road. Despite the use of Y *Verfahren*, the bomb dropped 3,000 yards short, bringing death and dreadful devastation to West Hendon. The following night, probably the first serious attack of the month, another 'Max' was successfully dropped on London. Again the target was an 'aero-engine factory at London-Edgware', but this time the bomb landed on Harrow with less serious consequences – in the region of 75 lost their lives at Hendon, but just one person was killed at Harrow.

The night of 15 February 1941 saw the *Luftwaffe* struggling to attack a number of targets, notably Liverpool and Humberside, and also saw Flt Lt John 'Cat's Eyes' Cunningham, as he was increasingly being called, and his new radar operator, Sgt Jimmy Rawnsley, get another kill. There was no doubt as to who he got – Cunningham reported seeing a big orange flame on the ground near Newton Abbot in Devon, and *Lt* Eberhard Beckmann's Heinkel 111 of 7/*KG* 27 crashed outside Totnes. Another Heinkel 111, flown by the *Staffel Kapitän* of 6/*KG* 4, *Hptm* Heinz Styra, fell victim to *Flak* and balloons while attacking Humberside; there were no survivors from either bomber. However, one German crew lost that night did all survive, while the RAF received an almost intact example of a Junkers 88 A-5.

Lt Herbert Florian and his crew from 8/*KG* 1 had been briefed to attack Liverpool, using *Knickebein* to fly from their airfield at Grevillers towards Calais, then over the Channel to the north of London towards their target. Unfortunately for them *Knickebein* was playing up, so they relied on taking bearings from beacons at Calais. Then their direction-finding equipment began playing up. The intelligence debrief gives an idea of how difficult it must have been flying at night in poor weather in February 1941, and tells what subsequently happened to the German crew:

> …shortly after 0100hrs, the aircraft arrived at a spot they thought from their bearings must have been Liverpool. They were above the clouds at 13,000 feet and encountered searchlights and severe AA fire. The latter was so accurate that they dumped their bombs through a hole in the cloud on where they thought the AA and searchlight emplacements were situated.
>
> One 500kg and one 250kg bombs were seen to explode but second 500kg bomb which was dropped on second run was not observed…

The intelligence report then takes great delight in stating that no bombs of 250kg or 500kg fell within 15 miles of Liverpool that night. However, subsequent post-war research shows that incendiaries were dropped at 1945hrs and again at 0148hrs, causing minor damage to houses and a fire at Bank Hall station, and that high-explosive bombs did land in the Commercial Road area causing damage to property, including a General Post Office garage, and seven casualties. The intelligence report then continues:

> …The crew then turned for home and flew on Beacon 82 [their airfield]… After flying for some time, they seemed to be directly over the Beacon but it was soon realised that the direction-finding equipment was unreliable. They then tried to get a fix from the wireless stations at Caen and Grevillers aerodrome but they found that the wireless was being jammed by other messages on this frequency and they became completely lost.

The Wireless Operator sent out the distress call sign but got no assistance... At this time, their height appears to have been around 3,000 feet and a little later they saw balloons above them and had an exciting time dodging the cables. The pilot was convinced that the aircraft was by now over the Continent... Some time before the aircraft came down, a beacon was seen flashing XD. This proved to the crew that they were not in the part of France near their aerodrome as no such beacon was known in that part of the country.

Later, the XD beacon was seen again near an aerodrome and as they were completely lost and running extremely short of petrol (only about 250 litres left), a red cartridge was fired, this being the German emergency request. The aerodrome replied with a red cartridge, which is German refusal of this permission, and the crew in desperation fired a second cartridge. The pilot then put the machine down on the aerodrome with its wheels down...

The aerodrome in question was Steeple Morden in Bedfordshire, and the crew were quickly captured. The bomber had apparently suffered a damaged engine due to anti-aircraft fire, and the starboard undercarriage collapsed on landing. However, the Junkers 88 was only superficially damaged and was brought on RAF charge, being used as a source of spares for a number of other Junkers 88 A-5s captured during 1941.

The night of 17-18 February would see the last major attack on London for that month before the target switched to Swansea and Cardiff. The weather still played its part and allowed *Pirateinsätze* against the usual targets such as airfields and industrial centres. During the attack on London, *Luftwaffe* losses were light and the loss of one bomber resulted in a vivid report in a local newspaper:

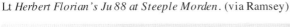

Lt *Herbert Florian's Ju 88 at Steeple Morden*. (via Ramsey)

An enemy bomber was brought down in the Home Counties on Monday night, one of the crew being killed [sic] and the rest captured. The pilot was a youth of twenty and was wearing the Iron Cross. He bailed out a few seconds before the plane crashed and was found injured a short distance away...

The 'youth of twenty' was 20-year-old *Lt* Günther Hübner, who was flying a Dornier 17 of 3/*KGr* 606 from Poulmic in Brittany. For similar reasons, his memories of that night are equally vivid:

Leutnant Günther Hübner, 3/KGr 606

We flew over the Channel Islands and left Cherbourg to our right. We then took a course over Brighton to London. We saw the big 'U' of the Thames and dropped our bombs. We changed course again and suddenly we were attacked from behind. It all went very fast. The cockpit was full of smoke and the right engine on fire. I was not able to keep the plane on course and we lost height rapidly. After his attack, we saw the night-fighter very near over us – it was a Beaufighter...

Sqn Ldr James Little of 219 Sqn had got airborne from RAF Tangmere about 30 minutes before the attack. He had quickly located the slow Dornier 17 and had to slow down by flying a series of 'S' turns behind the German bomber. In what would be the first radar-assisted kill for 219 Sqn, his combat report relates what happened:

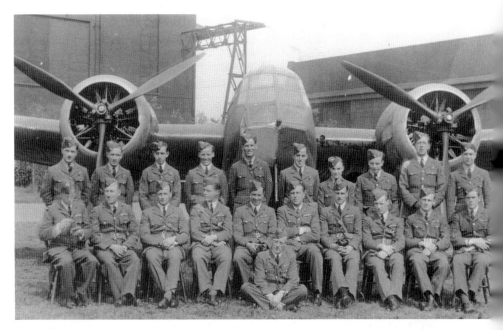

Sqn Ldr James Little (sitting fifth from the right) and his AI operator, Sgt Colin Pyne (standing on the extreme right) of 219 Sqn.

Sqn Ldr Little had 'Weapon' flashing which assisted in keeping on the tail of the Bandit as he almost lost sight of the Bandit in the 'S' turns – opened throttle slightly to close on Bandit and almost immediately reached minimum AI range – exhaust flames still appeared considerable distance ahead. Sqn Ldr Little coarsened pitch slightly as Bandit appeared to come back – quickly throttled back when clouds of flame came out of both exhausts, which pilot considered were bound to be seen by e/a. He decided to attack and opened fire at about 200 yds range aiming at centre of fuselage. This was immediately followed by flashes and sparks of dazzling intensity which appeared to come mostly from starboard side of e/a. Pilot was too dazzled to observe e/a afterwards and flew around continuing to fire at flashes. To avoid collision with Bandit's port wing, having dropped into the enemy's slipstream, Sqn Ldr Little pulled back stick slightly and e/a passed about 10 feet directly below him.

The German pilot continues:

...after some time I told my crew to bail out. As the last one I had some difficulties from getting out of my seat because the plane went out of control as soon as I let go of the stick. Finally I made it and the plane went down near my parachute. I landed in a field near the burning plane and broke my ankle. Soon there were Home Guardsmen around who took my pistol and brought me to a police station. The next night I spent in the barracks of some Guards Regiment. It must have been west of Windsor because my *Beobachter* told me later that he spent the night in the park of Windsor Castle...

The Dornier 17 had crashed at Bray, just to the west of Windsor. The newspaper relates what happened after the crash:

The wreckage was strewn over a wide area and what were apparently cannon shells and incendiary bombs exploding for some time. A fire-watcher and a farmer were guided to where the injured pilot lay by his groans. Through a woman interpreter, he told them in French that his companions had also bailed out.

A fire watcher and a farmer and his son were the first to find the pilot. They saw the parachute descending and a few minutes later they were guided to where he lay by his groans. Members of the Home Guard and police were quickly on the scene. The pilot was given treatment at a local hospital and afterwards taken away by a military escort. When the bomber crashed, its load of incendiaries and flares exploded and soon the machine was a burnt-out wreck. The orange glow in the sky could be seen for miles around.

A farmer who lives near the scene of the crash said to a representative of this paper, 'My son and I saw the plane circling around my house. It made a steep dive and fell in a field. A few seconds later the whole countryside was brilliantly illuminated by exploding incendiary bombs and flares in the machine. I could see exploding bullets shooting from the machine in all directions. Suddenly I saw a parachute descending a few yards from me. It landed in the field near the burning plane. My son and two other men heard the German airman's groans. His ankle was severely injured...'

The remains of Hübner's Do 17. (via Watkins)

The last week or so of February 1941 was dominated by the three consecutive night attacks on Swansea, starting on the night of 19 February. It gives a clear illustration of what the *Luftwaffe* could achieve – no bombers were lost as a direct result of enemy action during these attacks, and yet again the RAF's night-fighters could do nothing to interfere; it was not until well into March that the next confirmed success occurred. The reports of the three attacks make sobering reading as to the chaos a coordinated series of attacks could cause:

What the wreckage used to look like: a Do 17 Z camouflaged for night operations over the UK.

19-20 February: This raid started at 2010hrs. About 101 HE and several hundreds of IBs dropped. The latter were all promptly dealt with. One HE fell in Swansea High Street Station and damaged two platforms. A large crater between Skewen Signal Box and Swansea Valley Junction blocked the main Great Western Railway line and traffic has been diverted. A large UXB caused the closing of the Swansea District line near Cwmfelin. Telephone communications in the town were seriously affected but no incident concerning other utility services has been reported. 69 UXBs are causing serious dislocation of traffic. The Swansea General Hospital was slightly damaged and serious casualties have had to be evacuated to other hospitals. There is a UXB inside HM Prison. Casualties are reported as 24 killed and 54 seriously injured.

20-21 February: The attack commenced at 2005hrs and continued until about 2345hrs. Loco sheds, timber yards, a warehouse at the Prince of Wales Dock and Cowrie Lodge PAC [sic] Institution were amongst the buildings set on fire. The most serious fire occurred in Mayhill residential district but all fires were quickly brought under control. Two wardens' posts and an Auxiliary Fire Service station at Manseltown received direct hits and at the latter 10 casualties among the personnel have been reported. As on the previous night, damage was mostly confined to residential areas. Casualties so far known at 30 killed, 82 seriously and 29 slightly injured, excluding the personnel already mentioned. Full reports are awaited but it is known that all rendered homeless have been accommodated and the general situation is well under control. Comparatively little damage was done to industrial and business property.

21-22 February: The attack was mainly incendiary and began at 2010hrs but 51 HE were also dropped. The area affected was the centre of the town. Owing to the breakage of water mains on the previous night there was an early failure of water pressure resulting in extensive fires involving the Market, the Hospital, the BBC, a large number of shops, an Auxiliary Fire Service station, three schools, churches and private houses. It was found possible, however, to run 100 pump lines from the Docks and although 200 working fires were at one time reported all except one were under control after 0500hrs. In all there were 131 incidents. Public services, including the main trunk sewer and water supply, were all affected and the Food Office destroyed. There are no reports of damage to industrial targets. The casualties known are approximately 25 killed and 40 seriously injured. About 30 roads in the town area are reported to be blocked.

The total casualties for the three raids are 200 dead, 254 seriously injured and 129 slightly injured.

It was Cardiff's turn five days later, but the *Luftwaffe* did not achieve as much as they had by attacking Swansea three nights in a row. However, the first night of March 1941 would be a different matter for the Welsh capital.

On 6 February Adolf Hitler, it his latest War Directive entitled 'Directions for Operations against the English War Economy', had summed up the Blitz and allied naval campaign so far by saying:

Contrary to our former view, the greatest effect of our operations against the English war economy has lain in the high losses of merchant shipping inflicted by our naval and air forces. This effect has been increased by the wrecking of port installations, the destruction of large quantities of supplies and by the diminished use of ships when they are compelled to sail in convoys.

The effect of direct air attacks against the English armament industry is difficult to estimate, but the destruction of many factories and the consequent disorganisation of the armament industry must lead to a considerable fall in production.

The least effect of all (as far as we can see) has been that upon the morale and the will to resist of the English people.

The attacks of February 1941 were proof of the German intention to concentrate on British maritime and associated targets, and targets related to the British aircraft industry and there was no talk of terror attacks or breaking the will or morale of the British people. Hitler's gaze was already looking elsewhere towards the Balkans. The weather in the first two months of 1941 had seen a diminishing of the ferocity of air attacks, but with the approach of spring and an improvement in the weather, the next two and a half months would see the Blitz reaching a crescendo before an unexpected change in *Luftwaffe* bomber tactics occurred.

Ju 88s from an unidentified unit setting forth as night falls.

3

The Storm before the Calm
March-11 May 1941

March 1941 began with Cardiff being singled out for the first three major attacks of the month, albeit the attacking forces were much smaller than previously. Weather and the unserviceability of some airfields could account for this, as well as the move away of some *Kampfgeschwader* in preparation for the German attack on the Balkans, which commenced the following month – affected units were I and III/*KG* 2, III/*KG* 3, *KG* 51 and II/*KG* 4. Furthermore, much of *KG* 27 was now involved mainly in anti-shipping operations, as noted in a British intelligence reported dated 27 February 1941:

> This unit, which has previously been almost entirely engaged in night bombing, has been identified during the past few days in intensive reconnaissance work in the Western Approaches and off the southern coast of Eire. It is thought that its future activities may now be directed against seaborne targets...

Hptm Walther Herbold's I/*KG* 1 moved to Brest, where it too participated in similar missions, being subordinated to the newly formed *Fliegerführer Atlantik*, itself being subordinated to *Luftflotte* 3. The following month it would be redesignated III/*KG* 40, *KG* 40 later being synonymous with anti-shipping operations. At the same time, the phasing out of the Dornier 17 from most front-line units continued and saw elements of II/*KG* 2 commencing conversion training to the new Dornier 217 E.

V4+AK of 2/KG 1 shows its shipping successes – this unit would later become 8/KG 40. This is thought to be the aircraft of Oblt *Karl Kahra, the Staffel Kapitän, who would be killed in an accident in April 1942.*

The first two attacks (1-2 March and 3-4 March 1941) passed with very light *Luftwaffe* losses – one for each night. However, on the night of 4-5 March three aircraft were lost. One from 8/*KG* 77 simply disappeared (a probable victim of *Flak*), but 1/*KG* 28 lost two – one to *Flak* and one to a fighter. The demise of the first I/*KG* 28 loss, which was commanded by the 35-year-old *Staffel Kapitän*, *Maj* Dr Roman Auernig, was witnessed by another pilot of the *Staffel*:

Leutnant Wilhelm Neumann, 1/KG 28

Maj Roman Auernig was a former Austrian officer who had graduated in military history at the academy in Wiener Neustadt. He was a very close friend of mine. He was killed over the Bristol Channel by *Flak* from ships [sic]. About 200 metres ahead of my aircraft, his mines under his aircraft were hit and the plane exploded. The explosion lifted my aircraft more than 100 metres. Dr Auernig had been a very kind well-bred gentlemanly officer with much Austrian charm. In the streets of Nantes afterwards I received condolences from many French people when they had heard my friend had been killed.

The other loss was commanded by another friend of Wilhelm Neumann, his former *Beobachter*, *Lt* Otto Von Hanffstengel. Again, they went missing during the attack on Cardiff and it would be a few more days before their fate was ascertained. Three bodies were picked up from the sea 5 miles south-east of Bere Head in Devon, and were identified as *Lt* Hanffstengel, *Uffz* Otto Hinrichs and an *Uffz* Kretzschmar (which is assumed to have been *Gefr* Hermann Kura, the *Bordmechaniker*). RAF intelligence quickly worked out from documents found on the bodies that their unit was 1/*KG* 28, and the link with its previous designation, 1/*KGr* 126. As to when the aircraft was lost:

LtzS *Hanffstengel and* Lt *Wilhelm Neumann.*

...a W/T signals table for the period from 0400hrs to midnight on 1.3.41 shows that the men were still alive on this date. The condition of the bodies rather suggests that their aircraft came down on a later date, possibly during the operation on 4.3.41 when another aircraft of the *Staffel* was lost off Barry...

That the aircraft came to crash in the sea is believed to be as a result of Sqn Ldr Mike Anderson and Sgt Gordon Thomas of 604 Sqn, whose combat report reads as follows:

...Left Wallop 2039 landed Wallop 2158. Instructed to wait near Swanage 12,000 feet, was then controlled by Sopley and put onto vector 330. This was changed to a vector of 270 degrees and then back to 330. Red 3 was then told to flash weapon and climb to 18,000 feet. No contact was obtained on weapon and he was vectored five degrees three times at 345 when contact was obtained on weapon. E/a was followed for about 10 minutes turning to port before being seen at about 500 yds range on the same level setting course well to the right of fires on ground and was considered to be a He 111. Red 3 got right under bandit seeing exhausts then opened fire when level at about 100 yds range, his guns firing erratically. Bandit went into steep left diving spiral and was followed down to 14,000 feet finally being lost when travelling too fast for contact to be maintained...

Again, the days that followed were quieter due to poor weather, but saw an increase in successful *Pirateinsätze*. For example, on 6 March *Oblt* Paul Hollinde of I/*KG* 27 attempted to bomb the Bristol Aircraft factory at Filton on the outskirts of Bristol – the attack was declared a success by the *Luftwaffe*, but in fact his bombs fell 2 miles from their intended target. The following day saw *Oblt* Hermann Lohmann of *Stab* II/*KG* 27 carry out his second attack on the Parnall Factory at Yate; his first attack on 27 February had resulted in the deaths of fifty-two workers, and this second attack resulted in the deaths of three more, as well as causing extensive damage. Meanwhile at Newark, Nottinghamshire, *Lt* Günther Rudolph of 1/*KG* 4 and *Oblt* Ulrich Knauth of 6/*KG* 4 carried out a devastating attack on the Ransome & Marles works, a factory making ball bearings. Thirty-six workers lost their lives and forty-two were injured. However, not all attacks that day were successful:

Reconnaissance photograph of the Bristol Factory, Filton (Target 7352).

Oberleutnant Erich Kunst, 2/Kampfgeschwader 3

Oblt Erich Kunst. (Kunst)

The Do 17 flown by Kunst in the Battle of Britain. (Kunst)

Our mission was to carry out a weather recce in the area roughly covered by East Anglia to report cloud cover, cloud base and height. This was to enable single crews to attack targets such as the ball bearing factory at Chelmsford, harbour installations and RAF stations.

We started at 0600hrs – it was still pitch-dark – low-lying clouds and miserable weather. As we penetrated the dark clouds, we could see behind us the dawn coming and later the sun rising. We navigated with two radio beacons, but nearing the British coast the cloud cover became 7/10ths and we descended to 1,000 metres just below the cloud base. We covered our area with no opposition from fighters and when we neared Norwich the cloud cover was complete again. I climbed into the clouds intending to head for home. I asked Ophoff [*Bordfunker*] for correct bearings and he told me that he could not get any signal at all. Even our home base navigation aid did not answer. When he could not get in touch with our HQ by radio, he found out we had not been issued with the latest alternative frequencies and code tables, which were to change at 0800hrs.

In order to get a landmark for the shortest way home, we had to go down and got a visual between Great Yarmouth and Lowestoft, but I also detected some military installations – a radio transmitter station and some gun positions on the coast. We always had for such missions our normal bomb load of twenty 50kg bombs with us and we released the first ten on the radio station. This was a near miss. The second row of ten went right through the gun position when the Bofors started to let fly.

We flew by that time parallel to the coast. I turned right to the sea and dropped to sea level to avoid direct sight for the gun-layers behind the cliff. About 2 miles off the coast it happened. A red glowing Bofors projectile hit us coming from above. The starboard engine stopped, flames and smoke all over the starboard wing. I stalled the aircraft, feathering the starboard propeller, and tried to get height but I had to level out at about 1,000 feet. The flames and smoke vanished but I could not get the aircraft on a straight course. It banked to port and I could not do anything to correct it. I think that the ailerons on the starboard wing were also damaged. I told the crew that we could not make it home, that I could not land the aircraft and that we had to bail out very quickly since we were losing height all the time. The last words from Wendland [*Beobachter*] were 'Didn't I tell you *Oberleutnant* – the missing mascot!' He had lost our mascot – a little porcelain pig which had flown with us for sixty-nine missions – Wendland was quite sensitive and had muttered his disapproval and had not talked much for most of the flight.

Oeckinghaus [*Bordschütze*] left the plane the moment I gave the order to bail out through the upper hatch. Wendland slipped away through the lower hatch where Ophoff and I also had to go. He was still working on the radio, giving a farewell message on the emergency frequency. He then jumped out and when I left the aircraft the altimeter was reading 700 feet. My descent was a very short one. Pulling the handle, feeling the jerk of the 'chute opening and

Uffz *Herbert Oeckinghaus and* Fw *Willi Ophoff*. (Kunst)

splashing into the sea, seemed to be a matter of seconds. When I jumped, I saw all three 'chutes opened and after recovering from the shock I saw the aircraft crashing into the sea with flames and smoke all around.

Ofw *Herbert Wendland, on the extreme right*. (Kunst)

A Bofors gun similar to the one that shot down Kunst's Do 17.

A little while later I heard some feeble shouts for help but I could not see far because of the waves and thought of Ophoff who was the nearest to me – the other two must have landed further away. I could not do anything before freeing myself from the mess of the harness, the cords and the 'chute itself. It took quite a while to untangle myself and I started swimming to the coast. I splashed in the sea about a mile from the coast. I could see soldiers gesticulating on top of a cliff but the beach was empty. The water was extremely cold and when I eventually reached land after hours (in my imagination – in reality perhaps three-quarters of an hour), I saw soldiers coming towards me before I collapsed.

I came to in a basement room on a stretcher – naked but covered with a blanket. One soldier was rubbing my feet, the other tried to fill my mouth with a bad-tasting spirit (whisky as I learned later – I had never tried it until then). When I had recovered from the shock, I was given underwear, socks, boots, shirt and uniform of a gunner and taken to the Officers' Mess to meet the unit commander. I asked him about the fate of my crew and he told me that I would meet two of them later – he could not tell me what happened to Ophoff. When I asked why nobody had come to rescue me while struggling on the beach, he told me the local Engineer unit had to be called since the beach had been mined. So I had been lucky...

The British side of Erich's demise is equally dramatic:

Aircraft was observed by eyewitnesses to approach coast at about 800 feet. Coming in from the east over Gorleston Pier, it was immediately engaged by light AA fire, which consisted of Bofors, Bren and Lewis guns in the grounds of the Cliff Hotel. A stream of tracers hit the body of the ac which then caught fire. It banked away to the south, slowly losing height and ditched in the sea half a mile from the shore opposite the wreck of the 'White Swan' off Links Road.

Aircraft burned on the surface for two to three minutes and then sank. Two crew were picked up by launch while the other two swam for shore. One man disappeared from view 100 yds out and is presumed to have drowned. The other reached the shore in an exhausted condition. He was captured by members of 514 (Coastal) Regiment, Royal Artillery...

From now on the weather began to improve, allowing the *Luftwaffe* to attack one night after another with a major attack and a number of minor attacks. Still, German losses were light, and even then not every loss was due to British gunfire, as one German bomber pilot relates:

He 111s of KG 26 (and opposite) in Norway in the spring of 1941.

Oberleutnant Rolf Alander, Stab/KG 26

On 11 March 1941 I took off from Christiansand in Norway in order to find and attack a large convoy running north from Edinburgh. In the evening twilight I found the convoy approximately offshore from Aberdeen. I attacked the first freighter in the right row. Coming out of the dark in the north at low level, we dropped our bombs while climbing ahead of the target. Unfortunately I hit the mast top with the tips of the propeller of the starboard engine and the elevator so I immediately had to cut this engine. The He 111 H-5 was not able to fly on a single engine for long so I gave the order to drop surplus equipment and headed for the Netherlands. The port engine then lost power and I hit the water in complete darkness. The *Beobachter* sitting besides me was thrown head over heels through the cockpit glass into the sea. The rest of us were able to abandon the aircraft into the dinghy, but we were not able to find our comrade in the darkness; he must have already been dead. An hour later we were picked up by a trawler and brought to Dundee. This was the end of my 50th mission...

Rolf Alander, in a photograph taken in 1936. (Alander)

British shipping under attack by German aircraft.

As the month progressed, the intensity of the attacks increased and at last RAF night-fighters started to make themselves felt. On the night of 12-13 March 1941 the target was Liverpool/Birkenhead. Post-attack analysis by the British gives an indication of the intensity of the attack:

At about 2100hrs, flares were reported from all over the Merseyside area and the fall of bombs quickly followed. During the raid, which continued till about 0300hrs, the main weight of the attack fell on the dock areas, where some serious fires were started.

The damage inflicted was widespread although not vital. Dockside machinery and handling equipment suffered fairly considerably, two ships and a large floating crane were sunk (but should not interfere with shipping), three ships were damaged and the port was closed. Fires broke out in warehouses, sheds, timber yards and offices. A number of installations in the area were also hit and there were several serious fires. Among the key points damaged are three flour mills (Spillers, Ranks and Pauls) and two oil installations (Anglo-American at Ellesmere Port and Vacuum Oil at Birkenhead, which was practically destroyed). Two key point factories were hit, namely Lever Brothers at Port Sunlight and the Automatic Telephone Company's works at Edge Lane, but damage was light in both cases.

A smoke screen tries to hide Liverpool from a Ju 88 of 3/123. (via Wakefield)

Utility services also suffered fairly severely especially in the Wallasey area. In this borough, gas, water and electricity supplies had all failed at one period; the Corporation's gas works, electricity power station and water pumping station were all hit as well as many mains and cables and in addition the water boosting pumps were put out of action through the failure of electricity. It was hoped to restore gas supplies after four days but no reports of restoration of other supplies have been received. There was damage to the utility services at the Athol Street Gas Works in Liverpool, numerous mains and cables were hit and the electricity supply failed in five areas. Water mains were damaged and in places water had to be carted.

The telephone system was dislocated by the breakage of wires and the necessity for evacuating the exchange, which controlled two circuits and the trunk services.

The Port Office wireless station at Seaforth was put out of action but was later reported to be working normally.

A number of hits were registered on the railway system of the area and working was disorganised. Services on the Wirral Railway (serving the docks on the left bank) were suspended. An electrified line also came to a standstill when the current failed.

The university, Cotton Exchange and St Anne's School were damaged and damage was also done to two police stations on Merseyside and one in Cheshire. Three hospitals and the School of Art were damaged in Birkenhead and the maternity hospital in Wallasey was also affected.

264 people are known to have been killed on this night in Birkenhead, 198 in Wallasey and 49 in Liverpool besides some 500 seriously injured.

That night saw a record number of RAF night-fighters airborne, which were assisted by an almost full moon and little cloud. Defiants of 151, 255, 264 and 307 Sqns claimed three destroyed, two probables and one damaged, while the AI-equipped Beaufighters of 604 Sqn claimed one destroyed, one probable and one damaged. AA claimed a further three destroyed, one probable and five damaged. German losses were five aircraft crashing on or close to the UK. A further Heinkel 111 of *Stab* III/*KG* 26 flown by *Oblt* Herbert Kaden was reported lost without trace (probably the aircraft shot down by Fg Off Terry Welsh and Sgt Lawrence Hayden of 264 Sqn into the sea south of Hastings), while another from III/*KG* 26 ditched off Cherbourg with three wounded crew. One flown by *Fw* Herbert Richter of *Stab*/*KG* 27 force-landed close to

This is believed to be Fw *Herbert Richter's He 111 of* Stab/KG 27 *off St Malo after the Liverpool attack of 12-13 March 1941.*

the shore at St Malo in northern France, with all four crew wounded due to a night-fighter attack. One of these last two Heinkels was probably a victim of Polish pilot Sgt Franciszek Jankowiak and his gunner Sgt Jerzy Karais from the recently formed 307 Sqn; it was the first successful combat for this new squadron and, although he only claimed a damaged, it would now appear that this claim should have been destroyed:

Sergeant Franciszek Jankowiak, B Flt, 307 Sqn

I received an order for patrolling the line George South at 14,000 feet. I took off at 2150hrs. It was a moonlit night and visibility was good.

Sgt Jankowiak of 307 Sqn.

After patrolling the line for 10 minutes, I noticed above [Point] Garn an enemy He 111 on the background of white cloud in a SE direction 3,000 feet below and 600 yards in front of me.

I warned my air gunner and dived to 150 feet below He 111 and 50 yards from his right side. The air gunner gave a burst of about 3 seconds. Simultaneously, the lower rear gunner of the enemy aircraft returned the fire by a short burst but failed to hit the Defiant. I saw the bullets of my air gunner entering the enemy aircraft fuselage. I consider that the He 111 was damaged...

Another Defiant pilot, Fg Off Desmond Hughes of 264 Sqn, was far more positive about his kill, showing how effective a Defiant's quadruple .303 machine guns were:

Des Hughes of 264 Sqn, seen here as a Wing Commander in 1944.

...The e/a was approached under the starboard wing and was identified as an He 111. E/a was engaged from about 50 yds from this position with a series of one second bursts. First burst started small fire in starboard engine whilst the next two bursts set the engine thoroughly on fire. At this juncture, the reflector sight went out. Carrying on with night tracer, Sgt Gash transferred his attention to the cabin and fired several more one second bursts and the de Wilde ammunition could be seen bursting inside the cabin which forthwith filled with flames. The bandit then fell off in a left-hand spiral dive and plunged to earth where the bomb load exploded...

The pilot on the receiving end of this devastating attack was the only survivor:

Stabsfeldwebel Karl Brüning, 5/KG 55

We flew over the English Coast at 5,000 metres. The weather was good, the visibility good, few clouds and moonlight, so ideal flying weather. It seemed a quiet flight – no *Flak* or searchlights. For me as a pilot there was a special reason to be alert, as on account of my experiences one could reckon on night-fighter attacks. I put my crew on the alert especially to watch the night sky.

Stfw Karl Brüning. (via Saunders)

The remains of Karl Brüning's He 111. (via Saunders)

Then things took their course. Without my comrades noticing anything, all hell was let loose.

Surprised by so many hits, the Heinkel caught fire. Both engines were hit – they stopped at once. The oil temperature shot up and speed fell. I lost height quickly. I had no means of defence as I was completely occupied with the plane. Through the intercom I heard screaming and groaning of both my comrades, *Bordfunker* Steiger and *Bordmechaniker* Weisse, who seemed to be badly wounded. My left hand on the throttle and my left ankle were both wounded – they were outside the safety of the armour plate. My back and set were protected by an 8mm armour plate. I felt only a slight blow – I had no pain. My *Beobachter* seemed to be unhurt. I saw no possibility of bringing the plane down – jumping by parachute was the only possible way of hanging on to life. I gave Düssel the order to crawl back, to lift up the escape hatch and, after preparing their parachutes, to throw both comrades out. Whether they were dead or wounded I could not ascertain – it was the only way of giving them a chance of life. The *Beobachter* came back and said he could not reach them as the walkway was already on fire. I gave the order 'Ready to jump!' – Düssel immediately jumped out through the side hatch. He must, as I later thought, have jumped without his parachute as everything happened so fast.

I trimmed the machine carefully in order to be able to jump out myself. I examined my parachute carefully as it was my only way of escape. Then I opened the sliding roof to be able to jump from my seat – then I realised that I would be jumping into the flames. I left my seat in order to jump from the side hatch. Then I saw the night-fighter 10-20 metres in front – he was in the process of making a left turn to pull away to the rear to make a new attack.

Fw *Konrad Steiger*. (via Saunders)

Fw *Alexander Düssel*. (via Saunders)

As I was afraid of hitting the tail, I wanted to jump in front of the plane but I could not overcome the air stream. I lost my strength and let go. I was thrown about turbulently – several seconds must have passed when I opened the parachute. It opened immediately, and with rushing and lurching movements I fell towards the earth.

Below me I saw my plane spiralling earthwards in flames. At about 2,000 metres I saw the impact, an explosion followed – petrol and bombs had gone up. My landing went smoothly – incidentally my first parachute jump...

Some of the remains of Brüning's He 111.

An He 111 of KG 55 *heads for England.* (via Wakefield)

Another loss that night was the Heinkel 111 commanded by the *Staffel Kapitän* of 6/*KG* 55, *Hptm* Wolfgang Berlin. A victim of a Hurricane flown by Sgt Robin McNair of the recently formed 96 Sqn, the bomber crashed at Widnes and three of its crew of five were taken prisoner. Berlin kept a diary of events immediately before and after his capture, which RAF intelligence managed to see. Although it contained 'little of intelligence value, … [it] is of some general interest…' Understandably, Berlin's account of the shooting down is very vivid:

> It was about 2330hrs and my faithful He 111, the G1+OP, had just dropped her bomb load on the target. I was about to close the bomb doors when all at once there was a terrific crashing and banging in the aircraft and I saw tracer bullets flying past the cockpit left and right. A night-fighter had got onto us – nothing to boast of considering that there was a brilliant full moon. The starboard engine packed up at once and the left followed suit as the night-fighter flew at us for the third time. We were losing height and the starboard engine began to smoke. So I gave the order, 'Jump for it!' But only the pilot, the W/T operator and I were able to do so; the mechanic and the rear gunner lay dead at their posts. We discovered later that the former had his spine shattered and the latter had a bullet through his head.
>
> We bailed out at about 3,000 feet and I seemed to myself to be hovering over England in complete immobility. I saw the light of the explosion when the Heinkel crashed, then I realised that I should be careful if I did not want to be left hanging in a high-tension cable. I curled up my legs and was over it and a moment later landed with a bump in a field. I stood alone in the moonlight, thanking heaven that I had once again been spared and thought of my wife who would be so long without news of me. Then a young boy approached circumspectly and directly afterwards two older men who took me along to a nearby farm, where the farmer's wife offered me tea, which I accepted. I ate a few biscuits with my tea and with the wrapping I burned some papers which I did not propose that the English should have. Soon the room was filled with Air Raid Wardens and Home Guardsmen who were anxious to gape at a German airman and to collect souvenirs. But I had nothing to give them. Meanwhile the Police arrived, having been summoned by telephone. After a short examination, I was handcuffed – to make sure that I should not escape – and was taken to the Police Station at Widnes by car…

The remains of Berlin's G1+OP at Widnes.   *Another view of the remains.* (Parry)

Hurricanes of 96 Sqn, one of which was responsible for shooting down the Widnes He 111.
(via Thomas)

Another loss that night was due to anti-aircraft fire, but where the aircraft crashed was a mystery until 1979. *Fw* Günther Unger of 9/*KG* 76 took off from Chateaudun carrying four 250kg and ten 50kg bombs destined for Birkenhead Docks. He flew up the Irish Sea, then turned east over Anglesey so as to approach the mouth of the Mersey from the north-west. Reaching the target without incident, he was forced to carry out four runs over the target, then dropped the bombs only to notice a glow coming from the cowling of the starboard engine, which was soon ablaze:

Feldwebel Günther Unger, 9/KG 76

...I banked over Ellesmere Port so as to head out to sea and to prevent the aircraft from falling into British hands and ordered the crew to bail out. My *Bordmechaniker* released the cockpit and was first to leave, making a safe landing somewhere in the Wirral. By the time the *Bordfunker* and *Beobachter* had made their exits, I realised that both engines were still functioning and the plane was flying well.

For a brief moment I thought of trying to fly home alone but then acknowledged this was a folly with such a fire and I too bailed out. I was then over the sea and landed on the mud flats somewhere between New Brighton and Hoylake, floundering in the shallow water for over an hour before finding a way ashore, totally exhausted.

Fw *Günther Unger*. (via Price)

I climbed the steps to the top of the sea wall to find the streets deserted. My main worry was that I might be beaten up if enraged civilians got hold of me. Finally, I found a very small man in an Army uniform with Home Guard written across his helmet and carrying a rifle. I went up to him and said in my best schoolboy English that I was a German airman and wished to be taken into custody, but he wasn't interested. He turned and started to move away from me! I followed him – he wasn't going to escape from capturing me so easily! I pursued him along the street until he came to a second Home Guard, who was prepared to take me into custody...

As to Unger's Junkers 88, it was assumed to have crashed in the Irish Sea or into the River Dee. However, at 2310hrs that night a Junkers 88 crashed into trees and houses at Wychbold in Worcestershire, narrowly missing the Bristol to Birmingham railway line. Although at the time RAF intelligence acknowledged that a Junkers 88 of 9/*KG* 76 had crashed near Droitwich, post-war research has proven beyond doubt that this was Unger's Junkers 88, which came as a great surprise to the German pilot:

This was incredible because, when I bailed out, my Ju 88 was flying on a course for the Irish Sea to the west. The autopilot was working and I cannot explain how this plane could turn back. It is possible that the fire in the port engine destroyed the autopilot and the plane then made a long curve to the left and crashed near Wychbold...

Despite the best efforts of the British defences, they had inflicted minimal losses on the German bombers. It was thought, however, that the defences had been instrumental in successfully defending Liverpool, despite the obvious devastation recorded by contemporary British sources.

For the remainder of the month the *Luftwaffe* continued its assault with major attacks on Glasgow, London, Hull and Plymouth. German losses still remained light, even if night-fighter claims began to creep up – nine destroyed, one probable and four damaged on the night of 13-14 March, three destroyed on the night of the 14th-15th, two destroyed on the night of the 15th-16th, and one damaged on the night of the 16th-17th. Still such claims (which should be added to the anti-aircraft claims) were overly optimistic. For example, during the 13-14 March attacks, the *Luftwaffe* suffered five lost over England, one ditched off Cherbourg (but its crew were rescued), and four returned with varying degrees of damage and crew casualties. The defences had still failed to thwart the attacks.

Stab/KG 2-Oblt *Erich Eitze (POW, 2 October 1940),* Oblt *Hans Georg Peters (killed on 22 June 1941),* Oblt *Hans-Jürgen von Keiser (killed on 13-14 March 41), unknown.*

Flt Lt Desmond Sheen 72 Sqn, who claimed a Ju 88 during the night of 13-14 March 1941.

Gen *Ritter von Griem shakes hands with* Lt *Egon Artz of 2/KG 51, who was shot down and taken POW on 16 March 1941.*

Respite came towards the last ten days of the month, when poor weather hampered night offensive and defensive operations. However, such weather favoured the *Pirateinsätze*. Three aircraft would be lost in such attacks. On 22 March *Oblt* Fritz Danzenberg's Heinkel 111 of 5/*KG* 4 was damaged by *Flak* attacking the bomber airfield at Leeming in North Yorkshire, only to then hit a balloon cable, which brought the bomber down near Hull. Four days later, *Lt* Otto Peper of 6/*KG* 76 attempted a low-level attack against Andover airfield in Hampshire, only to be shot down by light *Flak*, crashing away from the intended target. Just one bomber would be shot down by the RAF during March's *Pirateinsätze*:

Oberleutnant Werner Lode, 4/KG 77

In January 1941, when we were based at Beauvais, I was ordered to attack a factory near Oldham, which produced aircraft parts. I could take off only if I thought the weather would be the best for such an attack. There were only one or two of the best crews in each *Staffel* who had such orders – that meant they did not have a special order for each attack.

I tried it several times but each time the weather over France or England was not good. Mostly we had thick cloud over France and just before the coast of Britain it was clear and we had to turn back because of the very good RAF fighters, and in a fight between a bomber and a fighter, the fighter every time

The badge of KG 77.

will be the winner. Alternatively, the weather forecast predicted thick cloud over England so we would start in bright sunshine in France and the cloud over England only started inland from the coast. The fighters were waiting on the coastline, so we had to turn back.

On 23 March 1941, in the morning the weather in France was very bad – much rain and clouds from ground up to 6,000 feet. The forecasters said to me the same weather would be all over England. We later learned this was a mistake.

I hurried up my crew and we took off at 1000hrs local time. Until Coventry, the weather was very good – that means there was thick cloud and we hoped that the clouds would still be from 100 feet over the target.

Suddenly near Coventry the cloud cover was only some single clouds and we were a good target – we had reached the back of the depression, so we turned back. In the meantime, to the south, similar weather had developed...

At just after midday Red Section of 238 Sqn, Flt Lt Edward 'Teddy' Morris and Sgt Frantisek Bernard, had scrambled from Chilbolton in Hampshire to patrol their base. They described the weather as 'very cloudy, broken cloud 300-9,000 feet. Visibility – very good above cloud. Poor in low haze'. Nevertheless, this did not prevent them from being vectored onto Lode's bomber:

Sergeant Frantisek Bernard, Red 2, A Flt, 238 Sqn

…When over Alton, I saw an e/a which I identified as a Ju 88. Red 1 ordered line astern and he made two attacks as I could not risk attacking without hitting Red 1. My first attack was from astern and above at 300 yards closing and I fired a short 2-second burst. Before I attacked I saw that the starboard engine had stopped as a result of Red 1's attacks. After my attack I saw the port engine emitting smoke. I broke away and saw the e/a through the last layer of cloud at 1,000-500 feet. I circled around and did not see the e/a again…

Werner Lode continues the story:

…After the first attack, our starboard engine and all our blind flying instruments were out of action so I could only fly by instinct in the clouds… I tried to get in the clouds to escape the fighters but the stick was trembling and we were then dropping like a stone. Several times I levelled out but finally we were too low and I was looking for a good crash-landing place.

There were at this time all over southern England big iron poles with steel cables across as a protection against us landing troops. I crashed through three such poles but the fourth stopped the plane just near an AA post. The engines then burst into flames and we had to hurry to get out. At first we couldn't open the top of the cockpit but then it was opened and the *Beobachter, Bordfunker* and myself could jump out. The rear gunner (also called the *Bordmechaniker*) was lying behind the plane dead. I think that during the crash-landing he was sitting in the gondola. We threw our documents and guns into the flames. Then an old (for us he seemed old) AA man came, shouting 'Hands up!' We were so shocked, all we could say was 'Scheisse!'…

Werner Lode's Ju 88 blazing away.

April 1941 began as March 1941 had finished, with poor weather hampering nocturnal attacks but favouring daylight *Pirateinsätze*. April Fool's Day saw a particularly audacious attack on the Dorset airfield of Warmwell. Three Heinkel 111s from 9/*KG* 27 led by *Oblt* Karl-Otto Münz[3] struck just after midday, leaving six personnel killed, one missing and ten injured (one of those wounded was Battle of Britain veteran pilot Sgt Alan Harker DFM), as well as destroying a Vickers Wellington, two Fairey Battles, a Boulton Paul Defiant, two Miles Magisters, a Spitfire and a Czech Zlin aircraft. The Germans returned unscathed, claiming to have destroyed numerous buildings and twenty-four aircraft. However, daylight bomber losses were unusually high that day, with an 8/*KG* 1 Junkers 88 flying into a hill in Shropshire, three Heinkel 111s from I/*KG* 27 being lost on anti-shipping missions (two to fighters and one to engine failure) and a 5/*KG* 77 Junkers 88 being shot down by fighters.

The first concerted attack was on the night of 3 April 1941, when Avonmouth and Bristol were the targets, Avonmouth being singled out the following night. 604 Sqn was relatively successful those two nights, claiming two destroyed and two probably destroyed. *Luftwaffe* bomber losses were just one on the first night, one destroyed and two damaged the second night. Curiously, although II/*KG* 54 admitted to two Junkers 88s damaged by night-fighters, 604 Sqn only claimed to have encountered Heinkel 111s. Only Fg Off Ed Crew's kill, reported by him as '…hitting the ground on what appeared to be boggy land in the vicinity of Bristol…', can be positively confirmed, when *Ofw* Herbert Rose's Heinkel 111 from *Stab* III/*KG* 26 crashed at West Hewish, Weston-super-Mare, with Rose and two others being captured and two crew killed. It was a memorable combat for the RAF pilot, even when he wrote about it 42 years later and after a very successful RAF career:

[3] Surprisingly, Münz never received any decoration for this attack and was later reported missing over Russia on 19 July 1941.

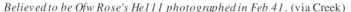

Believed to be Ofw Rose's He111 photographed in Feb 41. (via Creek)

Flying Officer Ed Crew, 604 Sqn

Ofw *Rose's He 111 after the encounter with Fg Off Crew*. (via Watkins)

I remember that particular He 111 as it was the first that Sgt Guthrie, my AI operator, and I got. We were flying R2252, according to my logbook. We were under Sopley GCI control at the time and we would have got AI contact at rather less than 15,000 feet since maximum range of AI Mk IV was height above ground or sea. The enemy aircraft did not take evasive action and I doubt whether he could have seen us as we approached in the normal way from behind and below. It was, I think, a starlit night without a moon, so we would not have got a visual very far away. I think we saw his exhausts first and then closed to get a faint silhouette against the sky. We fired a short burst of 20mm at about 100 yards and that was enough. It turned left and shortly afterwards passed me going in the opposite direction on fire.

The first major attack was against Greenock on the night of 7 April, which heralded the start of eighteen nights of major attacks the length and breadth of the United Kingdom. The post-attack analysis makes sombre reading:

Glasgow and Clydeside were subjected to a severe raid in which 50 [sic] enemy aircraft took part. The attacks started soon after 2200hrs. Bombs fell all over the city causing considerable damage. A heavy incendiary attack was made on Clydebank but, except at John Brown's Yard, the fires were quickly brought under control. Messrs Harland and Wolff's premises were damaged by HE at 0030hrs and at 0120hrs damage was caused at the shipyard of Charles Connell & Co, Scotstoun. Ship under construction was hit, one furnace was demolished and one damaged. Considerable damage was caused to the railways and at the LNER High Street Goods Station 60 wagons were badly damaged and a set of rails torn up. Five railway container vans and their contents were destroyed at College Street.

It is estimated that 4,000 people were rendered homeless and 16 rest centres were opened. Casualties amounted to 20 killed, 77 seriously and 236 slightly wounded.

RAF night-fighters were active, claiming five aircraft destroyed. In reality, two Heinkel 111s and a Junkers 88 were lost and can be positively attributed to RAF claims. However, one loss, a Heinkel 111 of 9/*KG* 26 flown by *Lt* Erwin Hartmann, was claimed by two pilots – Flt Lt John Cunningham of 604 Sqn and Flt Lt Derek Ward of 87 Sqn. Two nights before, Ward had unsuccessfully tried to intercept a dusk *Pirateinsätze* by three unidentified Junkers 88s against Exeter, where the bombers destroyed a Vickers Wellington, killing three and wounding a number. On this night, Ward was hoping to be more successful, but 87 Sqn's diary notes the reality:

> Many patrols without result from Charmy Down. Flt Lt Ward from Exeter was told there was a Hun near him and then saw a glow of light which he fired at. It went down in flames into the sea but apparently a Beaufighter had previously fired at it and the victory was credited to the Beaufighter.

The same night saw many targets being attacked across the United Kingdom. One attack was carried out by *Oblt* Erwin Moll and his crew from 3/*KG* 76; their mission was reported by War Reporter Harry Geim, whose post-attack report must have made exciting reading to the Germans:

> While strong forces of the *Luftwaffe* were attacking harbours and centres of the English armaments industry at night, other units had the task to attack English night-flying airfields. An example of special gallantry was the mission of *Oblt* Moll and his crew. They had been flying low-level over an English night-flying airfield for some time. With the aircraft's navigation lights switched on they got into landing English aircraft and carried out a brave low-level attack on some hangars. Five hangars received direct hits, two of them were completely destroyed by the resulting fires.

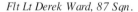

Flt Lt Derek Ward, 87 Sqn.

Well, we had already been worried about this crew, because they should have been back for half an hour. But finally they arrived. In the milky moonlight they flew a circuit of the aerodrome and then they landed. *Oblt* Moll, *Fw* Brähler, *Fw* Staude and *Fw* Franke climbed out of the Ju 88 and the first thing they did was stretching their stiff limbs, then they slipped off their flying suits.

Again this was a freezing cold night.

'I'll be damned!' called *Fw* Brähler, a Westphalian from Recklinghausen, who had gone round the plane in the meantime. 'Really, there are some hits in the fuselage and another one in the wing. But we did not notice that we had been shot at!'

And then they reported what had happened during their mission.

They crossed the English Channel and the coast at the ordered flying height. They had hoped that the cloud cover would break up over England but that was not the case, and so *Oblt* Moll, a blond Hanseatic from Lübeck, decided to go down through the clouds. It was not really safe to do this – over an enemy country, at night and with low clouds. When he was below the layer of clouds he noticed a searchlight somewhere in the darkness.

'Stop,' he thought, 'a searchlight means that there is something going on!' And he was right, because when he was flying direction searchlights he was able to make out very clearly three red lights which, from time to time, lighted up and disappeared again.

Very soon there were some more lights between the red ones, and at the same time there were more coloured lights darting around them in the sky.

Now the crew knew that they had found their target. Below them there was an English night-flying airfield, lights switched on. Three or four English aircraft, obviously night-fighters or bombers returning from a mission to Germany, were approaching the airfield. Their navigation lights could be seen very clearly.

What was there to think about? Without a moment's hesitation *Oblt* Moll switched on his 'festive lighting' so that those on the airfield would believe they were one of their planes. Then he got into line with the English aircraft and at low level he circled the airfield twice. While doing this the crew was able to have a close look at the airfield and remember every detail. It was a marvellous big airfield with five large, massive hangars and also some smaller buildings.

Indeed, it was not a very pleasant situation, because every moment the English could smell the rat, and then of course the Ju 88 would have been lost. Especially because they had some of the English aircraft on their tail, and with their navigation lights switched on they would be an easy target for the English guns.

But there was no other way to get to their target. So, *Oblt* Moll was flying two complete circuits together with the enemy planes until the English pilot flying in front of him approached the landing strip.

Oblt Moll told us about these exciting moments: 'I had this excellent chance to use my guns and shoot the landing English plane down. Or I could have dropped a bomb on his head or even on the runway. But as a consequence the lights would have been switched out and also it would have been very hard for me to find those five big hangars which were a much more important target for me.

So I did without this easy prey, circled around the airfield again and began the low-level bombing of the hangars. Because these were situated in a row at the edge of the airfield I was able to drop a well-aimed stick of bombs. At regular intervals the "eggs" tumbled down and all of them hit the target! Not one of them missed!

'Now I switched off the navigation lights very quickly, flew three more circuits of the airfield to have a close look at what had happened. One hangar was ablaze, a second one was also burning and had already collapsed. Fire-fighting teams were approaching from everywhere while the airfield was illuminated by the fire. Now I did not need the airfield lights any more which, by the way, had been switched off now.

'Then I noticed a single aircraft standing on the landing area. I turned round and we fired our machine guns at its big fuselage. But in the meantime it was high time to return back home.'

It was this brave crew's 31st mission to England, a crew that belongs to our specialists for difficult night missions and that has already taken part in the attacks on London, Birmingham, Liverpool, Sheffield and Bristol. However, this was one of their most gallant solo missions'.

Clearly propaganda, Andover airfield in Hampshire was a training base and targeted by a number of German bombers that night. On what was in fact his 41st mission, Moll reported attacking Andover just after midnight, but his notes are by no means as dramatic as the War Reporter's account. Nevertheless, RAF records confirm that Andover was attacked at 2245hrs resulting in the death of Plt Off John Cornelius-Wheeler and the wounding of two. Moll and his crew would fly just five more missions before they themselves were on the receiving end of an RAF night-fighter.

The following night, 8 April, saw *Oblt* Moll over England again, this time attacking a 'night-fighter airfield' – *Luftwaffe* records say it was near Norwich. However, the main focus of effort that night was the unfortunate city of Coventry. The British report reads as follows:

The attack started soon after 2200hrs with incendiary bombs on the south-eastern and central districts in which fires were started. Outbreaks occurred at Morris Bodies Ltd, Francis Barnett Ltd, Armstrong Siddeley Ltd and the Central Police Station, all of which were under control or extinguished by midnight when the activity abated. After a short interval the attack resumed with numerous high-explosive bombs and further incendiaries continuing intermittently until 0430hrs. Further fires were started amongst which was a fierce outbreak at the offices and foundry of the Daimler Company, and a tool room at Alvis Ltd was damaged by a high-explosive bomb. The Coventry and Warwickshire Hospital was hit and the King Henry VIII School and St Mary's Hall were damaged by fire. Water and gas mains suffered considerable damage and altogether some 110 incidents occurred. The casualties were 281 killed and 192 seriously injured.

The attack was particularly successful despite the best efforts of the defences. Defiants of 151 and 264 Sqns claimed six Heinkel 111s destroyed, one probably destroyed and one damaged; a Spitfire of 266 Sqn and a Hurricane of 310 Sqn on Cat's Eye patrols claimed a Heinkel 111 destroyed and a Junkers 88 probably destroyed, and radar-assisted Beaufighters of 604 Sqn claimed two Heinkel 111s damaged. The reality was four Heinkel 111s brought down over the United Kingdom, a Junkers 88 believed lost over the North Sea and a Junkers 88 crashed on its return to France due to the attentions of an RAF night-fighter – a clear case of over-optimistic claiming and, in a number of cases, duplicate claims.

The first combat came at 2155hrs and the result was clearly conclusive:

Squadron Leader Arthur Sanders, 264 Sqn

…When I had gained height and was over Beachy Head, Kenley Controller vectored me after an enemy aircraft that was flying inland at 16,000 feet. We had a very long chase after the e/a and when near or over the IAZ there was some pretty accurate AA fire. First burst boxed in our machine, so I requested that the guns were doused forthwith. We caught sight of the e/a at a range of 500 yards ahead and on the starboard side. I closed in to 350 yards and at this range my gunner, Plt Off Sutton, was able to put in a good 2-second burst into the fuselage of the ac behind the wing base. The De Wilde ammunition could be seen striking and bursting very clearly.

The e/a adopted no evasive action and as there was no return fire I was able to formate on it below and at a range of 50 yards. From this position Plt Off Sutton gave two more good bursts, the last from 200 yards. The e/a burst into flames and turned over and went straight down.

Neither my gunner nor I saw the enemy crew baling out…

Lt Julius Tengler of 9/*KG* 26 was on his 27th operational flight over the United Kingdom, his first having been as a second pilot attacking Portsmouth on the night of 5 December 1940. His *Flugbuch* reads as a perfect illustration of the length and breadth of the *Luftwaffe*'s Blitz offensive, with London, Sheffield, Liverpool, Manchester, Swansea, Southampton, Derby, Cardiff, Portsmouth, Birmingham, Bristol, Glasgow and Hull being the cities he visited. He had experienced a lot already, and his room mate, *Lt* Erwin Hartmann, with whom he had joined III/*KG* 26, had been lost the night before attacking Greenock, a victim of 604 and 87 Sqns. The British noted that the attack on Coventry came in two phases; Tengler was equipped with Y *Gerät*, which explains why he was at the vanguard of the attack:

Leutnant Julius Tengler, 9/KG 26

My crew this time had *Uffz* Zender as a trainee *Bordfunker* learning the Y *Gerät* with *Uffz* Faber. Y *Gerät* was the pathfinder device used by III/*KG* 26.

We started from Paris Le Bourget flying west-north-west over the Channel to pick up our Y beam from Cherbourg to Coventry. When on this beam the steering was automatic – I could leave my feet off the rudder pedals and all I needed to move the control column was my finger. The distance to the target was measured by a phase difference between the signal and electrical pulses from my plane. For calculation purposes, near to the target we should be on as steady a course, height and speed as possible. I think now we were a good target for night-fighters.

Maj *Viktor Von Lossberg*, Gr Kdr *of III*/KG 26, *taxies out*. *Note the single Y* Verfahren *mast behind his head.*

Von Lossberg at the controls of his He 111.

The Von Lossberg crew: Fw *Schuitzlein,* von *Lossberg,* Oblt *Rudi Mohrmann, and* Fw *Krause.*

Lt *Julius Tengler.* (Tengler)

Mark of the Lion: the badge of KG 26.

B3+IN of 5/KG 54 was shot down by a Defiant of 256 Sqn near Southport on the night of 7-8 April 1941. Günther Klemm and his Beobachter, Lt Heinrich Cöster survived, but two of the crew did not.

I remember it was a clear night and I could see in the moonlight the condensation trails from the planes ahead of me. Suddenly we were surprised by a burst of gunfire from behind (below or above, I don't know), which smashed the windows of the cockpit and wrecked one engine – I think in was the port one. Immediately after, the starboard engine caught fire. This proved deadly for Euerl [*Beobachter*] as he left the cockpit on this side. I opened the overhead escape hatch above me and tried to get out – this was the last thing I remember. The next thing I remembered was I was lying in a kind of ambulance together with (I think) Reitmeyer [*Bordmechaniker*]. He was wounded in the arm and I had shock. I was then in hospital for about twelve days.

Gefreiter Franz Reitmeyer, 9/KG 26

During the night-fighter's first approach I was shot through my left elbow and hand, and a leg was grazed by a bullet. One propeller did not turn any more and the other engine burned. I left the plane at about 13,000 feet, jumping through the gondola. Faber followed immediately after me – he had been shot through his leg. I saw Tengler slide against the tail unit and also Euerl, who went down with a burning parachute.

Gefr Franz Reitmeyer. (Reitmeyer)

Wolfgang Euerl, the only fatality.
(Reitmeyer)

Hubert Faber (fifth from right) and
Hans Zender (sixth from right), the
other two survivors from the
Tengler crew. (Reitmeyer)

The remains of the Tengler Heinkel…

The way Franz got out of the gondola seen from the inside (opposite) *and outside .* (via Wakefield)

...and what it looked like before its demise.

I made a smooth landing in a hedge. People approached from nearby farm premises. They were armed with farming tools but were friendly and a young, strong lad offered me a cigarette. Nothing could be seen of my crew. Some time later a jeep with WRAFs and soldiers arrived. After a short drive Tengler, Faber and I met again, though wounded. I did not see Zender again; he had only flown with us for training purposes. An ambulance took me to a military hospital where I was operated on immediately...

For Franz's family back in Germany, it would be a worrying time, especially when they received the following letter from Franz's *Staffel Kapitän*, *Hptm* Otto Stiller:

Dear Mr Reitmeyer!

Unfortunately I have to tell you that your son, *Gefr* Reitmeyer, did not return from a mission to England on 8 April 41.

Until today the *Staffel* has not been able to find out details about his whereabouts. However, there is still hope that your son is alive because reports about the fate of a crew always arrive very late.

As soon as any news will have come in about the whereabouts of your son you will be informed immediately.

As a member of *Leutnant* Tengler's crew your son has proved to be a fearless and brave soldier, having flown 26 missions. In recognition of his services he received the EK II an EK I, and he is proposed for the *Frontflugspange*.

The *Staffel* has lost a real airman and good comrade.

All the items which have been in the possession of your son over here will be forwarded to you via mail.

Hope to be able to inform you of good news very soon.

However, by the end of the month the news was more positive:

Dear Mr and Mrs Reitmayer

I am very happy to be able to tell you the most wonderful news of your life – your son, *Gefr* Franz Reitmayer, is alive. Today our headquarters has been informed that he is in British captivity. Unfortunately I cannot tell you more details, but I believe that you will be satisfied with the knowledge to meet him again safe and sound after the soon and final victory. The news received hitherto shows that German airmen in British captivity are treated well, and so there is no need to worry in this regard.

The aircraft probably had been shot down by a night-fighter north of London and the unwounded crew was able to escape by bailing out.

The *Staffel* and I, we all are glad of our comrades' fate.

Otto Stiller's prediction of a 'soon and final victory' would soon prove to be over-optimistic and he would be reported missing over Russia on 15 August 1941.

The *Luton News* reported the capture of one of the Tengler crew by 17-year-old Home Guardsman David Stedman:

…'I was going up the road alone when I saw a plane burst into flames when a fighter machine gunned it. It dived, crashed and continued to burn. I could see smoke and glow. I thought the plane could not be very far away so I decided to go that way on my bicycle. A man and a woman told me that a German parachutist had landed in a nearby park so I fixed my bayonet and went to see what was going on.'

David quickly found the German. He was lying on his back, practically unconscious, his parachute still attached to him. 'I told him he was all right,' said David, 'and he muttered something but I couldn't tell what it was.' Shortly afterwards David was joined by soldiers and an air raid warden and the airman was freed from his parachute with some difficulty. David and a soldier helped him to a car and he was driven away…

About three hours later the next victim fell at Wellesbourne in Warwickshire and was witnessed by a young man waiting to join the RAF:

At that time we lived a few miles away from Wasperton, south of Warwick. The night was quite clear and there was a steady stream of German aircraft… Much against my father's wishes, I watched much of this into the early hours of 9th April. Suddenly, just north of me there was a quite long burst of gunfire followed by a second burst shortly afterwards. The enemy aircraft burst into a ball of bright yellow flame and spiralled down to crash a few miles away…

This was a Heinkel 111 of 2/*KG* 27 crewed almost entirely by men whose surname was Müller. The body of *Oblt* Hans Müller (*Beobachter*) was found in the wreckage. *Ofw* Heinz Müller (*Flugzeugführer*), *Fw* Helmut Müller (*Bordmechaniker*) and *Fw* Georg Schäfer (*Bordfunker*) all bailed out and were captured. War Reporter *Sd Fhr* Wolf-Dieter Müller also bailed out, but it would appear that his parachute failed to open and his body was found during daylight. The cause of the crash was a Hurricane of 151 Sqn flown by rising night-fighter ace Plt Off Richard Stevens DFC, whose combat report matches what was seen from the ground:

An He 111 of 2/KG 27. The Müller aircraft was coded 1G+FK.

...Plt Off Stevens dived and closed to 75 yds making a quarter attack at 15,000 feet and hit belly of aircraft. A large explosion followed ... and the e/a dived. The port motor was alight and another burst into the centre section and fuselage caused flames to break out. The e/a was twisting and diving in a southerly direction and entered the cloud layer at about 5,000 feet. Plt Off Stevens followed and saw the e/a blazing ahead of him with bombs and incendiaries blowing up. It eventually crashed and exploded in a mass of flames...

Stevens's night did not end there, as about 20 minutes later he sighted another Heinkel 111. *Fw* Hans Kaufhold was on his 27th operational flight. He had been shot down and taken prisoner on 27 May 1940, only to be released following the French surrender. Because of his wounds, he did not recommence flying until after the Battle of Britain, and had then flown missions against Liverpool, London, Southampton, Glasgow, Bristol, Hull and Plymouth without incident. This night would be different, and he would have a remarkable story to tell:

Feldwebel Hans Kaufhold, 3/KG 55

It was a clear night and the moon was shining. When we reached Portsmouth at a height of about 4,000 metres, we were shot at by *Flak*. Then, just over Coventry, we were attacked by a Spitfire [sic]. The plane came out of the dark – the pilot must have seen us very well in the moonlight. He was in a good attacking position and during this attack the *Bordmechaniker* was wounded in the upper arm.

Fw *Hans Kaufhold.*

Kaufhold's He 111 before its demise…

....and after the crash.

After that, the Spitfire attacked from behind. Now it was my turn to shoot back. Everything happened so quickly, and at that time I was not able to communicate with the rest of the crew as the intercom connection had been broken.

The Spitfire attacked again from where he had attacked first but by that time we could not fight back. Our plane was burning and in the meantime the bombs had been dropped. The last thing I heard was someone saying 'Söllner! At 1,000 metres there are some clouds, so let's hide there!' Söllner was the pilot. After that, when I was watching the Spitfire, Herbert Link (the *Bordmechaniker*) indicated that we should bail out – the order had come from the *Kommandeur* (*Hptm* Otto Bodemeyer was the *Gruppen Kommandeur* of I/*KG* 55 and the *Beobachter*). However, I misunderstood him and in the meantime both in the cockpit had jumped by parachute, but we remained in the plane. Herbert had lost a lot of blood and was unconscious and we were still in the plane when it crashed. I cannot describe what happened next because I lost consciousness.

I think that when the plane hit the ground both of use were catapulted out. When I regained consciousness, I was lying in a meadow with my flying suit on fire. I jumped to my feet and put out the flames but my wrists, hands and face had been burned. I hurried to get away from the plane – the ammunition was exploding and later the fuel tanks exploded.

I followed a small path along to a road and heard footsteps approaching and I hid behind a bush. When I eventually reached a road I jumped into a ditch. I was in great pain from my burns and my lips had swollen. I heard shouting and dogs barking – soldiers were looking for us but they failed to find me. I sat as still as a rabbit in the ditch and the seekers passed me by.

Soon the Fire Brigade came but there was little that they could do. It became quieter and soon there was nobody around. I wondered what to do – the road was empty so I came out of the ditch and marched, or should I say limped, along the road. After a while a car came round a bend and stopped in front of me. An RAF officer stepped out and raised his revolver and shouted 'Hands up!', so I was captured for the second and last time during the war.

The following two nights would see the *Luftwaffe* target Birmingham and Coventry again. The importance of Birmingham was not missed by the Germans, the reason being articulated in a contemporary British report:

Birmingham has more key points than any other town outside London. It dominates the country's production of non-ferrous metal and machine tools and is very important in the finishing of steel goods and the manufacture of guns. There are three fairly noticeable concentrations of key points in the City and area:

1. In the south-east, the Acocks Green-Sparkbrook-Tyseley district

2. In the north-east, the Wilton-Nechells-Castle Bromwich district

3. In the north-west, the Smethwick-West Bromwich district

Birmingham had experienced forty-five attacks in 1940, most of them minor, but so far in 1941 had only been bombed twice, in January and March 1941. Of the two attacks, the one of 9-10 April was by far the worse:

At 2135hrs about 140 aircraft attacked the City. A large number of incendiary bombs were dropped on the north and eastern districts. The raid spread later over Aston, Stechford, Small Heath and King's Heath districts where high-explosive bombs caused considerable damage to factories and house property. The fires situation was aggravated by shortage of water; one major, 20 serious and 40 medium fires were still burning the following afternoon. Damage to mains was widespread and the electricity supply in the north-western part of North Bromwich failed. The key points affected were 25 factories including the Nechells Power Station and the Birmingham Corporation Gas Works. Other buildings damaged were five police stations, seven churches including the Cathedral, and four tram depots.

Despite the destruction, British defences had more luck this night, albeit that claims were over-optimistic with night-fighters claiming ten bombers destroyed, three probably destroyed and four damaged. Six bombers crashed on or near land while a further Heinkel 111 went missing; a number of aircraft returned damaged or with wounded or dead crew.

A well-known photograph of Sgts Thorn and Barker of 264 Sqn, taken the day after they shot down an He 111 of 5/KG 55 on 9-10 April 1941 – note the blacked-out Defiant behind. (Pelham)

The following night was similarly brutal both in the air and on the ground. Damage to Birmingham was less than the night before, the attack being described as developing 'slowly and was in no way comparable to that of the previous night'. However, Coventry reported suffering serious damage, with the Head Post Office being destroyed by fire and the telephone exchange, Council House, Police Court, two public shelters and a church being among the many buildings damaged. Sadly, 126 people also lost their lives. Night-fighters claimed eleven bombers destroyed, three probably destroyed and two damaged. This time claims were more realistic, with seven bombers crashing on or near land with a further four reported missing, one of which, a Heinkel 111 flown by *Lt* Caspar Graf von Krockow of 3/*KG* 55, ditched off the French coast at Trouville with the deaths of the pilot and two of his crew. Again, a number of aircraft returned damaged and with crews either dead or wounded.

Thorn and Barker's victim at Bushbridge in Surrey – only one of the crew survived. (Parry)

An unrecorded casualty from about this time was the He 111 of Maj *Von Lossberg of III/KG 26, which was damaged by* Flak *and its undercarriage collapsed on landing at Le Bourget.*

One of the successful night-fighter pilots was Fg Off Eric Barwell, flying a Defiant of 264 Sqn. In what would be his first combat of the night, the subsequent combat report relates what occurred:

> ...I was vectored after an e/a and, whilst at about 15,000 feet, saw the bandit 500 feet above me and about 1,000 yards ahead flying on the same course. I closed to 300 yards on the beam and slightly underneath and Sgt Martin opened fire...

Eric Barwell had been vectored onto a Heinkel 111 of the *Schulstaffel/KG* 26 flown by *Lt* Klaus Conrad. Equipped with Y *Gerät*, Conrad was at the vanguard of the attack on Birmingham, *KGr* 100 and III/*KG* 26 being the first units to attack; his aircraft was laden with eight 250kg bombs and incendiaries. He had flown in the region of 20-25 missions over the UK and this night, in addition to his normal crew, he was carrying a War Reporter, *Sd Fhr* Karl-August Richter, who was destined never to file his report of that mission, as Eric Barwell proves:

Fg Off Eric Barwell of 264 Sqn.

A Defiant of 264 Sqn, clearly showing the rear turret and its armament. (Pelham)

...He [Sgt Martin] got in about four good bursts of one or two seconds each whilst we were closing in from 300 to 50 yards and we both saw the de Wilde ammunition bursting in the fuselage and engines.

E/a took evasive action by putting his nose up and climbing so that even at 120mph when the Defiant was almost stalling, we were still overshooting.

As we passed underneath the enemy aircraft, it could clearly be distinguished as an He 111 and Sgt Martin had ceased fire as he had been blinded by the flashes of his ammunition. At this moment, the e/a suddenly dived away almost vertically into the cloud below and, although I followed him, I never saw him again... I now understand that the e/a crashed near the coast and that the crew bailed out, which neither I nor my gunner had observed...

Lt Klaus Conrad (right) after being awarded the EK II. (Conrad)

An He 111 flown by Klaus Conrad, but not thought to be the one he was flying on 10-11 April 1941. (Conrad)

After crossing the coast flying north-north-west and while in the vicinity of Redhill, the German crew reported being attacked from below and from the beam by a Defiant that hit both engines. They jettisoned their bombs (something witnessed by Eric Barwell, who reported seeing incendiaries hitting the ground between Redhill and Beachy Head) and, with the port engine seized, they crossed the coast heading for France only for the starboard engine to catch fire. Klaus Conrad therefore turned the aircraft back towards the British mainland and ordered his crew to bail out. The finale to this combat was witnessed by a member of the East Sussex Constabulary:

PC George Knott

> ...on the 10th April 1941 I was on duty at West Street Alfriston when I saw a German bomber aeroplane flying at about 700 feet in a southerly direction. The port engine of this plane was emitting sparks and flames and the plane appeared to be losing height. About a minute after the plane passed over me I saw a parachute leave it; this was immediately followed by two more. I at once went to the HQ of 261 Anti-Tank Battery stationed at Alfriston and drove them to the place on the Downs where I thought the parachutists had dropped. At 2200hrs three German airmen were arrested and after being searched for arms and documents were conveyed to Hailsham Police Station. The body of another airman was later found on the Downs in a very broken condition... The pilot of the aeroplane made a forced-landing at Seaford and was arrested by the military.

Klaus Conrad succeeded in force-landing on a golf course at Seaford, only for the Heinkel to hit aircraft defence wires and burst into flames. Unwounded, the German pilot succeeded in running away from the crash but was quickly captured.

Ofw *Hermann Platt, the only death among the Conrad crew.* (via Burgess)

The burnt-out remains of Conrad's He 111. (Saunders)

The following night it was the turn of Bristol and Avonmouth, which resulted in random destruction, including the St Phillips Bridge and Municipal Library, and 141 deaths. Night-fighters were active, claiming three destroyed, three probably destroyed and two damaged. Only one German bomber, from 9/*KG* 27, crashed on land, shot down by a Defiant of 307 Sqn, and probably also by a Beaufighter of 604 Sqn, as the times and locations match. A Heinkel 111 of 8/*KG* 55 crashed in the Channel on its return with the loss of its crew, and another Heinkel 111 from *Stab* III/*KG* 26 was abandoned by its crew over France on the return flight. A Junkers 88 of 5/*KG* 54 was also reported missing, possibly shot down by Fg Off Roderick Chisholm of 604 Sqn off Portsmouth.

A Ju 88 A of KG 54.

Loading 250kg bombs into night-camouflaged Ju 88s.

The two nights that followed were relatively quiet, albeit for one crew the relatively quiet would be deceptive:

Leutnant Lothar Horras, 3/KG 28

Take-off was planned for 13 Apr 1941 at 2300hrs. The *Kommandeur, Maj* Holm Schellmann, would start at 2230hrs and I would then go at 2300hrs. Target was the aircraft carrier *Victorious*, which at that time was in the Vickers Armstrong docks at Barrow in Furness. This was the second time I had been tasked to attack this target – the first time didn't come off due to bad weather. Our job was to attack the carrier at low level with one PC 1400 and one PC 1000 hung externally. Due to the long flight and short runway at Nantes, the take-off could only be possible with the assistance of a rocket-assisted take-off.

Lt *Lothar Horras at the controls of his He 111. To the left is* Gefr *Josef Brüninghausen.* (Horras)

The route was Nantes-St Malo-Scillies-south coast of Ireland-east coast of Ireland-northern point of the Isle of Man-Solway Firth, then low level to the *Victorious*. My usual aircraft was coded 'CL', but the one I flew was 'EL', a loaded spare in case one of us had problems starting. Since my starter failed, I changed to 'EL'.

The flight for the first attack went perfectly except that the *Kommandeur* radioed that the weather over the target was perfect, which meant that despite my flight deviations, I was well received over the target!

In the meantime, the weather was no longer so good – a rainstorm over the target – and during my first attack at 50 metres I was heartily greeted by light *Flak*, which shot quite well but didn't hit me. I turned and repeated the attack after 10 minutes. Visibility was better but the approach was not good enough and, without dropping my bombs, I flew past the target and turned for a new attack. On the third attempt the plane was hit for the first time, and just before I dropped the bombs part of the instrument panel flew past my ears. By means of a very slight change of course, the bombs were dropped amidships on the pier – at least that is how it looked to us as 12 seconds later the bombs exploded. A fire broke out – I don't know exactly what it was, probably stores on the pier.

Since I did not know if any damage had been done to my engines, I flew directly west...

Gefreiter Kurt Schlender, 3/KG 28

…One of my transmitters had been hit. Fortunately it was in a steel frame and some form of missile got caught in it. The main compass was out but we had otherwise escaped unscathed. Over the sea, we debated what we should do. If we returned overland, fighters would get us, so we decided to reach France by keeping well clear of the coast despite not having enough fuel. That was the lesser risk.

We were trying to gain height but since the main compass was out of action and we were navigating with the auxiliary compass, we were not making for the open sea but Anglesey and the Welsh mountains.

All was quiet on board. I had an altimeter and had noticed that we had reached 1,000 metres. My finger had been injured and I said to the *Bordmechaniker*, 'Can you put a bandage on that?' He came up from the floor, put the bandage on and went back down. Just then we heard from the cockpit, 'Did you notice anything just now? What was it?' Well, yes, something had whizzed past – it must have been the first mountain peak we had just skimmed.

We were flying in the clouds – visibility zero. Next thing there was a bang, fire and deadly silence…

Lothar Horras continues the story:

…I just missed the first peak and then hit the second. Since the *Beobachter* and myself were not strapped in, we flew straight through the cockpit, and when I came to I was right in front of a huge fire. My *Beobachter* had found me and dragged me out from under part of the engine – most of my injuries came from the engine. When the fire burned down, we found the body of my *Bordmechaniker*. We couldn't find the *Bordfunker* but he soon turned up…

Being the least injured, effecting a rescue was left to Kurt Schlender:

…I thought I was the only survivor and towards dawn, when the fire had subsided, I went to the far end of the crash site and there the pilot and *Beobachter* were sitting… The pilot had all but lost two fingers – they were just dangling from a tendon. There wasn't a lot of bleeding so I advised them to be cut off and put a bandage on. We all three debated and decided there was no other way. Then we debated what was to be done. We realised that we were high up in the mountains above the clouds and in all probability the crash had not been noticed. I suggested that I go down and try to get help – the others didn't really want to be left alone, but I said it had to be done or we would all starve to death…

By an incredible stroke of luck, I found the right way down. After a while I saw a small river bed and a house with smoke rising from the chimney. It was light by now so I waded through the river and after throwing away my gun in order not to appear too aggressive, I knocked at the door.

The door was opened by an elderly lady whom I told in very broken English that I was a German airman. She called her husband and they offered me a cup of tea. The husband stayed with me while his wife went to a neighbour who presumably had a telephone in order to call the military authorities. It didn't take long and a policeman came in. Some time later the door was opened again. First I saw a rifle with a bayonet being push through the opened crack of the door, then there was a head wearing a tin helmet – a Tommy! He looked around, gave me a friendly smile and said, 'Where is the German?' He looked again, realised it was me, placed the rifle in the corner, came up to me and said, 'Shake hands!'…

Two nights later, the *Luftwaffe* carried out a series of major and minor attacks the length and breadth of the United Kingdom, the main attack being against Belfast. This was the first operational flight that *Gefr* Josef Schmauz of 6/*KG* 53, who wrote the Foreword to this book, flew in a flying career that saw him being shot down by fighters once and *Flak* twice, finally ending when he was shot down a second time and badly wounded by an American fighter on 28 August 1944. The effectiveness of the Belfast attack was marred by cloud over Northern Ireland, which resulted in numerous secondary and diversionary targets being attacked. *Flak* claimed to have destroyed three bombers and damaged three others, while fighters claimed to have destroyed six and damaged one. Despite the effort expended by the *Luftwaffe*, losses were light – the *Staffel Kapitän* of 3/*KG* 53, *Hptm* Werner Höring, and his crew were taken prisoner when their bomber suffered engine failure over Yorkshire en route to Belfast, and *KG* 55 lost two aircraft, one crashing in Southampton, the other in the Channel. The final loss was a Junkers 88 from II/*KG* 54, shot down by Brazilian-born Flt Lt Cosme Gomm of 604 Sqn, whose aircraft recognition was slightly awry:

Officers from 604 Sqn outside the Officers' Mess at Middle Wallop – Cosme Gomm is on the right of the group standing at the back. Other officers identified are Sqn Ldr Piers Kelly, CO of 93 Sqn (sitting, third from left), Ed Crew (sitting fourth from left), and Hugh Speke (sitting, second from right).

...contact 10,000 feet well above to port. Climbed steeply and overtaking. At time of visual, e/a was 1,500 feet above but on converging course. Pilot saw one exhaust. Turned to port still climbing. Got to a little below and behind, saw four exhausts about 100 yards away. Saw outline of wings and recognised as He 111 by shape at wing root and dihedral... Fired – first rounds went below. Pulled nose up a little and immediately an explosion. Pilot pulled up as stuff hit windscreen. Saw e/a going straight down till it hit the ground at 2245hrs.

At exactly the same time, *Uffz* Albert Barth's Junkers 88 disintegrated and hit the ground at Holcombe Burnell in Devon, witnessed by an unnamed Special Constable:

I was about to retire when I heard machine gun fire and went outside and saw a glow in the sky. It got larger and larger until I thought it would hit the house. Finally the aircraft nose-dived into a hedge and went into the field a few hundred yards from me. Parts of the machine caught fire as they hit the ground with machine gun bullets bursting everywhere...

This night also saw another audacious attack on an airfield by five Heinkel 111s of III/*KG* 27. Briefed to attack the airfield at Braunton (the nearest town to Chivenor), between 0402 and 0428hrs German time, they dropped five SC 250, fifty-two SD 50 and 1,152 incendiary bombs. Their attack matches perfectly with the report filed by the CO of No. 3 (Coastal) Operational Training Unit:

It was a fine moonlit night, cloud level being about 2,000 feet. The red warning was received at 2258hrs but it was not until 0300hrs that the attack on the aerodrome developed.

One machine approaching from NW dropped stick of four large bombs to SE and just off the aerodrome.

The second machine attacked 15 minutes later along centre of aerodrome from south dropping sticks of HE along NE runway followed by a further machine from north direction which dropped a stick of HE straddling east to west of runway with seven bombs.

A further machine approaching from north to west dropped large number of incendiaries. Commencing 250 yards west of Control Tower, hangars, buildings and adjoining village of Chivenor.

The attack was believed to have been carried out by four separate machines, one at least and possibly three He 111s...

In addition to damage to the airfield, which rendered it unserviceable for a few days, three Bristol Beauforts, ten Avro Ansons, five Bristol Blenheims and a single Fairey Battle suffered varying degrees of damage.

The following night saw London being the focus for two waves of attacks in what would prove to be the heaviest attack of the war so far. By now, the mood of those on the receiving end was starting to turn ugly. It was this night and during the first attack that *Oblt* Erwin Moll's luck finally ran out, albeit not completely:

Oberleutnant Erwin Moll, 3/KG 76

Oblt *Erwin Moll (second from left) with his original crew, none of whom survived the Battle of France: Hans Fortmüller (killed on 1 June 1940), Heinrich Lang and August Flaig (both killed on 25 May 1940).* (Moll)

An all-out offensive against London was planned for 16 April 1941. So there were no nuisance sorties and together with our *Gruppe* we flew direction London. When I took off with my Junkers 88 to attack dockyards in the curve of the River Thames, it was relatively early because I had planned to fly two missions that night. When I crossed the English coast there was still a narrow band of light on the westerly horizon. Heavy *Flak* could be observed in the south of London. So I decided to fly round London in the west and to attack my target coming from the north. I was flying over the south-west of London when the *Bordfunker* and *Bordmechaniker*, who were observing the sky behind us, reported a night-fighter below left and climbing. They had been able to see it because the enemy aircraft was lit up by a searchlight. If it had climbed higher the pilot could have recognised our plane by the light of the horizon. So I immediately changed the course and approached the target directly, flying through the *Flak* barrage. Then we were also illuminated by searchlights. By changing course and airscrew pitch we quickly left the cone of light but now had to fear that the night-fighter had seen us. It was probable that the *Flak* had not recognised us because the underside of our planes had been painted black. I flew a 180° downturn but as soon as I had finished this manoeuvre there were two explosions in the area of the right wing. I suppose that we had been hit accidentally by two shells of a *Flak* salvo. When my *Bordmechaniker* called 'Starboard engine burning!', I switched it off. His next call was, 'Away with the bombs, they are burning!' So I pushed the button and dropped the bombs. After that I had some time to have a look at the wing and noticed that a large part of it was burning, but not the engine itself. In order to get as far away as possible from London I opened the throttle again. However, I was not able to read the instruments because of the flickering light of the flames.

After a few minutes I noticed a slow reaction of the aileron and concluded that the fire had damaged the control rods. So the heat possibly could have damaged the main spar, too, and this would cause the wing to break off soon. That is why I ordered the crew to bail out. The *Beobachter* and *Bordfunker* left the aircraft using the upper hatch, the *Bordmechaniker* bailed out through the hinged hatch in the ventral gondola. After my crew had left the plane I opened my seatbelt and climbed into the back of the canopy. Without thinking twice I decided to leave the plane through the gondola, more difficult but safer. With a short look back I said goodbye to my aircraft, drew up my legs and fell.

After going head over heels a few times, I pulled the ripcord. At first I thought I had damaged it and the parachute would not open. With a swearword on my lips I threw away the ripcord. Well, this was my first parachute jump. But after a few moments, to my relief I felt how the parachute was pulled out and opened up with a jerk so that I lost my flying boots. For a moment it was quiet but then the sounds of this nocturnal air battle could be heard. The most prominent noise was the roar of aeroplane engines, and I think this was my own Ju 88. When I looked down I noticed some fires below me, but these could have been caused by my bombs. The parachute began to rotate and when I looked up I saw the reason. The left strap of the harness had been cut, perhaps by a piece of shrapnel, so there was only one left. As I was at about 10,000 feet my hands got cold and I put them into the pockets of my flying suit and waited. Later I saw terraced houses, gardens and something that looked like a wood. When I was about 330 feet high I pulled my hands out of the pockets. A short time

The remains of Moll's Ju 88 in a Wimbledon back garden. (Parry)

later I fell past the wall of a house and landed on a concrete surface behind this house, next to a corrugated iron wall and a metal barrel. Because I did not have my boots any more the impact was quite hard and I just wanted to lie there. But then I heard voices coming nearer and I stood up. Three men appeared and one of them, who was wearing a helmet, asked me, 'What do you want?'

I answered, 'I must be led to the next military station.'

'Are you hurt?'

'I don't know – it hurts under my left foot. May I have a light?'

'We have to go inside the house for that.'

In front of the door there was a group of people. My escort stopped and the spokesman asked me, 'Are you German or Czech?'

'I'm German.'

'That's what I thought.'

Then someone pulled my hair from behind but immediately let go when everyone angrily called, 'Who was that?'

A woman standing in front of me stroked my hand to cheer me up and someone else offered me a cup of tea. I was really grateful for this friendly gesture. I gave my pistol to a Canadian soldier who had entered the room a short time after me. Here I found out that my foot was not hurt, just bruised. The people told me they were not afraid of the bombs. They were friendly and we had a chat until a police car arrived, which took me to the police station...

Two more crew members would survive, one being the *Bordmechaniker.*

Feldwebel Ewald Franke, 3/KG 76

We were one of the first aircraft to take off, as we were supposed to be flying two missions that night. Because of this, it was still fairly light. Shortly before we arrived over London I saw this British fighter that was flying a bit under and behind us. I told the pilot about it so he changed course 20 or 30 degrees. If I had been the pilot, I would have changed the course at least 180 degrees and the fighter wouldn't have found us so quickly again! It wasn't like that – we got shot down!

The incendiary bombs caught fire and both engines were hit so we were told to bail out. I landed on a big gas tank. I was captured and brought to a police station – people spat at me. I was then told that Otto Staude had been killed – I was very shocked as he was a very good friend of mine.

The aircraft that stalked then shot down Erwin Moll's bomber was crewed by Flt Lt Tony 'Dot' Dottridge and Sgt Trevor Williams of 219 Sqn. It was their first confirmed kill:

…Flintlock then gave him a vector of 190 degrees followed by a vector of 220 degrees and told he had a Bandit for him. Pilot was then told to vector 340 degrees and flash weapon which he did and AI operator obtained a blip. Flintlock then told pilot he was about 2 miles astern of Bandit and to increase speed by AI operator. Pilot closed to minimum range and saw the e/a who had a small white light on his tail. Pilot closed to 150 yards astern to try and recognise the e/a but failed to do so, being dazzled by the white light.

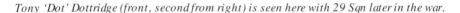

Tony 'Dot' Dottridge (front, second from right) is seen here with 29 Sqn later in the war.

By this time e/a was approaching a cone of searchlight and AA fire, our pilot following astern about 200 yards away, ASI at 180mph. E/a turned slightly to port to avoid searchlight and AA fire and proceeded around this concentration in a clockwise direction. Our pilot then challenged the e/a with front recognition lights and navigation lights but was not answered. He opened fire at a range of 150 yards, closing to 100 yards astern and delivered a 6-second burst. Cannon shells were seen to burst on the fuselage and starboard engine and starboard petrol tanks caught fire which, in about 10 seconds, enveloped the fuselage and the e/a lost height rapidly and finally dived vertically towards the ground, which it hit, exploded and a large fire started which lasted for several minutes.

There is no doubt as to the identity of their victim – the RAF crew broke off combat near Wimbledon, which was precisely where Erwin Moll's bomber crashed.

A further five German bombers would be lost during the second attack early the next morning – two to fighters and the remainder to *Flak*. Both night-fighter kills went to the Commanding Officer of 219 Sqn, Wg Cdr Thomas Pike, who would later become Marshal of the Royal Air Force Sir Thomas Pike KCB CBE DFC. However, he was not flying with his normal AI operator:

219 Sqn, 1941. Wg Cdr Pike is sitting ninth from the left. Pike's usual AI operator is Sgt Bunny Austin (sitting, extreme right). Flt Lt 'Dot' Dottridge is sitting seventh from right – his AI operator, Sgt Trevor Williams, is on the extreme right of the back row. (Williams)

Sergeant Terry Clark, 219 Sqn

Terry Clark, seen later in the war. (Clark)

I recall that evening quite well. I was in the Sergeants' Mess (late afternoon) when the telephone rang. The message wasn't to report to B Flight – you are flying with the CO tonight (his own navigator had gone sick). Panic set in! I would have rather stayed in the Mess and had a few pints. However, full marks to the CO – he was a first-class pilot (we navigators are choosy, you know!) and he put me at ease right away. Little did I know that I would be flying with a man destined to be Marshal of the RAF. I met him several times while he held that dizzy rank and he had not changed one bit – still a kind, charming man.

The following day after that interesting flight I returned to my Flight and apologised to my regular pilot, Fg Off Dudley Hobbis, for having bagged two (I felt that I had let him down as we had no luck). However, 27th April and 14th June 1941 saw two enemy aircraft destroyed. I felt I had redeemed myself with my pilot!

Their first kill was a Junkers 88 of 4/*KG* 1 commanded by the *Staffel Kapitän*, *Oblt* Erich Schlecht, which plunged vertically into the ground at Cranleigh in Surrey, killing all of its crew. Just under an hour later, and on the verge of returning to his base at Tangmere, something caught the British pilot's eye:

Wing Commander Thomas Pike, 219 Sqn

I then returned to Tangmere control and, while on a homing vector, saw two or three bombs drop quite nearby. I turned onto the line of bombs and flashed weapon. AI contact was obtained almost immediately at about 1,500 yards range. Tangmere was asked if there were any friendly aircraft nearby and the only likely one was ordered to turn and dive away. AI contact was maintained for a short chase of about 5 minutes, during which time the enemy appeared to take evasive action but not violently. By this time the moon had risen and, when about minimum range, enemy silhouette was seen. Two exhaust flames (one under each wing) were then seen and range was closed to 250-300 yards. A 4-second burst was given at this range and enemy exploded in the air. Burning fragments blew back and hit the

Beaufighter and two parachutes were seen to leave by the AI operator. The burning wreckage was watched while it fell and finally struck the ground.

One of the two parachutes belonged to *Uffz* Thomas Hammerl of 3/*KG* 28. He had joined his *Geschwader*, then designated *KGr* 126, at Marl in Germany on 12 August 1940, but did not fly his first operational flight until 2 October. Being part of IX *Fliegerkorps*, most of his missions had been dropping *Luftminen*, predominantly against coastal targets but latterly, like this mission, against land targets:

Unteroffizier Thomas Hammerl, 3/KG 28

Thomas Hammerl (right). (Hammerl)

Briefing normally took place about 2 hours before take-off. We prepared our maps, planned courses and made a note of frequencies and D/F beacons. Meanwhile the mechanics checked the aircraft and warmed up the engines. Bombs or parachute mine were already on board. The planes took off at 1-minute intervals. I do not know if we took off with the help of rocket pods or not. Our target was the India Docks east of London. My aircraft was the last one and we took off at 0105hrs direction D/F beacon Malo. We climbed until we were at 13,440 feet over the Channel. The mines were activated when we saw the English coast. It was a starlit night, the ideal condition for night-fighters.

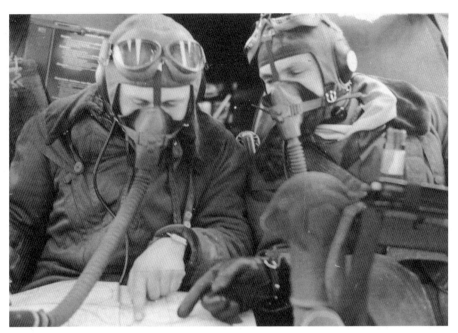

Gefr *Wolfgang Schüler (left, killed on 17 April 1941) and* Uffz *Thomas Hammerl*. (Hammerl)

Ofw Engel, the navigator and bomb aimer, was lying at the front in the glazed canopy when suddenly a *Flak* shell exploded, up and in front of us. The shrapnel rattled against our plane but caused no damage. But some minutes later there was a big bang – a night-fighter had attacked, unnoticed by us. The right engine jammed and had come off its bearers. The right wing and fuel tank had been torn open and were on fire. The cockpit was in flames, too. There was no chance to carry on, so we had to bail out. The navigator hurried back to his seat, folded it back and fastened his lap strap parachute. He opened the window and disappeared! In the meantime I tried to trim the aircraft and also called the *Bordfunker* and the *Bordmechaniker*, but did not get any answer. I do not know what had happened in the back of the plane. Because of the fire I was already slightly burned and finally was forced to bail out too. Moreover, the flare-pistol cartridges had also caught fire. In a Heinkel 111 one could lift the pilot's seat hydraulically, so I pulled the lever and there I was, opened the sliding hatch in the roof and left the plane. Seconds later I pulled the ripcord and floated into captivity. The parachute landed under a tree. When I unfastened the harness I noticed that I could not see anything with my right eye and the eyesight on the left was also limited. I was taken to a first aid post by a friendly Englishman and his son. My burns on hands and face were first treated at Guildford Hospital. From there I was taken to Royal Herbert Hospital in London, Woolwich – the treatment there was very good. *Fw* Engel had landed in front of a house and instantly got a cup of tea. Unfortunately, the *Bordmechaniker* and the *Bordfunker* did not survive the attack.

Three more bombers were lost to *Flak*. There were no survivors from the Junkers 88 flown by *Uffz* Horst Prätorius of 3/*KG* 77, while *Fw* Heinrich Brück and his crew from 3/*KG* 77 simply disappeared. However, all crew members survived from the final *Flak* victim, despite bailing out over a burning London:

Leutnant Günther Sissimato, 8/KG 77

The operations on 16 April 1941 were an attack on London in retaliation for an attack on civilian dwellings in Berlin.

Twice before I had bombed London – a granary and docks on the Thames. This night I flew at 4,500 metres (the ordered height), the second at a height of 3,200 metres. There were two reasons for this. On the first attack, *Flak* exploded at 3,500-4,000 metres so I concluded above this the night-fighters lay in wait. I felt that night-fighters were the greater danger. The second was I wanted to get back on the ground quicker as I was going on leave with my parents in Berlin.

After the first flight I saved time by not taking on more fuel. I only loaded new bombs and changed *Bordfunker* – *Fw* Gerd Wähler didn't feel well and as I could locate London and Juvincourt without the need for radio (burning London could be seen from Amiens and it was a clear night), I took *Gefr* Schuhmann for what would be his only operational flight of the war. Gerd remained behind. Just like the four left from the original eighteen crews at the start of the Battle of Britain, Gerd didn't survive the war.[4]

As much as the RAF would like to hear, I was not shot down by a night-fighter, it was *Flak* that got me. After dropping the bombs, I kept the speed, direction and height constant so my crew could observe the detonations. At this time I must have been located and hit. The plane immediately became like a torch and I ordered the crew to bail out. I myself was in a dilemma. Should I stay or abandon my 'BS' to its fate? My plane wasn't just a machine but had been a faithful friend. I would have rather stayed but felt it would be cowardly to flee my fate on the ground, having told my crew to bail out. I therefore said goodbye to my true 'BS', gave full power to both engines and bailed out. I heard 'BS' flying off and felt very lonely.

Overhead I heard the engines of planes, under me the *Flak* and detonation of bombs. I was blinded by the flashes and flares of ghostly fires shooting high from houses. For a few houses I could see their windows illuminated by the fires. The nearer I approached to the ground, the more infernal it became. I now felt the heat and felt the choking smoke, which made ghost-like clouds. As I was wearing a life jacket, I hoped I would fall in the Thames.

The rising hot air took me just over the Thames to where it was dark, and when I judged I was over land I made a three-point landing (legs-bottom-back of the head). A reception committee slowly approached carrying torches and guns. I was still numb from the knock on the back of my head and as dizzy as a groggy boxer. In the state between dream and reality, I spoke French and was treated kindly...

[4] Wähler was reported missing over Russia with 8/*KG* 77 on 10 October 1941.

The remains of Sissimato's 3Z+BS in Kensington. (via Watkins)

The following night was somewhat quieter for much of the United Kingdom, with Portsmouth being the focus of effort. Despite in the region of 250 aircraft participating, results were poor, as the post-attack report notes:

> At approximately 2140hrs flares, incendiary and high-explosive bombs were dropped, chiefly falling in the surrounding areas but a great many fell in the sea in Langstone Harbour. Although the raid appeared to be aimed at the Dockyard, little damage was done. There was some dislocation of utility services. The electricity supply to the Dockyard failed but was partially maintained by the Corporation Power Station until the normal supply was restored. Considerable damage was done to property including the Telephone Exchange when a parachute mine was dropped at Hayling Island.

The reason for this failure is attributed to the use of a 'Starfish' decoy site based on Hayling Island, which tricked the German bombers to drop their loads to the east of their intended target, hence the bombs falling into Langstone Harbour. The diary for the airfield of Thorney Island on the eastern shores of Langstone Harbour gives a vivid description of what happened:

> Red warning was received at 2125hrs. A constant stream of e/a was flying over the aerodrome at varying heights between 2100 and 0453hrs. The attack appeared to be a general one in this area. Enemy appeared to be uncertain of his position and seemed to be searching for his objective by means of flares and incendiaries. Due to this, the 'drome and Q Site were being constantly lit up and gun positions were all fully manned. When an aircraft dived to 300 feet, the AA positions were able to come into action and one Hispano gun fired 20 rounds into this at close range. The bulk of the Light AA was expended in extinguishing flares. During this period, 13 HE bombs and approximately 1,000 incendiaries fell on the Island and the immediate vicinity. Two HEs fell 100 yards south of Q Site and one landmine and five HEs fell in a village three-quarters of a mile away from the Q Site. One Blenheim aircraft sustained damage by splinters to front Perspex and one wing. One shelter was damaged by HE bomb falling within 5 yards. The Officers' Mess and COs' outhouse were slightly damaged by incendiaries. No damage to Q Site, no injuries to personnel. One e/a, Ju 88, brought down on south landing ground and totally destroyed, occupants killed.

In addition to the Junkers 88 of 2/*KG* 54, which crashed on Thorney Island, another from 8/*KG* 77 crashed in the Solent. The latter was flown by 22-year-old *Lt* Karl Höflinger, who on 8 January 1941 had carried out a lone daylight attack on the Standard Motors factory in Coventry, and had been awarded the *Ritterkreuz* on 7 March. He and his crew, *Ofw* Karl Odelga, *Ofw* Karl Vogelhuber and *Fw* Karl Herfort, were all killed.

The burial of Ofw *Heinrich Meyer and his crew of 2/*KG 54 *at Thorney Island after they were shot down by* Flak *and crashed on the airfield, 17-18 April 1941.* (Saunders)

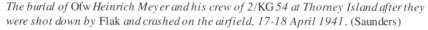

Crews of KGr *100 take a meal between their two attacks on the night of 19-20 April 1941.* (Schick)

A night off followed before London was again subjected to three waves of attacks. German losses were light – just one claim by a night-fighter and one confirmed claim by *Flak*. Numerous bombers returned damaged and a few crashed on their return as a result of *Flak*, as one pilot reports:

Unteroffizier Hans Schaber, 5/KG 30

We soon found our target because as soon as we flew over the Dutch coast we saw to the west a burning fire. That had to be London. Our orders were to fly round London from the north, then south as far as the Thames, follow the river eastwards and then attack the Port of London. Over the British coast we were received by searchlights. However, it was easy to avoid them. I made a small change in the engine revolutions and the beam went out so we concluded that the searchlights were guided by listening devices.

Uffz *Hans Schaber.* (Schaber)

Uffz *Hans Schaber at the controls of his Ju 88.*

The flight to the target and the attack itself did not bring any difficulties – there was little defence. Gliding in, we came to the target and I pressed the button and dropped our dangerous load. The plane shot upwards as she was now 2 tonnes lighter. Time to get out of this uncomfortable territory!

One or two minutes passed – we flew in the direction of home and, as always, I checked the instruments. It was then I saw that the oil temperature of the port engine was very high and rising. I passed the message on to my comrades. We were at 2,000 metres and I tried to gain more altitude, but soon the engine began to stutter and I went to single-engined flight. England was behind us. I told the *Bordfunker* to send a message that we were flying on one engine.

Because the single engine was causing us to crab in flight, the bomb release mechanisms were offering a lot of air resistance. They could be jettisoned as the bolts had an explosive charge. I did this and they flew off, but one of them became stuck on a cable and was wobbling underneath the wing.

It was not too far to the Dutch coast and after 30 minutes we crossed it at 1,000 metres height. Just another 10 minutes and we would reach our airfield. During this time nobody spoke. I was busy with the plane, the *Bordfunker* was constantly in touch with base, where everything was prepared for a belly landing – free runway, fire brigade and ambulances. The other two had to keep watch as one had to be wary of enemy night-fighters.

At that time it was forbidden to land with undercarriage down with a Ju 88 flying on one engine. We reached the base, the lights were turned on. However, since our departure the wind had changed. We had departed towards the east and now we had to land from the south so I had to fly with one engine three-quarters of the way around the airfield. I lowered the undercarriage, headed the plane for the runway and applied a little power. Shortly before we crossed the edge I was surprised that a horn sounded, which meant that the undercarriage was not down. I warned all to hold tight as the undercarriage could collapse, but on touch-down it stopped – the undercarriage was down. I did not use the brakes and we rolled clear of the runway and came to a halt...

Andenken

an den

Oberfeldwebel der Luftwaffe

Wolfgang Haselsteiner

von Haibühl

welcher am 19. April 1941 bei
einem Nachteinsatz über London
nicht zurückgekehrt ist und den
Fliegertod erlitten hat.

R. J. P.

Mein Jesus Barmherzigkeit
(300 Tage Ablaß.)
Süßes Herz Maria sei meine Rettung
(300 Tage Ablaß.)
Barmherziger Jesus gib ihr die enige
Ruhe!   (300 Tage Ablaß)
(Man bittet diese Ablässe dem lb. Ver-
storbenen zuzuwenden.)

Kanzleibuchdruckerei A. Hörmann, Neukirchen bl. Blut

Dein Grab im fernen Feindeslande
Ist uns wohl eine schwere Pein.
Doch nimm dies Wort zum Unterpfande
Dein Grab soll nicht verlassen sein;
Allabends, wenn die Glocken summen,
Zieht liebend unser Geist dorthin
Und streut dir betend Andachtsblumen
Aufs Heldengrab mit frommen Sinn.

*A card produced by the family of Ofw Wolfgang Haselsteiner, killed attacking London on
19 April 1941. A member of 1/KG 76, he was killed when his Ju 88 was shot down by
Flak and crashed at Slinfold in Sussex.*

The remainder of the month, when the weather permitted, saw attacks on harbours and
port installations, with Plymouth being attacked five times and Liverpool once.
Plymouth was targeted three nights in a row, starting on the night of 21 April, during
which much damage and devastation was caused. It was estimated that 400 civilians
were killed over those three nights and 256 seriously injured, the greater proportion
being killed on the first two nights. It was a similar story for the last two attacks of
the month – two nights in a row starting on 28 April, with forty being reported killed
the first night and 100 the second. The attack on Liverpool on the night of 26 April
was a different matter, as the official report states:

> A desultory attack commenced at 2253hrs with incendiary and high-explosive
> bombs. The raid was not on a heavy scale and little damage was done. Only two
> casualties were reported from the Liverpool area.

Claims against the attackers were minimal over this ten-day period – four bombers
claimed as destroyed, two probably destroyed and five damaged, plus twice the number
claimed again by AA. The reality was more like six German bombers directly lost to

The funeral of Lt Gerd Tocha of 3/KG 28. On 30 April 1941 he was fatally wounded attacking a ship, but managed to fly back to Nantes.

Flak and fighters with the same number again being damaged and crashing or crash-landing on their return. The next ten days would see a flurry of activity from the German side before, inexplicably as it would seem to the British at that time, the intensity of attacks dropped off dramatically.

The first bomber to appear over the United Kingdom on 1 May 1941 was near Weymouth at lunchtime, flown by *Oblt* Ernst Heinrichs of *Stab* II/*KG* 54:

> At 1300hrs a single enemy aircraft dropped five high-explosive bombs on the Whitehead Torpedo Company's factory and also machine-gunned the site. The resulting fires were soon extinguished but the damage, although not serious, will slightly affect production. There were seven casualties, one of which was fatal.

A locally published account describes in greater detail what happened, and the effect that Heinrich's attack had:

> Fortunately the attack occurred during the lunch hour, when approximately 100 men and women were in the Mess Room at Concert. The weather was cloudy and overcast and although a warning was given at 1225hrs, at 1230hrs the workforce heard the sound of machine gun fire, then a Junkers 88 glided in low over Chesil Beach and, on reaching the Works, it dropped five bombs. The bombs fell on the AM (Admiralty) Workshop, the new Fitting Shop, and the Gyro Shop.

Oblt *Ernst Heinrichs.*
(via Creek)

On a second run over the Works the plane was met by machine gun and pom-pom fire from defences in the neighbourhood of the Works and on this occasion five bombs were dropped about 300 yards from the Works.

A Luftwaffe recce photo of Weymouth taken in March 1941. (via Hansen)

Four of the bombs from the first drop exploded and they were estimated to have been some 50kg each. A fifth bomb of 250kg was of the armour-piercing type, but fortunately it failed to explode. [The] damage was considerable, with a complete loss of wall and roof coverings to many of the Assembly Shops, to the Stores, and to the Experimental Department. Although there was considerable collateral damage to all parts of the Works there were only nine casualties within the factory site and none of them were seriously hurt. However, one person was killed outside the Works as he walked along Portland Road near the Ferrybridge Hotel, when he was struck by a piece of flying debris.

The 250kg bomb that failed to explode caused considerable consternation among the workforce. Captain Cock of the 8th Dorsets sent a detachment down to the Works to lead a search for the UXB and it was eventually located lying on its side in the AM Shop, buried beneath the debris. By 1630hrs Mr Gourley, of the 143rd Section Bomb Disposal Unit, was at the Works and, having decided that the fuse could be removed, Mr Gourley, Captain Cock, and Captain Ernie Lloyd of the Whitehead Home Guard bravely set to work to defuse the bomb. By 1800hrs it had been made safe.

Owing to the presence of the UXB, the Factory closed for the remainder of the day. Work was quickly transferred to other areas of the site, or to the Torpedo Depot at Bincleaves, and by 8 May final assembly of 18-inch torpedoes was again under way... [By kind permission of Mrs D. F. Hollings]

Briefed to attack 'a torpedo store at Portland', Heinrichs approached his target at Wyke Regis over Lyme Bay before streaking back out to sea. His attack fatally wounded 17-year-olds Tom Good and Walter Trevor, and the net result of his attack was that torpedo production had to be dispersed away from Wyke Regis. Although claimed by AA as damaged, Heinrichs returned unscathed and on 24 June 1941 would be awarded the *Ritterkreuz* for his exploits. However, he would never wear this award as he was lost attacking shipping off the Irish coast on 28 May. Two of his crew from 1 May were also lost – *Ofw* Iggo Iggena and *Uffz* Herbert Mandl, his *Beobachter*, *Fw* Fritz Karsch, being replaced by the *Gruppen Adjutant*, *Oblt* Karl Brand, for his final mission.[5]

[5] Karsch would survive the war, being commissioned and ending as an *Oblt* in *Stab* II/*KG* 6. He would be awarded the *Ehrenpokal* and *Deutsches Kreuz in Gold*.

An unidentified Ju 88 A-5 camouflaged for night operations.

That night it was Liverpool's turn for a minor attack, which resulted in scattered bombing across the city. Two German aircraft were lost. The Junkers 88 of *Gefr* Alexander Klokowsky of 1/*KG* 54 was badly damaged by *Flak* over the United Kingdom and the crew were forced to bail out near Le Havre, the pilot and two of his crew being killed. The second loss was a Heinkel 111 of 4/*KG* 27, shot down off the South Coast by Fg Off Arthur Hodgkinson and Sgt Bert Dye of 219 Sqn:

Leutnant Helmut Ballauf, 4/KG 27

That night we started at about 2100hrs, the target was Liverpool. We flew at about 10,000 feet. It was a clear night. At about 2245hrs I asked my crew to look out for the English coast; the white band would give us the exact position. At that same moment a night-fighter must have been behind us. Nobody noticed it. It fired at our plane and there were some explosions to the rear. I dived and gave the order to bail out. I bailed out at about 3,000 feet, got clear of the airscrews, opened the parachute and landed in the sea. A short distance away I saw a big fire burning on the sea – the fuel from my plane. I inflated my life jacket and swam for about half an hour. Suddenly I saw a shadow coming towards me – it was an air-sea rescue boat. They had seen the fireball on the water and were looking for survivors. They picked me up – I think there were four men in the boat. They treated me very correctly. I told them there were four of us in the plane and they searched until dawn. I think our position was 2 or 3 miles off Selsey Bill. In the morning they brought me to a little town – I think it was Littlehampton. A policeman took me to the police station and from there I was transferred the same day by a military car to an interrogation camp near London.

That same night almost saw the loss of one of the RAF night-fighters. Fg Off Ian Joll and Sgt Arthur O'Leary of 604 Sqn had just identified their prey as a Heinkel 111 and thought that they had not been spotted:

> ...Closed to 100 feet and about 100 yards behind and identified as He 111. When short burst of fire from lower rear gun position of e/a. This just missed pilot and hit the operator in right leg and also the radio.
>
> E/a immediately started violent turns. Pilot lost the silhouette and followed him on the exhausts for about six turns. E/a then steadied up and flew straight and level. Pilot then closed in to same as before, raised nose until e/a came gradually into sights and fired full burst which went straight into fuselage. There were a few flashes in the fuselage about the gun positions. E/a put its nose down slowly and fighter passed over the top and never saw it again. Three or four minutes later saw a white flare on the ground. There were one or two searchlights to the south-east.
>
> Radio was completely dead. Operator came forward and reported he was wounded. Pilot tried without success to get a signal from a flare path so climbed up again. Operator offered to try to get the Middle Wallop AI beacon and pilot and operator arranged a code on the emergency hooter. After about 10 minutes, pilot identified Colerne beacon and came home on the AI beacon on a course of 125.
>
> Operator was found to have five bullets in right leg. This is second time he has been wounded when flying in this same machine. Pilot remarks that Sgt O'Leary displayed great courage and fortitude in successfully homing the aircraft while wounded. It was entirely due to this that he was able to bring the machine back to base.

No German bombers returned that night claiming to have shot at a night-fighter, but it is thought that the lucky Heinkel 111 was from *KGr* 100. Unsurprisingly, Sgt O'Leary was awarded the DFM for his actions.

The following two nights saw Liverpool and Merseyside receiving fairly devastating attacks. It would appear that just two *Geschwader* from *Luftflotte* 3 were involved on the first night, and the scale of the involvement of *Luftflotte* 2 cannot be said for certain:

> A heavy attack commenced at 2230hrs caused fairly heavy civilian and general damage. A number of fires were caused in the Docks, creating dislocation and difficulties in transportation. Actual damage to installations were not severe except in Queens Dock. The Mersey Dock and Harbour Board offices were destroyed. Several railway lines were blocked but restricted service into the docks was maintained. Tramways were also disorganised but buses were kept running almost normally. The ventilation plant of the Mersey Tunnel was slightly damaged. The water, gas and electricity systems suffered considerable damage. Telephones were interrupted owing to two exchanges being temporarily vacated because of damage to blackout. The main transmitter of the Seaforth Wireless Station was put out of action until the 4th.

Three bombers were lost during this attack, one to a Defiant, one to an AI-equipped Beaufighter and one to AA fire. The first to be shot down was a Junkers 88 of 8/*KG* 77 flown by *Fw* Franz Beckmann. Flt Lt George Budd and Sgt George Evans of 604

Sqn reported that their kill crashed on land near Lyndhurst, which matches exactly with where Beckmann's bomber crashed. The intelligence report on the crash makes interesting if not amusing reading:

> After a short briefing by the *Staffel Kapitän*, *Hptm* Günther Wagner, three aircraft from 8/*KG* 77 took off from Juvincourt at 5-minute intervals. The 3Z+DS was held up by engine trouble and took off last at 2100hrs.
>
> The objective of the whole *Gruppe* was the Docks at Liverpool and the 8th *Staffel* had been allotted the area between pinpoints 796165 and 800130. 4 x 250 kilo and 5 x SC50 kilo bombs were carried.
>
> Course was set to make landfall just west of the Isle of Wight and the crew then intended to fly northwards until level with the northern limit of the target, which would then be approached from the east.
>
> Further interrogation regarding the combat adds little to the details in the Preliminary Report; the crew were taken unawares and the aircraft hit before evasive action could be taken.
>
> With the exception of the pilot who was killed, the crew bailed out and having landed in the wilds of the New Forest found some difficulty in giving themselves up.
>
> The W/T operator, who had lost his flying boots on leaving the aircraft, landed in a pond in a wood. After wandering for some time, he encountered a white ghost which shook him considerably until it materialised into a Forest pony.
>
> A little later he reached a road and tried several times without success to stop motorcars. Finally, when a large ambulance appeared, he stood in the centre of the road, waved his arms until the driver stopped and shouted 'Soldat Germain!' The driver flashed his torch and after a quick look let in his clutch and made off.
>
> The airman finally succeeded in giving himself up to a Military Policeman and some soldiers near a large military camp.

The next aircraft to be shot down was commanded by *Oblt* Horst Hempel of 9/*KG* 77. Hit by AA fire, he and his crew all bailed out successfully and his Junkers 88 crashed near Cobham in Surrey. The last casualty of the night was a Junkers 88 of 1/*KG* 30 flown by *Fw* Erwin Geiger. He and his crew were found to have been quite experienced. They had taken part in the first attack of the war by I/*KG* 30 on 16 October 1939 after having flown in Poland with *KG* 1. They had apparently missed the Norwegian Campaign, having been injured in a crash the day before it commenced. Now with 9/*KG* 30, they were able to take part in the bombing of RAF Driffield on 15 August 1940, but apparently the experience was so bad that Geiger was taking off operational flying until November 1940, by which time 9/*KG* 30 had become 1/*KG* 30. Their demise was thought to have been due to *Flak*, but matches with a claim submitted by Fg Off Guy Edmiston and Sgt Albert Beale of 151 Sqn. Again, the crew were all captured and the intelligence report makes amusing reading:

> On the night of 2/3 May, 12 aircraft from I/*KG* 30 were to start from Eindhoven to attack the dock area at Liverpool just opposite to Birkenhead. The 4D+BH was the only aircraft of the 1st *Staffel* operating, the remainder being drawn from the 2nd and 3rd *Staffeln*.

Fw *Geiger's Ju 88 lies on the beach at Weybourne in Norfolk.*

After the crews had been briefed by the *Staffel Kapitän* of 2/*KG* 30, the 4D+BH, carrying 1 x 1000 kg and 1 x 500 kg mines, was sent on ahead with orders to report back on weather conditions for the remaining aircraft of the *Gruppe*.

Maj [Walter] Seeburg, an assistant Operations Staff Officer on the aerodrome staff at Eindhoven, was acting as gunner of this aircraft and was apparently making this flight solely for the sake of experience which, he certainly gained. The usual *Bordmechaniker* [sic], *Uffz* Schmidt, was annoyed at having to stay behind but no doubt now feels more cheerful...

The following night, the bombing and the losses were much greater:

A strong force of enemy aircraft estimated at 290 commenced to attack at 2230hrs. The cumulative effect of this and the two previous raids was widespread destruction. Sheds were extensively damaged over a large section of North Dock. In Liverpool South Dock damage to quay installations was not so severe. A number of ships were reported either sunk, on fire or seriously damaged. All rail traffic into and out of the Docks was brought to a standstill. In addition there was also dislocation of road transport. In Bootle traffic was further complicated by the fact that two important bridges were smashed. In Liverpool, the Clarence Dock Power Station received several direct hits and was put out of commission until the 5th. The Lister Drive Power Station experienced trouble with the feeders and a generator was put out of commission. The water supply failed extensively but were restored fairly fully on the following night. Gas supplies were maintained at reduced pressure. The Liverpool Trunk Exchange was put out of action, two other exchanges were badly damaged and the telegraph service was completely stopped. Casualties reported were 406 killed and 641 seriously injured.

This report surprising fails to mention one dreadful incident. The 7,000-ton cargo liner SS *Malakand* was berthed in Huskisson No 2 dock laden with in the region of 1,000 tons of munitions destined for the Middle East. A deflated barrage balloon slipped free of its moorings and became tangled in the *Malakand's* rigging. It then fell onto the deck and burst into flames. The crew immediately set about extinguishing the fire, but flames from nearby burning sheds then quickly spread to the ship. The crew tried in vain to fight the new flames but it was hopeless and they tried to scuttle the ship to prevent an explosion. Despite succeeding in doing this, a few hours after the all clear the *Malakand* exploded, destroying the whole dock and damaging the overhead railway lines. Plates from the ship were blown 2$\frac{1}{2}$ miles away, one of which landed on a car, killing a newly married couple. Amazingly, only two other civilians lost their lives in the explosion.

Night-fighters were active, claiming ten destroyed, one probable and three damaged, while AA claimed a further three destroyed and numerous damaged. Seven bombers can be positively attributed to night-fighters, one collided with a barrage balloon cable, and one suffered engine failure.

One crew that night had completed seven operational flights over the United Kingdom against Greenock, Hull, London, Glasgow, Portland, Plymouth and Liverpool, but this attack on Liverpool would be their last:

Gefreiter Bernhard Winterscheidt, 8/KG 26

That night we were on a special mission. The Y *Gerät* beam was put from Le Havre to Liverpool – our target. We carried a single 1,000kg blockbuster attached to the outside of the hull. We were lucky that it was damaged when we were attacked and it did not explode.

We were over the southern coast at 6,000 metres when a night-fighter, which we could not see, fired at us from the front bottom left. The port engine and fuel tank immediately caught fire so we had to bail out. Two of the crew, Bernhard Möllers and Otto Kaminsky, were killed. The pilot, Georg Macher, survived the jump but was wounded in the left thigh and taken to Chichester hospital...

Macher bailed out first, followed by Kaminsky, the *Beobachter*, sadly, in the chaos he forgot to put on his parachute and was killed. The other crew members bailed out of the rear hatch and it appears that Möller hit the fuselage as, when his body was found, his skull and both legs were broken despite the parachute being open. They had been shot down by a Beaufighter of 219 Sqn crewed by Flt Lt Tony Dottridge and Sgt Trevor Williams:

Sergeant Trevor Williams, 219 Sqn

We were over the Channel under ground radar control when I picked up the He 111 on my set and brought Tony Dottridge in close enough to identify the He 111. We both had a good look before attacking from astern and slightly below. The tactics were to get as early as possible to this position without being seen and then to gently pull up the nose with a good burst of cannon. It worked this time and the He 111 went down on fire...

Who shot down a Heinkel 111 of 3/*KG* 53 is less certain. Sgt Arnold Hill and Sgt Ernest Hollis of 25 Sqn filed a claim for a Heinkel 111 destroyed near Holt in Norfolk, as did

Sgt Trevor Williams files a combat report while his pilot, Flt Lt 'Dot' Dottridge, is on the phone. (Williams)

Sgt Henry Bodien and Sgt Douglas Wrampling of 151 Sqn, who claimed to have destroyed a Heinkel 111 over the Wash. The former's combat report explains the uncertainty:

> Attack was opened from dead astern with four cannon and four machine guns firing .303. Pilot saw tracer bullets disappear into aircraft and others bounce off into the air and also off the starboard engine. Quite a lot of sparks and what appeared to be red-hot particles appeared. No return fire was experienced. E/a turned over on port side and went into a steep dive. Sgt Hill followed for nearly 10,000 feet but had to pull

The remains of Lt Hans Glänzinger's Ju 88 of Stab II/KG 54 in Cheshire, 3-4 May 1941. (Parry)

Night-camouflaged Ju 88s of II/KG 54. (via Creek)

out as dive was too steep. He called up GCI and said he thought he had 'got him'. He made several circles of the spot but as there were fires on the ground and many searchlights, he could not pick out anything that looked like a burning aircraft.

The Austrian pilot's account also doesn't help in confirming who shot him down:

Leutnant Alfred Von Plank-Bachselten, 3/KG 53

I was shot down over England by a night-fighter after a raid on Liverpool. I was flying over The Wash when my *Bordfunker* told me that a night-fighter was attacking us and the bullets were all around us. During this attack, my *Bordfunker* was killed while the rest of us didn't even get a scratch. The reason for this was armoured plating behind my back. The port engine was badly damaged and also the Perspex in my cockpit. Shortly after the attack, the temperature of the port engine shot up and I was forced to shut it down and thought I'll fly home on one engine and get the Iron Cross for bravery but it was not possible to hold the altitude so I was forced to make an emergency landing with the undercarriage up.

After our landing, we found out that the *Bordfunker* was dead, and after we recovered his body we tried to get the plane to explode but the charge didn't work so we soaked our maps with fuel and set them on fire. We then destroyed all of our papers, took a machine gun to try and get someone to take us to an airfield by telling them we were British aircrew. At first we came to a small town but there was nobody around. Near the town was a hill with a light beacon on top – I think this was to help British planes find their base. After having shot out the light, a Home Guardsman came and asked us to follow him. He did not believe my story that I was an Allied flyer. He called a policeman who was very friendly and took us to his home, serving us tea...

Bombs would drop again on Liverpool for the following four nights, but the main target for the night of 4 May 1941 was Belfast. Again, night-fighters claimed three destroyed, two probables and three damaged. German losses, all of them Junkers 88s, match quite well with three shot down by night-fighters, two suffering engine failure due to fuel shortage and two lost to unknown causes. Two of those lost crashed into houses – one from 8/*KG* 1 crashed into the Butchers Arms public house at Eastgate in Lincolnshire, killing three of the German crew, publican Cyril Lappage and his wife Fanny, Minnie Cooper and her daughter Violet Jackson, and three soldiers, as well as injuring six more. A hour later Sgt Ken Hollowell and Sgt Richard Crossman of 25 Sqn shot down a Junkers 88, which crashed into 13-15 High Street, Idle, Bradford. In 9 High Street, Sarah Boyd was killed, her husband John dying of his injuries exactly a month later. In No 13, 12-month-old Elsa Green was killed, and in No 15 Herbert Jowett was killed, and another two civilians injured. The German crew all survived:

Oberleutnant zur See Reinhard Metzger, 2/106

A Ju 88 of 2/106. (via Creek)

We took off from Schiphol with nine Ju 88s to bomb Belfast Harbour. Our airfield was attacked by RAF bombers as we were starting up, then while we were circling over the airfield another bomber squadron came – we saw them beneath us.

When we crossed the English coast there were no defences, no balloons, no searchlights, no fighters – that was very suspicious. I said to my crew that this was going to be a hard trip – either England had surrendered or, which was more possible, it was a trap. As I said this, I saw the last plane in our *Staffel* being attacked by fighters and going down in flames. A few minutes afterwards, another plane went down on fire.[6] Things were getting serious.

We had been ordered to fly at 3,500 metres. However, in case we were attacked we flew in the higher regions so we could dive away. As far as I remember, it was not a Defiant that attacked us but a Beaufighter. I ordered Jänichen and Beeck to bail out to reduce weight. I cut away all things heavy and threw it out of the plane, even the machine guns and ammunition, and Jürgens and I wanted to fly back to France. The starboard wing had been hit and the skin had gone, the engine was on fire so we had switched it off. After all of this, the plane was under control and we thought we could get home.

Suddenly I saw a fighter beneath us and he attacked us with machine guns. Three other fighters were above us but they did not attack. The most dangerous one was the one coming from below. The only thing I could do was to hide behind the armoured plate and try not to get wounded or killed. All the Perspex was riddled and there was no chance of continuing. The plane went into a spin and burst into flames. It was difficult to get out of the plane because of the centrifugal forces. Today I wonder that we did get out without any panic.

I landed on a school roof to the north of Idle and was taken prisoner by a woman schoolteacher. I don't remember very much of my first hours in England as I was wounded and had to be taken to hospital.

Fred Barker

I heard this plane overhead. Its engines were racing and dying away – it was obviously in trouble. There was then a whooshing sound and the plane burst into flames. I then realised that it had dropped in our yard, which was about 80 yards from where I was standing. I ran up High Street but as soon as I opened the shop, I was met by flames. Three people [sic] died as a result of the crash. The aircraft hit the end of a row of cottages and two people in the end cottage were killed by fire. In the third cottage, the owner decided that night that he would sleep downstairs, presumably because he thought he would be safe from air raids, but with the plane falling it broke the window and splashed fuel into the house which set the man alight...

---

[6] *Oblt zS* Werner Pyrkosch and his crew from 2/106 were the only other loss from this unit that night – it is assumed that they crashed in the North Sea.

The next three nights saw attacks being mainly directed again either against Glasgow or Liverpool. The damage inflicted on Glasgow and Clydeside was widespread and included a distillery, which resulted in thousands of gallons of whisky going up in flames. During the attacks on Glasgow, the RAF claimed to have shot down six bombers and damaged three on the night of 5 May, and eight destroyed, one probable and four damaged on the night of 6 May; AA guns claimed one the first night and two the second night. German losses on the first night were five bombers missing (including one that ditched off the French coast, its crew being rescued), as well as a reconnaissance Junkers 88 of 2/122 (which was possibly lost carrying out a damage assessment) and three bombers damaged, while on the second night five bombers were lost. There were a number of German aircrew who remember the second night particularly well.

Hptm *Eugen Eichler's He 111 of 1/*KG *4 near Newcastle, which had crashed in the early hours of 6 May 1941.* (Parry)

Hptm *Eichler, seen here as a POW in Canada.*

Just before midnight, Fg Off Victor Verity and Sgt Fred Wake of 96 Sqn claimed to have shot down a Heinkel 111 at Morpeth. At precisely that time, a Heinkel 111 of 2/*KG* 53 crashed at Morpeth[7]:

[7] Some sources state that this aircraft was shot down by Fg Off Robert Day and Fg Off Frank Lanning of 141 Sqn.

Unteroffizier Karl Simon, 2/KG 53

On the night of 6-7 May 1941 we were on our way from Vitry-en-Artois to Dumbarton. During the flight into England we were attacked by a Defiant night-fighter in the area of Newcastle and repeatedly shot at and hit many times. We could not get away from him – the Defiant was very persistent! A fire started in our plane, just behind the pilot, and was presumably caused by damaged supply leads. Nearby were oxygen bottles and there was also my parachute, which was shot to pieces. The oxygen bottles exploded and blew a hole in the fuselage wall.

Uffz *Karl Simon (left) next to his pilot,* Uffz *Karl Rassloff.* (via Norman)

The fire in the aircraft could not be extinguished and I could not bail out. In these circumstances, Rassloff, an excellent pilot, decided to make an emergency landing in the moonlight and with relatively good visibility. He succeeded in making a good belly-landing and one of the crew was injured. I was able to radio an emergency report of our landing and hoped that our HQ would inform my mother that we had all survived being brought down.

Because the burning plane was in danger of exploding, we all distanced ourselves from the wreck at the double and delivered ourselves to a nearby house, allegedly a hospital. After a short time, the police came and took us away...

About 2 hours later, a Junkers 88 slithered to a stop on Holy Island, having been fatally damaged by a Defiant crewed by Fg Off Robert Day and Fg Off Frank Lanning. The crew all got out, set fire to their aircraft and patiently awaited capture:

Unteroffizier Hans Schaber, 5/KG 30

Uffz *Hans Schaber.* (Schaber)

It had been quiet in the plane – only the *Beobachter* asked or said anything. Soon we saw searchlights, *Flak* and old and new fires in England. Most of our journey was over the sea. Our course was set for Berwick-upon-Tweed – the evening was good so we could watch the English coast on our left. In the vicinity of The Wash we saw a convoy going south-east... When I was east of Berwick, I set the course westwards and reminded Werner Arndt, our gunner, whom we had nicknamed Maurice, to watch out for night-fighters...

The Schaber crew with their Ju 88. (Schaber)

We flew south of Edinburgh and were nearly in the north of Glasgow. The mouth of the Clyde and the Port were easily recognisable. I wanted to turn more towards the south-west to reach our attack course when the *Bordfunker* called, in an anxious voice, 'Night-fighter behind us!'...

We dived – that was my reaction. We dived at 70 degrees but he had shot at us. I saw on the port engine a small fire and heard a dull explosion. 'He is following us!' called the *Bordfunker*. Now I flew a half turn so that the Ju 88 dived on its back steeply. Then I pulled up and flew vertically the opposite direction and we lost our hunter. We had reached a speed of 750kmph and we had to drop our bombs quickly – we lost them somewhere to the north-east of Glasgow...

The German crew were initially optimistic about getting back, but it soon transpired that the bomb doors had stuck open, the port engine was losing coolant and was overheating, and it appeared that there was a problem with the starboard engine. Hans ordered all unnecessary equipment to be jettisoned, but by the time they had reached Berwick-upon-Tweed and had dropped to 200 metres. The crew decided they had to crash-land rather than ditch or bail out. Hans continues:

...I turned towards land and said, 'We are going to land on the beach.' Nöske replied, 'By night and in such bad light?' He had a better view than me and said the beach was narrow and by cliffs. If I could coax the engine a little longer, maybe there will be a more suitable place further along. The beach became broader and flatter. I set for landing but the strong easterly wind pushed us further over land. I turned on the landing lights and to our horror there was a tower ahead of us. Once more full power and out to sea – we now hung like a ripe plum on a tree. The plane hardly responded any more. Now I lowered the plane – I called to get rid of the cabin roof, which we did by pressing a lever. I then touched down on the sand – I tried to avoid bouncing and the sand flew into the open roof into our cabin. We came to a stop and just left a slight trail in the sand behind us.

A crash-landed Ju 88 of KG 30. (Quehl)

I turned the electrics off – the lights went out and there was silence. Now we had to destroy the plane as she must not fall into the hands of the enemy. For this purpose there was an explosive charge fixed between our seats. I sent the crew behind the dunes, took the explosive capsule, removed the rubber seal and screwed it in; I pulled out the line and ran for cover. It should have exploded within 3 minutes but nothing happened. It was forbidden to go back, but after 10 minutes I went back. In the dark I felt the capsule but could not detect a fault...

However, there was a fault, and now desperate times required desperate measures:

...Our flare pistol was still there. I loaded it, opened the fuel tank, put the pistol barrel into the tank and fixed it in as best as possible with the chain of the fuel cap. Now I tied a line to the trigger, went 25 metres away and pulled. A flame of about 5 metres shot out of the tank and the fire then went out. I repeated the procedure without success. After a short discussion we decided to use a machine gun and shoot the last drum of ammunition into the plane. This we did from the top of the nearest dune, but even that did not work. We were surprised that we were not interrupted in our work! Now came our last effort. I climbed once more into the cabin to check if the fuel tanks were intact. They were still working, so I pumped all the fuel into one tank until it overflowed. We soaked the parachute with petrol and threw it into the cabin and the overflowing tank. With the flare pistol, I fired from a short distance and all burned...

As Hans Schaber was struggling to set fire to his plane, much further south a Heinkel 111 of 7/*KG* 27 was being attacked by Sqn Ldr Charles Pritchard and Sgt Ben Gledhill of 600 Sqn:

Ben Gledhill, seen here with 125 Sqn later in the war.

Leutnant Ekkehard Wüllenweber, 7/KG 27

Our home base was Orleans. In the afternoon we flew to Caen for refuelling and bomb loading (four 250kgs and a number of incendiary bombs). The course was straight to Glasgow. After dropping the bombs, return flight to Orleans with a reduced speed because of fuel shortage on a 6-hour flight. It was all quiet until we observed flashes and beams from the ground signalling in a certain direction, to which we did not pay much attention. Suddenly my *Bordfunker* reported, 'Night-fighter behind!' At the same time we were attacked by tracers directly through the body of the plane. Damage to the plane caused strong vibrations so I made a slight turn to port, losing height in order to escape the fighter. Seconds later a second attack set the plane on fire just behind the cockpit and the intercom went dead. The *Beobachter* was apparently dead, so I had no choice but to get out through the canopy above the pilot's seat, having suffered burns to my face and on my arms.

Fortunately, I missed the fuselage and pulled the parachute handle. I landed in a meadow near Oborne and was taken prisoner at a railway house...

The following night it was Liverpool's turn again, after which the city would have nearly three weeks' respite from the attentions of the *Luftwaffe*. Hull was also attacked successfully. Again, the effects were dreadful:

Approximately 186 enemy aircraft attacked the Merseyside area when Bootle was the main target. The raid began at 0023hrs and by 0410hrs 22 fires were reported from Seaforth along the line of Docks to Huskisson Dock. The fire situation was not reasonably in hand until 1700hrs on 8 May. Six fires were still burning on 10 May. 20,000 people were estimated to be homeless as a result of the raid. The North End System (Gladstone and Sandon Docks) suffered severe damage. All movement of vessels in this system was temporarily stopped owing to the gutting of a power station at Canada Pier Head and to the collapse of the Canada-Brocklebank Bridge, which blocked the passage. The Leeds & Liverpool Canal was seriously damaged for a distance of 3 miles and is likely to be out of use for a considerable time. The Athol Street gas works was hit again resulting in complete failure of gas in Bootle.

Despite the devastation to Liverpool and a number of other cities that night, night-fighters and AA guns put up a spirited defence. Guns claimed the destruction of six and fighters claimed seventeen destroyed, three probably destroyed and ten damaged. Both non-radar-equipped and radar-equipped fighters were very active, while single-seat fighters were also active. The first combats were against night intruders of I/*NJG* 2, which, as usual, were looking for unwary British aircraft near their home airfields. At the same time, Havocs of 23 Sqn and Defiants of 264 Sqn were doing the same to the German airbases. Four Hurricanes of 87 Sqn also set out to do similar at the airfield of Maupertus. Two of them didn't have to go that far:

Sqn Ldr Gleed again on his way over to Maupertus with Sgt Thorogood sighted a Do 17 Z flying north at about 12,000 feet. Sqn Ldr Gleed turned and stalked it for a few minutes hoping to bring it down nearer to the coast. The e/a opened fire first and after a few attacks, Sqn Ldr Gleed shot it down into the sea in flames...

Sqn Ldr Ian Gleed of 87 Sqn.

Sgt 'Rubber' Thorogood, 87 Sqn.

The identity of Gleed's victim is unknown, but the next confirmed kill is known. Fg Off George Howden and Sgt Fielding of 600 Sqn reported their first confirmed kill as follows:

> Fg Off Howden was vectored onto a bandit travelling due north. After a series of dummy runs, weapon was flashed and on second attempt a fair blip was obtained. This improved on operator directing pilot and a visual was obtained before maximum range was reached. Aircraft was identified as hostile. Attack was made from dead astern and slightly below. Two bursts were fired at 300 yds closing to 200 yds. Starboard engine was seen to catch fire and e/a crashed in a long turning dive, exploding on hitting the ground.

Oberleutnant Johannes Maron, Stab/KG 27

This night I have the special job, taking off 15 minutes earlier than the rest of the *Geschwader* to mark the target with incendiary bombs, the target this night being the shipyards of Liverpool. I was an experienced *Beobachter* and commanded the plane – it was my 56th mission over the UK.

You need experience to mark a target in the dark, although this night was rather bright and we nearly had a full moon. Over England we could easily see every road, field, house and tree from a height of 3,500 metres – also the balloons around Cardiff and in the distance Swansea. I took off at about 2100hrs from Tours. We reached and crossed the Channel without incident and arrived over Poole, turning north to Bristol and Liverpool.

This night I wondered why no *Flak* guns were active – even the notorious batteries of Portland were silent. Furthermore, no searchlights were switched on except three beams from different positions, which moved towards me. As I was the only plane in the air at that time, I supposed that I was their target. We had been informed that there was a new system of defensive tactics by the RAF and I experienced it for the first time this night – night-fighters were active and one of them was being directed towards me.

I warned the crew to look out and ordered the *Bordschütze* down below into the gun position of the belly of our He 111. The *Bordfunker* had to look out of the top position for enemy aircraft coming from behind. After some time, the *Bordfunker* shouted, 'Night-fighter from above behind the aircraft!' and began firing with his machine gun. It was of no use – bullets hit the starboard wing and pierced the cockpit. The crew reported they hadn't been hit but smoke was affecting them. Some of our incendiary bombs had caught fire and the starboard wing was glowing dark red. We dropped all of our bombs and the pilot dived as steeply as possible, but this was no help. I ordered Dietrich, Eggers and Hilger to bail out and wished them luck. The pilot Ronge and I tried to extinguish the now blazing flames on the starboard wing by twisting and turning and losing height quickly. We had been attacked at 10-12,000 feet but now I could see the silvery sparkling Bristol Channel, so gave the pilot the order to bail out. I intended to follow immediately – he had to get out first because on his side (port) there was no fire. I want to point out that all of this happened in a calm and considerate manner – there was no panic at all.

I was the last one out and we were already very close to the ground – at about 600 feet I opened my parachute and landed in a small field surrounded by hedges near a small village. When I looked around (I was unhurt), I saw three soldiers with guns coming towards me asking me to put my hands up. At the same time I noticed the other parachutes from the rest of the crew approaching the ground. I could see the Heinkel burning on a nearby hill...

As Johannes Maron stated, the moonlight was particularly bright that night, which allowed Defiants of 96, 255 and 256 Sqns to file claims for seven bombers destroyed, two probably destroyed and eight damaged. Of the twelve German bombers lost that night, six can be positively matched to Defiant claims. One was a Heinkel 111, claimed by Plt Off Don Toone and Fg Off Bob Lamb of 256 Sqn, whose victim was seen to blow up on the water's edge at Bootle:

Leutnant Heinz Dunkerbeck, 3/KG 55

…That night the target was the harbour installations of Liverpool. We took off from Le Bourget and passed Land's End and St David's Head to avoid the English night-fighters. After dropping the bombs and having flown on a southerly course for a few minutes, we were attacked by a Boulton Paul Defiant night-fighter, which was flying on a parallel course. All those crew members in the rear of the aircraft were killed instantly by the first bursts of fire because there was no side armour plating. The intercom was also put out of action. The Defiant continued the attacks with the forward firing guns until the starboard engine caught fire. When the fire had spread I gave my *Beobachter* a sign to bail out through the hatch in the ventral gondola. After a few minutes I opened the upper Perspex hatch and bailed out to the left.

I landed on a block of concrete near Crosby on the River Mersey, where I was captured by soldiers. Because of the hard landing I limped, so they took me to a first aid post. After I had been served a cup of tea there, I was taken to a police station. There I was put into a cell. About an hour later an RAF officer entered the cell and declared that he was the one who had shot me down. He had prepared a letter of confirmation for his 'kill' and wanted me to sign it. I did what he had asked for.

The bright moonlight was both a blessing and curse for the night-fighters, and two were shot down by return fire. Sqn Ldr George Gatherall and Fg Off Dennis Wallen of 256 Sqn were either shot down by the Junkers 88 they were attacking or an over-zealous gunner from their own squadron; they landed safely at Widnes. Sgt James Wright and Sgt John Vaughan of 604 Sqn were also lucky:

Beaufighter R2101 coded NG-R of 604 Sqn, which was abandoned by Sgts Wright and Vaughan on 8 May 1941.

Intercepted Raid 197 commencing interception 0346hrs. GCI report aircraft probably destroyed. Winchester Observer Corps report crash in sea at 0408hrs. During pursuit, e/a fired at Blazer 30 wounding pilot in right hand and forearm. Pilot fired and saw e/a crash in sea in flames. Pilot returned to base but Beaufighter caught fire and crashed 0410hrs. Pilot and operator bailed out and are safe except for pilot's wounds.

At last, night-fighters were beginning to make an impression, but still the devastation caused by the German bombers was dreadful. The following night, which would turn out to be the penultimate night of the Blitz, the *Luftwaffe* targeted Nottingham and Hull, but Derby, Sheffield and Plymouth were visited by smaller formations of bombers. The attacks on Plymouth and Sheffield barely got a mention in British reports, while weather interfered with the attack on Derby. Hull was then attacked by a number of aircraft, which failed to find their primary targets. Hull had been attacked the night before and the British report shows how bad things must have been:

200 enemy bombers were operating on this night when at 0024hrs a further raid began, which was even more severe than that of the previous night. 200 incidents were reported, mostly in the centre of the city and the Docks. Damage was particularly heavy in East Hull. Fires were intense and concentrated, one of the worst being at Oil Importers premises from which running oil was alight in Main Street. Commercial buildings in the neighbourhood were already on fire and rescue work was seriously hindered.

The Fire Brigade HQ was practically demolished and direct hits were also sustained by a Divisional Fire Station and the Guildhall. All tram routes in the city were put out of action by damage to the overhead wire, and the tracks on several roads were blocked and the Hull-New Holland ferry was suspended.

In the two nights' raiding, 370 people lost their lives and some 30,000 people in Hull were made homeless out of a population of some 300,000.

It was a similar story at Nottingham, with 209 incidents and nearly 200 civilians killed. AA guns claimed to have shot down three bombers, while night-fighters claimed twelve bombers destroyed and four damaged. Six were lost attacking Britain, most of them being involved in the attack on Hull, and a further two Junkers 88s from II/*KG* 54 were lost over or near France. Aircraft from I/*KG* 54, III/*KG* 54 and *Stab*/*KG* 55 also reported being damaged by fighters. Defiants of 255 Sqn were particularly successful in the Hull area, claiming six aircraft destroyed. It was New Zealander Flt Lt Richard Trousdale and his fellow Kiwi gunner Sgt Francis Chunn who, it is believed, shot down one of the most photographed Blitz crashes, a Heinkel 111 of 6/*KG* 55 flown by *Fw* Gerhard Ender[8], which had been briefed to attack Sheffield:

---

[8] Ender was fatally wounded, and *Bordfunker Uffz* Bruno Schakat was killed when his parachute caught on the tail.

Fw *Ender's He 111 before…*

…and after.

Fw *Ender's He 111 in various states of dismantlement.* (via Watkins)

David Kirkwood

Suddenly, one damaged Heinkel flew low and circled back over Farnton Wood, heading straight over the fields and just missing the end of the farm buildings towards the house. Two airmen had been seen to bail out successfully, another had his parachute caught on the tail as the injured pilot looked for a place to crash-land the aircraft... I felt the rushing draught of air as the Heinkel passed only yards from the house, seeing the dead crewman being dragged behind the aircraft as it skimmed the hedges before crash-landing in the field just beyond the house.

By this time father had dashed inside and, armed with a 12-bore shotgun, ran across the road towards the plane, quickly finding the injured pilot crouching in a ditch. In the meantime my mother had cycled to the village in order to telephone the police, who then alerted the Army...

The following night saw a subtle change in German tactics, with numerous airfields being attacked while individual aircraft carried out attacks against specific industrial targets. Key Points such as the Pobjoy Air Motors & Aircraft Ltd factory at Northfleet in Kent and Airspeed Ltd at Christchurch in Hampshire were attacked, the latter by a Junkers 88 of II/*KG* 54. Only one German aircraft was lost, a 9/*KG* 1 Junkers 88 shot down by 219 Sqn, despite fighters claiming to have destroyed three and damaged two more. Embarrassingly, one of the claims not listed was when Fg Off Roderick Chisholm of 604 Sqn shot down Fg Off Robert Woodward of 600 Sqn; both Woodward and his operator, Sgt Alfred Lipscombe, bailed out safely.

Fw *Heinrich Müller, one of the survivors of Ender's crew.*

If the night of 9 May 1941 was relatively quiet for both sides, the night of the 10th would be totally different, with London experiencing a devastating series of attacks on what would effectively be the final night of the Blitz.

With good weather forecast and little activity during daylight, it was not until 2254hrs British time that the pathfinders of *KGr* 100 reported dropping their bombs. From then until 0524hrs, when a Junkers 88 of II/*KG* 54 released its load, London was subjected to a concerted and terrible air attack, as the British report shows:

This was a very severe raid though not in most respects as heavy as the two April raids. The main weight of the attack fell on the Central and City areas but bombing was very widespread affecting 60 boroughs in London as well as the eastern approaches.

The main problem was the incendiary bomb, and the fire situation, aggravated by a serious water shortage, became grave. Damage to residential, commercial and public property was very extensive.

Damage in the docks as a whole is assessed as substantial but not severe. The India Docks suffered the most damage; none of the docks escaped entirely, but damage was chiefly to warehouses, sheds and yards and was not vital. The ability of the port as a whole to handle traffic is probably little affected.

The river wall was damaged at Southwark and the embankment at Chelsea. Tower Pier and the floating pier at Billingsgate were hit. The river, however, remained open except for a very few restrictions.

There was very great dislocation of transport, especially railways. Many reports of damage to tracks and of interruption to services have been received and a summary of only the most important items is given. At one time all the termini were closed apart from Marylebone and the latest reports are that St Pancras, Broad Street, Fenchurch Street, Cannon Street, Victoria and Waterloo are still closed. Holborn Viaduct and the stretch Blackfriars-Elephant was entirely blocked. Eleven stretches of the London Passenger Transport Board were closed and on the 12th, though there was a considerable improvement, peak services were reduced by 50% owing to lack of current. There was heavy damage in Feltham Marshalling Yard where the up and down main lines and 16 sidings were destroyed. Freight exchanges in the west remained open, however.

Road transport was also greatly disorganised owing to the blocking of many roads; the obstructions, however, were mostly temporary such as fires, debris or the presence of fire appliances. Perhaps the greatest cause of delay was the closing of all routes through the City. There were many blocks also in the neighbourhood of Elephant and Castle. Vauxhall Bridge and Southwark Bridge were closed to traffic and only three river bridges in Central London (Tower, Westminster and Lambeth) remained open. Blackwall Tunnel also was blocked.

Utility services on the whole stood up to the attack well. Gas was the most affected. Five gas works were damaged, many mains were hit and others flooded. Supplies were cut off from almost the whole of Southwark, Bermondsey and north Camberwell but apart from these boroughs, and many small areas in Poplar and Clerkenwell, supplies were everywhere satisfactory.

As for water, pressure was low in most boroughs as a result of the breaking of 47 large mains and about 100 smaller ones, but only in Islington and Camberwell was it necessary to resort to water tanks.

Electricity suffered less. Although six power stations were reported hit and Central Electricity Board and other cables put out of commission, interruptions in supply were temporary and confined to a few districts to the east.

Telephone services were seriously interfered with. Some damage was caused to the transmission equipment of the Trunk and Toll Exchanges in Faraday Buildings and, coupled with damage to 40 trunk and 50 junction cables, seriously affected services between London and various parts of the country including 10 main centres, eg Manchester. The work of repair is proceeding under difficult conditions. There was minor damage to other exchanges.

The following report on food losses were received: 'Only a small amount of meat was apparently affected and the flour position is good. Some 1,000 tons of sugar were destroyed and about 25,000 chests of that commodity as

SC 1800 bombs, two of many dropped over London on 10 May 1941.

well as 14,000 boxes of butter are endangered. 16,000 gallons of milk were lost when a train was derailed'...

This was just part of the story. More than 2,100 fires were reported, fourteen hospitals were affected, and in the region of 1,360 civilians killed and 1,600 injured.

From the *Luftwaffe* perspective, the bombers attacked in two waves, with *Luftflotte* 3 reporting 291 attacking in the first wave and sixty-seven in the second; the precise number committed by *Luftflotte* 2 is uncertain, but 571 bomber sorties were apparently flown that night, and a number of other targets were also attacked by single aircraft.

AA guns claimed just two bombers over London, while another Heinkel 111 of 9/*KG* 55 was shot down attacking an aluminium factory at Birmingham. Night-fighter sorties were in the region of 325 and consisted single-seat, radar-assisted and non-radar-assisted aircraft. Claims were twenty-three bombers destroyed, seven probably destroyed and ten damaged. Yet again, claims were over-optimistic. In the first wave *Luftflotte* 3 reported that it lost two aircraft from III/*KG* 27 (one over the target area) and one from I/*KG* 55 – a further Heinkel 111 from II/*KG* 27 was abandoned over Orleans, and another from I/*KG* 55 ditched in the Channel and its crew were rescued. A Heinkel 111 of I/*KG* 27 also returned badly damaged by a 'Bristol Blenheim'. The second sortie saw the loss of two aircraft from III/*KG* 55 with a further aircraft ditching, and apparently a Junkers 88 crashed on take-off. Losses for *Luftflotte* 2 are less precise, but I/*KG* 28 lost one aircraft and two were lost by *KG* 53. Numerous aircraft were reported as damaged, some returning with wounded or dead crew members. RAF losses were just one, when Plt Off Frantisek Behal of 1 Sqn was apparently accidentally shot down by Fg Off Ed Crew of 604 Sqn and killed when his Hurricane crashed near Croydon.

Luftwaffe *reconnaissance photographs of aluminium factories at Birmingham showing Birmetal (Target 712, left) and James Booth (Target 714, right).*

The memories of those Germans who survived the night are still vivid. One of the first losses was from 2/*KG* 28 and was witnessed by a pilot from another aircraft from the same *Staffel*:

Leutnant Wilhelm Neumann, 1/KG 28

The *Gruppe Technisches Offizier* (*TO*) was *Lt* Otto Krüger. He was shot down over London by a Defiant [sic] about 100 metres in front of my aircraft. I could see them getting out by parachute. Otto's parachute on landing became entangled with the roof of a house and, by swinging out, he landed through the window into the dining room for tea. I succeeded him as *TO*...'[9]

[9] Neumann would be shot down attacking ships on 25 June 1941.

Credit for this loss has been given to four RAF night-fighters – two Hurricanes from 1 Sqn, another from 242 Sqn and even a Havoc from 85 Sqn – but the account of Wilhelm Neumann would discount the Havoc.

Another loss was from 3/*KG* 53:

Leutnant Walther von Siber, 3/KG 53

Lt *Walther von Siber (right). In the middle is* Oblt *Hans-Georg Ziegler, also of 3/KG 53, who was reported missing over the UK on 27-28 February 1941.* (Von Siber)

...My first mission was on London, other targets were Birmingham, Liverpool, Sheffield, Derby, Hull, Glasgow, Nottingham, etc. I also flew special sorties on merchant ships, harbour supply facilities at the English east coast, armament industry in the area of Nottingham and Norwich, and aircraft on night-flying airfields.

As a reprisal attack for the English air raid on Berlin, the *Gruppe* attacked London with twenty-three Heinkel He 111s twice that night. The only aircraft lost was our own A1+CL. It was a full moon and a very clear night. I can remember that we had been on our bombing run on the parliament/government quarter when the first salvo of a night-fighter (probably a Spitfire) hit our He 111. In a fraction of a second we jettisoned the bombs, opened fire with our defensive armament, and took evasive actions – but to little or no avail. The second burst was very effective and our Heinkel caught fire.

Now the *Beobachter* tried to find out about the state of the plane and the situation of the crew because there had been no answer to my questions and only groans could be heard over the intercom. Petrol was on fire in the central part of the He 111. *Fw* Fischer reported that *Uffz* Schurff and *Ofw* Meister were dead and that *Fw* Wylezol was wounded, hanging in his harness, and not able to get through the flames. Because of the blazing heat Fischer could not help, so I ordered him to bail out over land. I wanted to try to ditch the aircraft in the Channel. This way I could possibly rescue my crew and reach the French coast in our dinghy. Unfortunately I was not able to carry out this decision. Combat damage and fire had caused the loss of controls and the aircraft began to turn left and finally got into a spin. Luckily I had asked Fischer before he had bailed out to open the hatch over my pilot's seat, so eventually the movements of the spin threw me out of the plane. However, I do not know if I had pulled the ripcord consciously or not, but I came round again when the parachute opened up. I was captured by members of the Home Guard.

Again, who shot this aircraft down cannot be said for certain – some sources say it was Sgt Josef Dygryn of 1 Sqn, others say Sgt Percy Copeland of 151 Sqn. However, the RAF pilot that shot down the Heinkel 111 of 5/*KG* 53 near Ashford is certain:

Hauptmann Albert Hufenreuther, 5/KG 53

Hptm *Hufenreuther (front, third from right)*.

Together with four of my crew, I was shot down about midnight on 10/11 May 1941. It was to be our last mission against England before the *Gruppe* had to move somewhere else. In captivity, I learned it was to the east for the Russian Front.

That night there was good – too good – visibility when we dropped our bombs on London. Searchlights everywhere probing their beams into the sky, our pathfinders had thrown flares to help us find the targets, fires and smoke rose up from the ground, continuous fire from the *Flak* guns demonstrated what had been installed against us, and amongst the smoke balls from the exploding shells and the light beams there were hundreds of German bombers and some British night-fighters playing cat and dog with us.

After having released the bombs, we turned south to make for home. At that moment a night-fighter must have got behind us. When I saw the first tracer bullets to the left of my cockpit, it had already happened. The port engine trembled, instruments went crazy and within a short time the engine stopped. The only thing we could still do was to feather the propellers. The starboard engine was OK and by trading height for speed, we tried to get home...'[10]

Flying Officer Roger Boulding, 74 Sqn

A Spitfire of 74 Sqn.

It was one of those full-moon efforts when an elaborate plan for the defence of London was tried out. The ack-ack was restricted to a height of about 12,000 feet over central London, outside of which it was unrestricted except for (in theory!) a narrow corridor between two vertical searchlights. Outside the ack-ack were the regular night-fighters under close control, and at 500-foot intervals over the central area were individual day-fighters relying on their own eyes only, and I was one of these.

[10] 11 May was an unlucky date for *Hptm* Hufenreuther, as exactly a year earlier almost to the hour, when with *Stab* I/KG 53, he had been shot down by a French fighter near Reims, had crash-landed and been captured. He had been released in July 1940 and after a short time in the HQ in Berlin, had only just returned to his *Geschwader*.

On my first trip, after patrolling for some time over what seemed an enormous pyramid of flame, I had some trouble with the revs and, as it was nearly the end of my patrol, I decided to head basewards. Then, in spite of the glare of the exhausts, I saw in the brilliant moonlight just ahead of me the unmistakeable shape of a Heinkel 111. I closed from astern and just below, opening fire with a short burst, which hit him and created an immense cloud of fireworks. He dived hard and I followed. This put him against the dark background of the earth and me silhouetted against the moonlit sky, and gave his top rear gunner the opportunity to have squirt every time I got anywhere near him lining up for another go – very uncomfortable. Eventually I lost him after he had indulged in some very hairy low-level stuff across Kent in the dark.

Hufenreuther's He 111. (Boulding)

Some of us went to have a look at the Heinkel a few days later. He was most fortunate to have finished up after a wheels-up landing with small trees embedded in his leading edges but not in the nose. We went to the hospital outside Canterbury where the crew were taken, but I was told they were all badly injured so did not meet them.

Ironically enough, in June 1941 I was shot down during a sweep over France and spent the rest of the war behind the wire in Germany. C'est la guerre!

Another German crewman lucky to survive that night was 42-year-old *Lt* Martin Reiser, a *Beobachter* with 9/*KG* 55. Reiser had fought in the Great War, and had flown a number of missions with *Oblt* Johann Speck von Sternberg, who, just 3 hours before, had been shot down by *Flak* near Birmingham and was by now dead. This was Reiser's 26th operational flight against London, his 118th of the war and the second flight that night. He and his crew were unlucky to be intercepted by a Defiant of 151 Sqn crewed by Flt Lt Desmond McMullen and Sgt Stanley Fairweather:

NCO members of Hptm *Wolfgang Langer's crew from* 7/KG 27: *Fw* Erwin Ortmann, *Uffz Karl Bersack and* Uffz *Heinz Krause. Langer's He 111 would be shot down off Seaford by Plt Off Alan Grout of 29 Sqn at 0200hrs on 11 May 1941; there were no survivors.*

… the gunner sighted an He 111 but lost it immediately afterwards. The pilot picked it up again, however, travelling south very fast at 17,000 feet. With plug pulled, the Defiant overhauled and two long bursts were fired from under the port wing at 75 yds range. Both engines of e/a emitted dense smoke and the aircraft turned north, losing height in a series of 'S' turns. There was no return fire. Two more bursts from the starboard side were fired upon which e/a caught fire and spiralled down. Searchlights then illuminated both aircraft which helped Defiant.

Two of the crew bailed out and the machine crashed in flames. A fix was obtained and the position appeared to be within five miles of Tunbridge Wells…

Martin Reiser was the only survivor from his crew and his Heinkel 111 was the last bomber to crash on mainland Britain that night. As the sun rose on 11 May 1941, London counted the cost and prepared for more. However, inexplicable as it would seem, there would be no repetition that night. Although the ICI Ltd factory at Billingham-on-Tees was attacked, the German targets had changed:

It will be seen that nearly the whole of the German effort on this night was against RAF aerodromes and stations and no fewer than 22 were hit…

The remains of Oblt *Johann Speck von Sternberg's He 111 at Earlswood, Warwickshire.* (Parry)

The shattered remains of Lt Martin Reiser's He 111 *at Withyham, Sussex.* (Saunders)

Seen here in its factory codes, Wk Nr 2958 *was assigned to 2/KG 55 and crash-landed at Chartres after attacking London on 11 May 1941.* Uffz *Heinz Bornstedt and* Uffz *Walter Hofmann were both wounded.*

Luftflotte 3 acknowledged that, for some reason, the targets that night for 241 bombers were twenty-two airfields and a series of other lesser targets, including factories at Coventry and Manchester; of the six aircraft lost that night (which included a Messerschmitt Bf 110 *Jabo* of 2/*Schnellkampfgeschwader* 210), five were brought down by *Flak*.

The nights that followed saw a reduction in effort by the *Luftwaffe* and, apart from an attack on Birmingham on the night of 16 May 1941, targets remained airfields and coastal targets in support of the breakout of the battleship *Bismarck*, which was eventually sunk on 27 May. Although there would be other lesser Blitzes against Britain, *the* Blitz was over.

One of the lucky ones: Lt Hans Thurner (left) of 9/KG 55 survived the Blitz only to be killed in action over Normandy on 10-11 June 1944. (Gruber)

Epilogue
11 May-22 June 1941

'In view of the four weeks' recuperation which the German long-range bomber force has enjoyed, it is considered that the units in central Germany and on the Western Front are now ready to undertake large-scale operations.'
ASO Summary No 212, 21 June 1941

The day after this comment was made, Germany launched Operation 'Barbarossa', the invasion of the Soviet Union. Those bomber units left on the Western Front were now a shadow of what had been there six months before.

German attacks continued with what units had not yet been withdrawn to the east. The trouble now was that AI-equipped night-fighter squadrons were increasing in number and they were becoming increasingly effective, and losses, especially of experienced crews, were mounting.

One crew from 7/*KG* 27 had been in constant action since August 1940. *Lt* Helmut Einicke had flown in the region of eighty-two operational flights. His *Bordfunker* explains what was happening at the end of May 1941:

Lt *Einicke's 1G+GR, lost on the night of 28 May 1941.* (Einicke)

Unteroffizier Hans Mühlhahn, 7/KG 27

It was 6 o'clock in the morning on 27 May 1941 when the NCO of the day sounded the alarm. We were based at Orleans airfield in France. We had been flying night missions on targets in Britain with our He 111 Ps until three weeks ago.

During the past few days our ground crew had removed the temporary black colour for night sorties from the aircraft. We had been given a break and some of us had received new uniforms. Unnecessary baggage had to be packed and sent home. There was a rumour going round persistently that we should be transferred to Italy or Africa.

However, a few minutes after we had been alerted, the crews were ready for action. But this time, which was unusual, we did not meet in the briefing room. The bus took us directly to the airfield. Here we were sitting around and waited for things to come. But there was no order to go into action and it was about midday when we returned to our billets again. In the afternoon we listened to the *Wehrmachtsbericht* and heard that the battleship *Bismarck* had been attacked by strong forces of the RN and the RAF and that her crew had scuttled the ship at about 1035hrs in the morning.

Now we knew why we had been alerted – to attack the English Fleet. It was about 1700hrs when all crews were ordered to meet in the briefing room. Here our *Staffel Kapitän* announced the sinking of the *Bismarck* and read out the combat orders. We were to attack the ships of the English Fleet which were, according to reports, on their way back to British waters. Flying very low, our *Kette* had the order to search for the enemy between England and Ireland (St George's Channel) and to attack with 250kg bombs.

The planes received their temporary black under-surfaces again and at about 1900hrs our *Kette* took off for the mission. We did not feel especially well because who really likes the idea of attacking a naval formation at low level? However, we were searching for the ships until it was pitch-black in the target area, but without success. Our secondary target was the harbour of Plymouth, which we had been ordered to attack from 6,560 feet. The *Kette* broke up, the aircraft climbed up to the ordered flying height and dropped the bombs. We all returned safely to our home base.

The following night would see coastal targets again being attacked:

Lt Helmut Einicke, 7/KG 27

Lt *Helmut Einicke*. (Einicke)

Task:	1. Attack on harbour facilities and ships in Liverpool 2. Test flight for *Knickebein* beam
Time of take-off:	28 May 41, 2308hrs
Load:	Full fuel load Six 250kg HE bombs
Time of attack:	29 May 41, 0120hrs
Flight route:	Orleans-Cherbourg-on radio beam to Liverpool
Altitude:	Depending on weather and defences
Altitude during bombing run:	Left up to our own decision

We crossed the French coast at about 3,300 feet east of Cherbourg. From there we climbed up to 11,800 feet flying the radio beam. Because of different wind forces it took about an hour until we were able to keep the aircraft constantly on *Knickebein* course.

There was the usual *Flak* and also night-fighters. But the crew did not observe the night-fighter that attacked us later. There was the normal sound of exploding *Flak* shells but suddenly, at 0112hrs, the noise of eight shots in regular intervals could be distinguished. Petrol was leaking out of the starboard

An He 111 of 7/KG 27 gets airborne for England. (Einicke)

wing-tip and the aircraft began to burn. I pushed forward the control column and dived down 3,300 feet in the hope of extinguishing the fire – but without success. When I pulled the plane out of the dive again the fire had reached the engine. So I ordered my crew to report and bail out. The *Beobachter* hooked to his parachute and jumped first through the side window. The *Bordfunker* reported and jumped next. Although I called several times I got no reply from the *Bordmechaniker*. Then I unbuckled and trimmed the plane to go in a climb, opened the sliding hatch above my seat and stood up looking to the rear of the aircraft. There, in the light of the fire, I could see the *Bordfunker* who had become entangled with his harness. He had already jettisoned the sliding dorsal gunner's windscreen and after a few moments I saw him jump into the dark night – with spread-out arms, disappearing between elevator and tail fin. I followed him and fell through a broken-up cloud layer.

I waited for a while until I pulled the ripcord to avoid being blown in the direction of the sea. When I eventually hit the ground the impact was so hard that I sprained my right knee. The pain was so bad that I first thought everything had been broken.

With my utility knife I destroyed my flying helmet and cut a few handkerchiefs out of my parachute. Then I thought about my situation. It was not possible to escape with my hurt leg, and I did not want to fall in the hands of the civilian population. So I cut a walking stick from a hedge and limped in the direction of the next *Flak* battery. After some hours I was captured by two soldiers of the Home Guard.

My crew and I were all taken to the police station in Mold. There my *Bordmechaniker* told me why he had not answered my call. While the aircraft was diving after the night-fighter attack, his parachute had fallen into the rear of the plane. So he was forced to disconnect the intercom and to creep into the rear to get back his chute. At the same moment he had fastened his parachute he was thrown out of the plane and landed exactly at this police station in Mold.

The *Bordfunker*'s recollections are similarly dramatic:

What was waiting for the Einicke crew: a Beaufighter of 604 Sqn. (via Wakefield)

Unteroffizier Hans Mühlhahn, 7/KG 27

I climbed down from my seat to set the correct frequency when there was a terrible bang in the plane and it was as bright as day. I hit my head on the radio equipment and felt that something hot was running down my back. Later I concluded that it must have been a small AA shrapnel. A little bit dazed I tried to climb back to my seat again. There I noticed that the plane was going into a right spin. From my seat I was able to see the mess; a long tongue of fire came out of the right wing.

I was not able to talk to my pilot – the intercom had failed. There was only one hope: to bail out from my station, the dorsal gunner's position. When I wanted to push back the sliding windscreen I noticed that an AA shell had already done this for me. The windscreen had been shot away. While trying to get out I had a quick glance at the altimeter. It read 12,130 feet and it was 0112hrs. The first try to leave on the port side of the aircraft failed. My harness had got entangled in parts of the machine gun. With all my strength I tried to get free and finally succeeded. In fractions of a second I was free; there was a hissing sound when I fell past the tail plane. Now I had time and counted from 1 to 23, as I had learned. But where the hell was the handle of the ripcord? Eventually I found it and pulled. There was a swoosh behind me, a bang and a jerk, which pulled the flying boots off my feet, and I was hanging on my parachute.

Darkness around me. At some distance beams of searchlights wandered through the sky like ghosts. The AA batteries were also quite busy and I was afraid of being wounded just hanging on my chute. And there was the big question: where do you come down – on water or land? Just in case, I had one hand at the life jacket's bottle of compressed air, the other one at the buckle of my harness. Then everything happened very fast. In the darkness I saw tree-tops and at the same moment my feet hit the ground. A blow on the buckle and I was free. I had landed on a meadow.

When I took off my flying helmet I felt something sticky on my fingers. After some examination I found a torch in my life jacket, switched it on and found that the sticky feeling was my own blood. And now I also felt the pain – there was an injury to my head. My wristwatch read 0119hrs. So I had been hanging on my chute for 7 minutes. However, I had landed somewhere in the British Isles, near Liverpool. Only thirty-six years later I was able to find out that I had come down in Nercwys, a small settlement near Mold.

I shouted and tried to get some attention. One reason was that I hoped members of my crew had landed near where I was. But I did not get any answer. So I drew my pistol and fired until the magazine was empty. Again no answer.

Now I tried to get to a settlement or, at least, to meet some people. I left my parachute where it was – it was of no use any more. After a short walk across a field I reached a hedge, which I climbed. Because of the blackout there was darkness all around me, no gleam of light. I decided to take the path on my left and after several hundred yards I met two men. One of them, in uniform, was my age, the other one about 40 years. They took hold of me and led me to a house nearby.

Here, six or seven people were sitting in a larger room, their night's sleep disturbed by the air raid. I gave my pistol and one of my first aid packs, which I had in my flying suit, to the younger man in uniform. An elderly woman dressed my wound and offered me tea and bread. I had a few sips but was not able to eat anything, because I was sure that my way into captivity had begun right now.

After some time, about an hour, with this nice family who had had taken care of me so well, I heard a vehicle stopping in front of the house and then several policemen entered. They searched me thoroughly for weapons and took me to the waiting vehicle. The driver was an elderly woman, in uniform with a steel helmet on her head. They took me to the police station in a small town. In the guardroom a doctor was waiting for me. He examined my head injury and dressed the wound once more. I tried to find out the whereabouts of my crew but did not get any answer. They wanted to know the number of crew members and I told them there had been four. Then I was taken into a cell and they left me and my thoughts alone. You could still hear the AA guns and our aircraft on their way back home. Now I was a Prisoner of War.

Next morning in my cell – I had not got a wink of sleep that night – I was given something to eat. When I asked if members of my crew had been found I got an answer that I thought was positive. That came true in the afternoon when Army soldiers collected us at the police station. My crew was complete again, though we all looked the worse for wear. A long way into captivity began for me, as POW serial No 20948...

The confusion as to who shot down this Heinkel 111 was also shared by the British. Wg Cdr Charles Appleton of 604 Sqn filed a combat report that concluded:

…My first visual was of the exhausts and the second and third occasions I could see both the exhausts and the silhouette. My operator, realising the danger from

Officers of 604 Sqn: Wg Cdr Charles Appleton is seated, third from the right, apparently talking to Hugh Speke (standing on the extreme right).

searchlights, kept us in contact about 3,000 feet away and dead astern of the target. We finally got our fourth visual on a range of 1,200 feet. I closed to 200 feet and opened fire from dead astern. Hits were seen on the fuselage and then there was a large explosion. The e/a dived in flames to the ground where it continued to burn. The place was Mold, Flintshire.

However, Anti-Aircraft Command received the following report:

Mersey guns opened fire at 0110hrs at a height of 7,000 feet and fired four rounds. The gun site responsible and other gun sites in the vicinity saw the bursts, which were immediately followed by a flash and a flaming mass which dived towards the earth and is presumed to be the aircraft found at Buckley near Mold, Flintshire...

Such was the disagreement that Lt Gen Frederick Pyle, the General Officer Commanding in Chief, wrote to CINC Fighter Command disputing the RAF's claim. It is not known for certain how this ended, but the RAF maintained that this kill was theirs. With the Blitz now over, it appears that the lack of aircraft to shoot down was becoming a cause for argument!

Conclusion

From the German invasion of France and the Low Countries on 10 May 1940 to exactly one year and one day later, Britain had stood alone against Nazi Germany and more importantly the *Luftwaffe*, and had survived.

The RAF had proven itself in the Battle of Britain, forcing the German bombers to fly their attacks by night. This itself was a problem for the RAF as it had few night-fighters and, of those, even fewer had AI radar. Even then, first-generation AI radar was nowhere near as effective as later versions. As we have seen, it was not until late November 1940 that the first German bomber was shot down by an AI-equipped night-fighter. Thus, the majority of British claims against German night-bombers were by generally inaccurate AA fire or by aircraft that had proven themselves to be inadequate as day-fighters. Furthermore, the last night of the Blitz saw more single-seat day-fighters claiming German bombers than AI-equipped night-fighters, albeit many of the claims were wildly over-optimistic or multiple claims (in one case a quadruple claim!).

Despite what many might think, German intelligence as to what to bomb was generally good. As we have seen with the bombing of the BMARC factory at Grantham, the *Luftwaffe* generally knew what they were targeting and, thanks to blind bombing systems such as *Knickebein* and X *Gerät*, were able to attack targets the length and breadth of the United Kingdom with a high degree of accuracy, despite British attempts to jam or bend the beams.

An He 111 of 2/KGr 100. (Schick)

Attaching protective covers to a He 111, France 1941.

Of the Blitz, in 1941, Air Chief Marshal Sir William Sholto Douglas, CINC Fighter Command, optimistically stated that:

> If the enemy had not chosen that moment to pull out we should soon have been inflicting such casualties on his night-bombers that the continuation of his night offensive on a similar scale would have been impossible.

One can argue against this in that by May 1941 the *Luftwaffe* was still able to put a massive force of bombers over a single target for hours on end, suffering minimal (and in some cases no) losses to British defences. One can agree that the *Luftwaffe*'s Blitz did give Britain an impetus to counter the German attacks, and by 1943 this had been almost honed to perfection – the impact of night-fighters and improved radar-predicted AA guns was evident, especially when what became known as the 'Baby Blitz' began in January 1944.

A Beaufighter VI of 409 Sqn. Formed in June 1941 to combat the night threat, by 1942 the Squadron was equipped with a much better AI radar.

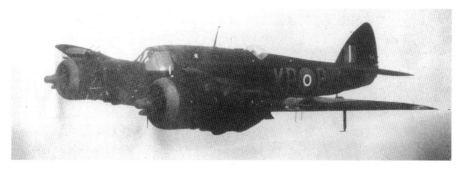

The arrival of the Mosquito inflicted even greater carnage during subsequent Blitzes.

So did the *Luftwaffe*'s Blitz fail? Looking at what German bombers did to London and such cities as Liverpool, they generally achieved their aim for the night of the attack, but had they continued to attack the same target night after night that target would have ceased to function as part of the British war machine. However, by switching to another target for another night gave the original target and the defences time to recover or recuperate – a simple case of German selection and maintenance of aim failing, as it had in the Battle of Britain.

The main reason the Blitz did fail was 'Barbarossa' and Hitler's gaze falling on the Balkans and the Mediterranean – with *Luftflotte 2* gone, what was left in *Luftflotte* 3 was not enough to continue an effective renewed Blitz campaign – reduced bomber numbers attacking the same targets, and now up against improved defences, would never have the same effect. Furthermore, the promise of newer or improved bombers

The Do 217 first flew operationally against the UK from July 1941. Its first loss was during a daylight attack on the 16th when Lt Anton Wieners of 4/KG 2 was shot down by Plt Off Robert Masters of 234 Sqn.

An attempt to counter the night-fighter menace: an He 111 fitted with a downwards-firing 20mm cannon.

such as the Dornier 217 fell short of what was really required – a bomber that could fly faster, higher, carry more bombs and defend itself.

It cannot be forgotten that those who lived through the Blitz suffered greatly. Pre-war estimates were that aerial bombardment would result in a predicted 600,000 civilian deaths; thankfully the Blitz saw less than 10% of that figure. Soon it would be the turn of the German civilians to experience what Britain had during the Blitz – their suffering would be much more and the death toll considerably and dreadfully higher.

Another loss: this Ju 88 A-4 of 3/KG 30 became lost attacking Birkenhead on the night of 23 July 1941 and landed at RAF Broadfield Down near Bristol.

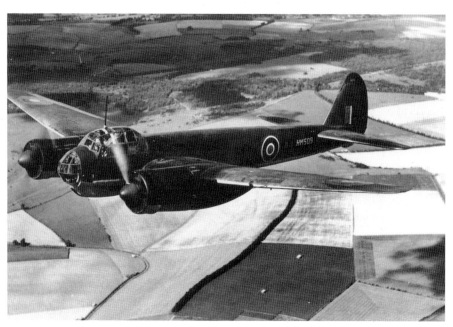

This Ju 88 A-5 was formerly M2+MK of 2/106 and landed in error at RAF Chivenor on the night of 26 November 1941.

Heinkel 111s of an unknown unit preparing for another nocturnal mission.

Appendix 1
Dramatis Personae

Prologue

19 June 1940

Stab II/*KG* 4; He 111 H-4 8747 5J+DM

Maj Dietrich Frhr Von Massenbach (*B, Gr Kdr*)-POW
Oblt Ulrich Jordan-*F-TO*-POW
Ofw Max Leimer-BF-POW
Fw Karl Amberger-BM-POW

Shot down by Flt Lt R.M.B. Duke-Woolley/AC D, Bell and Sgt A. Close/LAC L. Karasek of 23 Sqn and crashed at Blakeney Creek, Cley, Norfolk, 0045hrs

30 September 1940

2/*KG* 77; Ju 88 A-1 2142 3Z+DK

Oblt Friedrich Oeser-*F*-POW
Ofw Gustav Gorke-*B*-POW
Uffz Georg Klasing-*BM*-+
Gefr Rudi Hulsmann-*BS*-POW

Shot down by Sgt P. C. Farnes of 501 Sqn and crash-landed on Gatwick Race Course, 1500hrs

Chapter 1

1 November 1940

8/*KG* 55; He 111 P-2 1571 G1+JS

Lt Hans-Adalbert Tüffers-*F*-POW
Uffz Ernst Hawerstreng-*B*-POW
Uffz Richard Bubel-*BF*-+
Uffz Josef Juvan-*BM*-+

Shot down by *Flak* and crashed at Matlock Gardens, Hornchurch, Essex, 2145hrs

9 November 1940

2/*KG* 1; He 111 H-3 3335 V4+IK

Lt Max Probst-*F*-POW
Gefr Reinhard Geisinger-*B*-+
Uffz August Krüger-*BF*-+
Fw Rudolf Gey-*BM*-+

Shot down by *Flak* and crashed at Johnson Road, Bromley, Kent, 1928hrs

13 November 1940

8/*LG* 1; Ju 88 A-1 6157 L1+LS

Fw Willi Erwin-*F*-POW
Uffz Herbert Wermuth-*B*-POW
Fw Erwin Zins-*BF*-POW
Gefr Hans Bossdorf-BM-+

Shot down by Flt Lt W. J. Leather and Plt Off R. A. Johnston of 611 Sqn and crash-landed at Woodway Farm, Blewbury, Berks, 1445hrs

23 December 1940

3/*KGr* 100; He 111 H-2 2641 6N+DL

Fw Georg Deininger-*F*-Inj
Fw Helmut Uhlmann-*B*-Inj
Uffz Kurt Ott-*BF*-Inj
Ogefr Hans-Werner Hohlfeld-*BS*-Inj

Damaged in combat with Flt Lt J. C. Cunningham/Sgt J. Phillipson of 604 Sqn and crash-landed near Cherbourg

Chapter 2

16 January 1941

32 Sqn; Hurricane I P2984

Fg Off Jan Falkowski-Inj

Suffered engine failure during night sortie; pilot bailed out and ac crashed on Hayling Island, Hants

19 January 1941

1/*KG* 1; He 111 H-3 3325 V4+FH

Hptm Gustav Friedrich Graf zu Castell-Castell-*F-St Kap*-+
Ofw Günther Janson-*BF*-+
Stfw Xavier Kroiss-*BM*-+
Gefr Günther Lenning-*BS*-+
Ofw Heinz Schubert-*B*-+

Shot down by *Flak* and crashed at Wyckham Farm, Steyning, 2009hrs

29 January 1941

9/*KG* 30; Ju 88 A-5

Oblt Friedrich-Karl Rinck-*F-St Kap*-POW
Ogefr Ernst Stiller-*B*-POW
Ofw Wilhelm Rüther-*BF*-POW
Uffz Ferdinand Wissing-*BM*-POW

Damaged by *Flak* and crash-landed at
Pilley's Lane, Boston, Lincs, 1530hrs

17 February 1941

3/*KGr* 606; Do 17Z-3 3472 7T+JL

Lt Günther Hübner-*F*-POW
Lt Rolf Dieskau-*B*-POW
Gefr Walter Arnold-*BF*-POW
Uffz Ernst Tietjen-*BM*-POW

Shot down by Sqn Ldr J. H. Little/Sgt C. C.
Pyne, 219 Sqn, and crashed at Oakley
Court, Bray, Berks, 2030hrs

Chapter 3

7 March 1941

2/*KG* 3; Do 17 Z-2 3391 5K+MK

Oblt Erich Kunst-*F*-POW
Ofw Herbert Wendland-*B*-POW
Fw Willi Ophoff-*BF*-+
Uffz Herbert Oeckinghaus-*BS*-POW

Shot down by *Flak* and crashed in sea off
Gorleston-on-Sea, 0815hrs

11 March 1941

Stab/*KG* 26; He 111 H-5 3655 1H+AA

Oblt Rolf Alander-*F-St Kap*-POW
Uffz Peter Wähner-*B*-M
Fw Werner Meyer-*BF*-POW
Fw August Dether-*BM*-POW

Hit mast of ship during convoy attack off
Aberdeen; ditched 12 miles off Firth of
Tay, 2045hrs

12 March 1941

5/*KG* 55; He 111 P-4 2994 G1+GN

Stfw Karl Brüning-*F*-POW
Fw Alexander Düssel-*B*-+
Fw Konrad Steiger-*BF*-+
Ofw Willi Weisse-*BM*-+

Shot down by Fg Off F. D. Hughes/Sgt F.
Gash, 264 Sqn, and crashed at Dene Farm,
Ockley, Surrey, 2130hrs

12 March 1941

6/*KG* 55; He 111 P-4 2989 G1+OP

Hptm Wolfgang Berlin-*B-St Kap*-POW
Ofw Karl Single-*F*-POW
Fw Xaver Diem-*BF*-POW
Fw Leonhard Kuznik-*BM*-+
Fw Heinrich Ludwinski-*BS*-+

Shot down by Sgt R. J. McNair, 96 Sqn,
and crashed at Milton Road, Widnes,
2210hrs

12 March 1941

9/*KG* 76; Ju 88 A-5 7188 F1+BT

Fw Günther Unger-*F*-POW
Fw August Meier-*B*-POW
Uffz Franz Bergmann-*BF*-POW
Ofw Willi Dierk-*BM*-POW

Shot down by *Flak* and crashed at The
Croft, Wychbold, Worcs, 2210hrs

23 March 1941

4/*KG* 77; Ju 88 A-5 7103 3Z+DM

Oblt Werner Lode-*F*-POW
Ofw Josef Billesfeld-*B*-POW
Uffz Edwin Waraczynski-*BF*-POW
Uffz Franz Wallner-*BM*-+

Shot down by Flt Lt E. Morris and Sgt F. A.
Bernard, 238 Sqn, and crashed at Parsons
Farm, Poling, West Sussex, 1236hrs

8 April 1941

9/*KG* 26; He 111H-5 3628 1H+ET

Lt Julius Tengler-*F*-POW
Gefr Wolfgang Euerl-*B*-+
Uffz Hubert Faber-*BF*-POW
Gefr Franz Reitmeyer-*BM*-POW
Uffz Hans Zender-*BF*-POW

Shot down by Sqn Ldr A. T. D. Sutton/Plt Off F. C. Sutton, 264 Sqn, and crashed at Bendish House, Witwell, Herts, 2212hrs

9 April 1941

3/KG 55; He 111 P-4 2962 G1+DL

Ofw Heinz Söllner-*F*-POW
Hptm Otto Bodemeyer-*B-Gr Kdr*-POW
Fw Hans Kaufhold-*BF*-POW
Fw Herbert Link-*BM*-POW

Shot down by Plt Off R. P. Stevens, 151 Sqn, and crashed at Roes Rest Farm, Desford, Leics, 0145hrs

10 April 1941

SchuleSt/*KG* 26; He 111H-5 3592 1H+ID

Lt Klaus Conrad-*F*-POW
Ofw Hermann Platt-*B*-+
Uffz Karl Schwarzer-*BF*-POW
Gefr Walter Eckardt-*BS*-POW
Sd Fhr Karl-August Richter-POW

Shot down by Fg Off E. G. Barwell/Sgt A. Martin, 264 Sqn, and crashed on Blatchington Golf Course, Seaford, 2200hrs

14 April 1941

3/*KG* 28; He 111 H-5 3802 1T+EL

Lt Lothar Horras-*F*-POW
Ofw Bruno Perzanowski-*B*-POW
Gefr Kurt Schlender-*BF*-POW
Gefr Josef Brüninghausen-*BM*-+

Damaged by *Flak* and hit mountain at Llydmor, Aber, Caernarvonshire, 0530hrs. *B* was hung for murder on 18 December 1946 while a POW in Canada.

16 April 1941

3/*KG* 76; Ju 88 A5 7172 F1+DL

Oblt Erwin Moll-*F*-POW
Fw Kurt Brähler-B-POW
Fw Otto Staude-*BF*-+
Fw Ewald Franke-*BM*-POW

Shot down by Flt Lt A. R. Dottridge/Sgt G. T. Williams, 219 Sqn, and crashed 100 yards north of Wortel Road, Denmark Hill, Wimbledon, 2134hrs

17 April 1941

2/*KG* 28; He 111 H-5 3573 1T+EK

Uffz Thomas Hammerl-*F*-POW
Ofw Albert Engel-*B*-POW
Gefr Wolfgang Schüler-*BF*-+
Gefr Richard Mattern-*BS*-+

Shot down by Wg Cdr T. Pike/Sgt W. T. M. Clark, 219 Sqn, and crashed at Petworth Road, Wormley, Surrey, 0230hrs

17 April 1941

8/*KG* 77; Ju 88 A-5 5131 3Z+BS

Lt Günther Sissimato-*F*-POW
Gefr Paul Schuhmann-*BF*-POW
Uffz Walter Meissler-*B*-POW
Uffz Georg Abell-*BM*-POW

Shot down by *Flak* and crashed at
Observatory Gardens, Campden Hill Road,
Kensington, 0205hrs

1 May 1941

4/*KG* 27; He 111 P-2 2604

Lt Helmut Ballauf-*F*-POW
Fw Franz Förster-*B*-+
Uffz Rolf Averberg-*BF*-+
Fw Heinrich Platt-BM-+

Shot down by Plt Off A. J. Hodgkinson/Sgt
B. E. Dye, 219 Sqn, and crashed in sea
south of Shoreham, Sussex, 2245hrs

3 May 1941

8/*KG* 26; He 111 H-6 4064 1H+DS

Uffz Georg Macher-*F*-POW
Uffz Otto Kaminsky-*B*-+
Gefr Bernhard Möllers-*BM*-+
Gefr Bernhard Winterscheidt-*BF*-POW

Shot down by Flt Lt A. Dottridge/Sgt G. T.
Williams, 219 Sqn, and crashed at Oakhurst
Farm, Sidlesham, West Sussex, 2245hrs

4 May 1941

3/*KG* 53; He 111 H-4 3235 A1+LK

Lt Alfred Plank Von Bachselten-*F*-POW
Gefr Blasius Regnat-*B*-POW
Gefr Bruno Kauhardt-*BF*-+
Uffz Walter Richter-*BM*-POW

Either shot down by Sgt A. M. Hill/Sgt E.
J. Hollis, 25 Sqn, 0025hrs, or Sgt H. E.
Bodien/Sgt D. Wrampling, 151 Sqn.
Crash-landed ay Sharrington, Norfolk,
0104hrs

5 May 1941

2/106; Ju 88 A-5 0656 M2+DK

Oblt zS Reinhard Metzger-*B*-POW
Oblt Ernst Jürgens-*F*-POW
Ofw Hans Beeck-*BF*-POW
Fw Heinrich Jänischen-*BS*-POW

Shot down by Sgt K. B. Hollowell/Sgt R.
G. Crossman, 25 Sqn, and crashed at 13-15
High Street, Idle, Bradford, 0045hrs

6 May 1941

2/*KG* 53; He 111 H-5 3550 A1+CK

Uffz Karl Rassloff-*F*-POW
Gefr Emmerich Lehrnbass-*B*-POW
Gefr Walter Schmidt-*BM*-POW
Uffz Karl Simon-*BF*-POW
Gefr Heinz Quittenbaum-BS-POW

Shot down either by Fg Off V. V. S.
Verity/Sgt F. W. Wake, 96 Sqn, or Fg Off
R. L. F. Day/Fg Off F. C. A. Lanning, 141
Sqn, and crash-landed at St George's
Mental Hospital, Morpeth,
Northumberland, 2359hrs

7 May 1941

5/*KG* 30; Ju 88 A-5 7177 4D+EN

Uffz Hans Schaber-*F*-POW
Gefr Heinz Nöske-*B*-POW
Ofw Paul Graupner-*BF*-POW
Gefr Werner Arndt-*BS*-POW

Damaged in combat with Fg Off R. L. F.
Day/Fg Off F. C. A. Lanning, 141 Sqn, and
crash-landed on Holy Island, 0240hrs

7 May 1941

7/*KG* 27; He 111 P-2 2513 1G+BR

Lt Ekkehard Wüllenweber-F-POW
Fw Karl Ebert-*B*-+
Ofw Theo Kowolik-*BF*-+
Fw Johannes Ottlik-*BM*-+

Shot down by Sqn Ldr C. A. Pritchard/Sgt
B. P. Gledhill, 600 Sqn, and crashed at
Foxwell Farm, Oborne, Dorset, 0345hrs

8 May 1941

Stab/*KG* 27; He 111H-2 1647 1G+NA

Oblt Johannes Maron-*B*-POW
Ofw Heinrich Ronge-*F*-POW
Fw Heinz Dietrich-*BF*-POW
Uffz Heinrich Eggers-*BM*-POW
Ogefr Helmut Hilger-*BS*-POW

Shot down by Fg Off G. Howden/Sgt
Fielding, 600 Sqn, and crashed at Stock
Lane, Langford, Weston super Mare,
0012hrs

8 May 1941

3/*KG* 55; He 111 P-4 2874 G1+LL

Lt Heinz Dunkerbeck-*F*-POW
Fw Fritz Kitzing-*B*-POW
Uffz Joachim Salm-*BF*-+
Uffz Alfred Hentzsch-*BM*-+
Flg Cornell Mildenberger-*PK*-

Shot down by Plt Off D. Toone/Fg R. L.
Lamb, 256 Sqn, and crashed at Bagillt
Police Station, 0140hrs

11 May 1941

5/*KG* 53; He 111 H-5 3976 A1+JN

Hptm Albert Hufenreuther-B-POW
Fw Richard Furthmann-*F*-POW
Uffz Karl Gerhardt-*BF*-POW
Uffz Josef Berzbom-*BM*-POW
Gefr Eggert Weber-*BS*-POW

Shot down by Fg Off R. Boulding, 74 Sqn,
and crash-landed at Kennington, Ashford,
0006hrs

11 May 1941

3/*KG* 53; He 111 H-5 4002 A1+CL

Lt Walther Von Siber-*F*-POW
Fw Karl-Josef Fischer-B-POW
Uffz Adolf Schurff-*BF*-+
Ofw Helmut Meister-*BM*-+
Fw Edmund Wylezol-*BS*-+

Shot down by night-fighter and crashed at
Gore Farm, Upchurch, Kent, 0200hrs

Epilogue
29 May 1941

7/*KG* 27; He 111 P-2 1419 1G+GR

Lt Helmut Einicke-*F*-POW
Uffz Hans Hartig-*B*-POW
Gefr Konrad Baron-*BM*-POW
Uffz Hans Muhlhahn-*BF*-POW

Shot down by Wg Cdr C. H. Appleton/Plt
Off P. F. Jackson, 604 Sqn, and crashed at
Buckley, near Mold, Flintshire, 0113hrs

Appendix 2
Luftwaffe Bomber Order of Battle
November 1940-June 1941

Bold entries indicate major targets

November 1940

Luftflotte 2 (Brussels)

IX *Fliegerkorps* (Soesterburg)

Stab/KG 4	He 111	Soesterburg
I/KG 4	He 111	Soesterburg
II/KG 4	He 111	Eindhoven
Stab/KG 30	Ju 88	Eindhoven
I/KG 30	Ju 88	Eindhoven/Gilze-Rijen
II/KG 30	Ju 88	Gilze-Rijen
III/KG 30	Ju 88	Schiphol
KGr 126	He 111	Nantes (became I/KG 28 late December 1940)

II *Fliegerkorps* (Ghent)

Stab/KG 2	Do 17	St Leger/Cambrai-Sud
I/KG 2	Do 17	Epinoy
II/KG 2	Do 17	St Leger
III/KG 2	Do 17	Cambrai-Sud
Stab/KG 3	Do 17	Le Culot
I/KG 3	Do 17	Le Culot
II/KG 3	Do 17	Antwerp-Deurne
III/KG 3	Do 17	St Trond
Stab/KG 53	He 111	Lille-Nord
I/KG 53	He 111	Vitry-en-Artois
II/KG 53	He 111	Lille Vendeville
III/KG 53	He 111	Lille Mouvaux

Luftflotte 3 (Paris)

I Fliegerkorps (Beauvais)

Stab/KG 1	He 111	Amiens-Glissy/Rosieres-en-Santerre
I/KG 1	He 111	Montdidier
II/KG 1	He 111	Rosieres-en-Santerre
III/KG 1	Ju 88	Grevillers
Stab/KG 26	He 111	Beauvais
I/KG 26	He 111	Beauvais
II/KG 26	He 111	Amiens
III/KG 26	He 111	Poix Nord
Stab/KG 77	Ju 88	Laon
I/KG 77	Ju 88	Laon
II/KG 77	Ju 88	Rheims
III/KG 77	Ju 88	Laon/Juvincourt (21 Nov 40)
Stab/KG 76	Ju 88	Cormeilles-en-Vexin
I/KG 76	Do 17	Beauvais (moved away by mid-November 1940)
II/KG 76	Ju 88	Creil (moved away December 1940)
III/KG 76	Do 17	Cormeilles-en-Vexin (moved away November-mid-December 1940)

IV *Fliegerkorps* (Dinard)

KGr 100	He 111	Vannes
KGr 606	Do 17	Lannion/Brest Poulmic
Stab/KG 27	He 111	Tours
I/KG 27	He 111	Tours
II/KG 27	He 111	Bourges
III/KG 27	He 111	Rennes
I/LG 1	Ju 88	Orleans/Bricy
II/LG 1	Ju 88	Orleans/Bricy
III/LG 1	Ju 88	Chateaudun

V *Fliegerkorps* (Villacoublay)

Stab/KG 51	Ju 88	Paris/Orly
I/KG 51	Ju 88	Villaroche
II/KG 51	Ju 88	Paris/Orly
III/KG 51	Ju 88	Bretigny
Stab/KG 54	Ju 88	Evreux
I/KG 54	Ju 88	Evreux
II/KG 54	Ju 88	St Andre
KGr 806	Ju 88	Caen
Stab/KG 55	He 111	Villacoublay
I/KG 55	He 111	Dreux
II/KG 55	He 111	Chartres
III/KG 55	He 111	Villacoublay

January 1941

Luftflotte 2 (Brussels)

II *Fliegerkorps* (Ghent)

Stab/*KG* 2	Do 17	Cambrai-Sud
I/*KG* 2	Do 17	Epinoy
II/*KG* 2	Do 17	Merville (from 7 January 1941)
III/*KG* 2	Do 17	Cambrai-Sud
Stab/*KG* 3	Do 17	Le Culot
I/*KG* 3	Do 17	Le Culot
II/*KG* 3	Do 17	Antwerp-Deurne
III/*KG* 3	Do 17	St Trond
Stab/*KG* 53	He 111	Lille-Nord
I/*KG* 53	He 111	Vitry-en-Artois
II/*KG* 53	He 111	Lille Vendeville

IX *Fliegerkorps* (Soesterburg)

Stab/*KG* 4	He 111	Soesterburg
I/*KG* 4	He 111	Soesterburg
II/*KG* 4	He 111	Eindhoven
III/*KG* 4	He 111	Leeuwarden (from mid-January 1941)
Stab/*KG* 30	Ju 88	Eindhoven
I/*KG* 30	Ju 88	Gilze-Rijen
II/*KG* 30	Ju 88	Gilze-Rijen
III/*KG* 30	Ju 88	Schiphol (from 13 January 1941)
I/*KG* 28	He 111	Nantes

Luftflotte 3 (Paris)

I *Fliegerkorps* (Beauvais)

Stab/*KG* 1	He 111	Amiens-Glissy
I/*KG* 1	He 111/ Ju 88	Montdidier
III/*KG* 1	Ju 88	Grevillers
Stab/*KG* 26	He 111	Beauvais
I/*KG* 26	He 111	Beauvais
II/*KG* 26	He 111	Amiens (moved away to Mediterranean 8-26 January 1941)
III/*KG* 26	He 111	Poix Nord
Stab/*KG* 77	Ju 88	Laon
I/*KG* 77	Ju 88	Laon
II/*KG* 77	Ju 88	Rheims
III/*KG* 77	Ju 88	Juvincourt

IV *Fliegerkorps* (Dinard)

*KG*r 100	He 111	Vannes
*KG*r 606	Do 17	Lannion
Stab/*KG* 27	He 111	Tours
I/*KG* 27	He 111	Tours
II/*KG* 27	He 111	Bourges
III/*KG* 27	He 111	Rennes
I/LG 1	Ju 88	Orleans/Bricy
II/LG 1	Ju 88	Orleans/Bricy (until 14 January 1941)
III/LG 1	Ju 88	Chateaudun (until 10 January 1941)

V *Fliegerkorps* (Villacoublay)

Stab/*KG* 51	Ju 88	Paris/Orly
I/*KG* 51	Ju 88	Villaroche
II/*KG* 51	Ju 88	Paris/Orly
III/*KG* 51	Ju 88	Bretigny
Stab/*KG* 54	Ju 88	Evreux
I/*KG* 54	Ju 88	Evreux
II/*KG* 54	Ju 88	St Andre
*KG*r 806	Ju 88	Caen
Stab/*KG* 55	He 111	Villacoublay
I/*KG* 55	He 111	Dreux
II/*KG* 55	He 111	Chartres
III/*KG* 55	He 111	Villacoublay

February 1941

Luftflotte 2 (Brussels)

II *Fliegerkorps* (Ghent)

Stab/*KG* 2	Do 17	Cambrai-Sud
I/*KG* 2	Do 17	Epinoy
II/*KG* 2	Do 17	Merville (moved away by end of February 1941)
III/*KG* 2	Do 17	Cambrai-Sud
Stab/*KG* 3	Do 17	Le Culot
I/*KG* 3	Do 17	Le Culot/Hammemille
II/*KG* 3	Do 17	Antwerp-Deurne
III/*KG* 3	Do 17	St Trond
Stab/*KG* 53	He 111	Lille-Nord
I/*KG* 53	He 111	Vitry-en-Artois
II/*KG* 53	He 111	Lille Vendeville

IX *Fliegerkorps* (Soesterburg)

Stab/*KG*4	He 111	Soesterburg
I/*KG*4	He 111	Soesterburg
II/*KG*4	He 111	Eindhoven
III/*KG*4	He 111	Leeuwarden
Stab/*KG*30	Ju 88	Eindhoven
I/*KG*30	Ju 88	Gilze-Rijen
II/*KG*30	Ju 88	Gilze-Rijen
III/*KG*30	Ju 88	Schiphol (moved away mid-February 1941)
I/*KG*28	He 111	Nantes
3/*KüFlGr*106	Ju 88	Schiphol

Luftflotte 3 (Paris)

I *Fliegerkorps* (Beauvais)

Stab/*KG*1	He 111	Amiens-Glissy
I/*KG*1	He 111/ Ju 88	Amiens-Glissy
III/*KG*1	Ju 88	Grevillers
III/*KG*26	He 111	Poix Nord, to Grevillers 2 February 1941, to Le Bourget 19 February 1941
II/*KG*76	Ju 88	Beauvais/Chateaudun (7 February-7 March 1941)
Stab/*KG*77	Ju 88	Reims
I/*KG*77	Ju 88	Reims
II/*KG*77	Ju 88	Reims
III/*KG*77	Ju 88	Juvincourt

IV *Fliegerkorps* (Dinard)

KGr 100	He 111	Vannes
KGr 606	Do 17	Lannion
Stab/*KG*27	He 111	Tours
I/*KG*27	He 111	Tours/Brest (24 February 1941)
II/*KG*27	He 111	Bourges
III/*KG*27	He 111	Rennes

V *Fliegerkorps* (Villacoublay)

Stab/*KG*51	Ju 88	Paris/Orly
I/*KG*51	Ju 88	Villaroche
II/*KG*51	Ju 88	Paris/Orly
III/*KG*51	Ju 88	Bretigny
Stab/*KG*54	Ju 88	Evreux
I/*KG*54	Ju 88	Evreux
II/*KG*54	Ju 88	St Andre
KGr 806	Ju 88	Caen
Stab/*KG*55	He 111	Villacoublay
I/*KG*55	He 111	Dreux
II/*KG*55	He 111	Chartres
III/*KG*55	He 111	Villacoublay

Luftflotte 5 (Oslo)

Stab/*KG*26	He 111	Aalborg-West (from mid-February 1941)
I/*KG*26	He 111	Aalborg-West (from start of February 1941)

March 1941

Luftflotte 2 (Brussels)

II *Fliegerkorps* (Ghent)

Stab/*KG*2	Do 17	Cambrai-Sud (moved away end March 1941)
I/*KG*2	Do 17	Epinoy to Merville (moved away 14-end March 1941)
III/*KG*2	Do 17	Cambrai-Sud (moved away end March 1941)
Stab/*KG*3	Do 17	Le Culot (moved away end March 1941)
I/*KG*3	Do 17	Hammemille (moved away end March 1941)
II/*KG*3	Do 17	Antwerp-Deurne (moved away end March 1941)
III/*KG*3	Do 17	St Trond (moved away end March 1941)
Stab/*KG*53	He 111	Lille-Nord
I/*KG*53	He 111	Vitry-en-Artois
II/*KG*53	He 111	Lille Nord

IX *Fliegerkorps* (Soesterburg)

Stab/*KG* 4	He 111	Soesterburg
I/*KG* 4	He 111	Soesterburg (2/*KG* 4 moved away 9 March 1941)
II/*KG* 4	He 111	Eindhoven to Soesterburg (moved away end March 1941)
III/*KG* 4	He 111	Leeuwarden
Stab/*KG* 30	Ju 88	Eindhoven?
I/*KG* 30	Ju 88	Gilze-Rijen
II/*KG* 30	Ju 88	Gilze-Rijen to Eindhoven
I/*KG* 28	He 111	Nantes
3/*KüFlGr* 106	Ju 88	Schiphol

Luftflotte 3 (Paris)

I *Fliegerkorps* (Beauvais)

Stab/*KG* 1	He 111	Amiens-Glissy
I/*KG* 1	He 111	Amiens-Glissy (moved to Brest and re-formed as III/*KG* 40 end March 1941)
II/*KG* 1	Ju 88	Rosieres-en-Santerre (from 18 March 1941)
III/*KG* 1	Ju 88	Grevillers to Amy
III/*KG* 26	He 111	Le Bourget
Stab/*KG* 76	Ju 88	Chateaudun/Creil (arrived mid-March 1941)
I/*KG* 76	Ju 88	Chateaudun (arrived mid-March 1941)
II/*KG* 76	Ju 88	Chateaudun/Beaumont
III/*KG* 76	Ju 88	Chateaudun/Cormeilles
Stab/*KG* 77	Ju 88	Reims to Juvincourt
I/*KG* 77	Ju 88	Reims to Beauvais to Juvincourt (Berry-Au-Bac) (23 March 1941)
II/*KG* 77	Ju 88	Reims to Beauvais (9 March 1941)
III/*KG* 77	Ju 88	Juvincourt

IV *Fliegerkorps* (Dinard)

KGr 100	He 111	Vannes
KGr 606	Do 17	Lannion
Stab/*KG* 27	He 111	Tours
I/*KG* 27	He 111	Brest/Tours (24 March 1941)
II/*KG* 27	He 111	Dinard
III/*KG* 27	He 111	Rennes (to Orleans-Bricy 23 March 1941)
III/*KG* 40	He 111	Bordeaux (formed from I/*KG* 1)

V *Fliegerkorps* (Villacoublay)

Stab/*KG* 51	Ju 88	Paris/Orly (moved away end March 1941)
I/*KG* 51	Ju 88	Villaroche (moved away end March 1941)
II/*KG* 51	Ju 88	Bretigny (moved away end March 1941)
III/*KG* 51	Ju 88	Bretigny (moved away end March 1941)
Stab/*KG* 54	Ju 88	Evreux
I/*KG* 54	Ju 88	Evreux
II/*KG* 54	Ju 88	St Andre/Evreux
KGr 806	Ju 88	Caen
Stab/*KG* 55	He 111	Villacoublay
I/*KG* 55	He 111	Le Bourget
II/*KG* 55	He 111	Chartres
III/*KG* 55	He 111	Le Bourget/ Villacoublay

Luftflotte 5 (Oslo)

Stab/*KG* 26	He 111	Aalborg-West to Stavanger
I/*KG* 26	He 111	Aalborg-West

April 1941

Luftflotte 2 (Brussels)

II *Fliegerkorps* (Ghent)

Stab/*KG* 53	He 111	Lille-Nord
I/*KG* 53	He 111	Vitry-en-Artois
II/*KG* 53	He 111	Lille Vendeville

IX *Fliegerkorps* (Soesterburg)

Stab/*KG* 4	He 111	Soesterburg
I/*KG* 4	He 111	Soesterburg
III/*KG* 4	He 111	Leeuwarden
Stab/*KG* 30	Ju 88	Eindhoven
I/*KG* 30	Ju 88	Gilze-Rijen/Eindhoven
II/*KG* 30	Ju 88	Gilze-Rijen
I/*KG* 28	He 111	Nantes (moved temporarily to *Luftflotte* 3)
KuFlGr 106	Ju 88	Schiphol (whole *Gruppe* from 20 April 1941)

Luftflotte 3 (Paris)

I *Fliegerkorps* (Beauvais)

Stab/*KG* 1	He 111	Amiens-Glissy
II/*KG* 1	Ju 88	Rosieres-en-Santerre
III/*KG* 1	Ju 88	Amy
III/*KG* 26	He 111	Le Bourget
Stab/*KG* 76	Ju 88	Creil
I/*KG* 76	Ju 88	Chateaudun to Beaumont
II/*KG* 76	Ju 88	Beaumont/Creil/Beaumont
III/*KG* 76	Ju 88	Cormeilles
Stab/*KG* 77	Ju 88	Juvincourt
I/*KG* 77	Ju 88	Juvincourt/Laon
II/*KG* 77	Ju 88	Beauvais
III/*KG* 77	Ju 88	Juvincourt

IV *Fliegerkorps* (Dinard)/*Fliegerführer Atlantik* (Lorient)

*KG*r 100	He 111	Vannes
*KG*r 606	Do 17	Lannion

Stab/*KG* 27	He 111	Tours
I/*KG* 27	He 111	Tours
II/*KG* 27	He 111	Dinard/Bourges
III/*KG* 27	He 111	Orleans-Bricy
III/*KG* 40	He 111	Brest Lanveoc

V *Fliegerkorps* (Villacoublay)

Stab/*KG* 54	Ju 88	Evreux
I/*KG* 54	Ju 88	Evreux
II/*KG* 54	Ju 88	St Andre to Bretigny (14 April 1941)
*KG*r 806	Ju 88	Caen
Stab/*KG* 55	He 111	Villacoublay
I/*KG* 55	He 111	Le Bourget to Melun Villaroche
II/*KG* 55	He 111	Chartres
III/*KG* 55	He 111	Villacoublay

Luftflotte 5 (Oslo)

Stab/*KG* 26	He 111	Stavanger
I/*KG* 26	He 111	Aalborg-West

May 1941

Luftflotte 2 (Brussels)

I *Fliegerkorps* (Ghent)

Stab/*KG* 3	Ju 88	Le Culot
I/*KG* 3	Ju 88	Le Culot
II/*KG* 3	Ju 88	Le Culot
Stab/*KG* 4	He 111	Soesterburg
I/*KG* 4	He 111	Soesterburg
III/*KG* 4	He 111	Soesterburg
Stab/*KG* 30	Ju 88	Eindhoven
I/*KG* 30	Ju 88	Eindhoven
II/*KG* 30	Ju 88	Gilze-Rijen/Aalborg (*Luftflotte* 5)
Stab/*KG* 53	He 111	Lille-Nord
I/*KG* 53	He 111	Vitry-en-Artois
II/*KG* 53	He 111	Lille Vendeville
I/*KG* 28	He 111	Nantes
KuFlGr 106	Ju 88	Schiphol

Luftflotte 3 (Paris)

I Fliegerkorps (Beauvais)

II/*KG* 1	Ju 88	Rosieres-en-Santerre
III/*KG* 1	Ju 88	Amy
III/*KG* 26	He 111	Le Bourget
Stab/*KG* 76	Ju 88	Criel
I/*KG* 76	Ju 88	Beaumont
II/*KG* 76	Ju 88	Criel
III/*KG* 76	Ju 88	Cormeilles
Stab/*KG* 77	Ju 88	Juvincourt
I/*KG* 77	Ju 88	Laon
II/*KG* 77	Ju 88	Beauvais
III/*KG* 77	Ju 88	Juvincourt

IV *Fliegerkorps* (Dinard)/
Fliegerführer Atlantik (Lorient)

III/*KG* 40	He 111	Brest/Lanveoc
*KG*r 100	He 111	Vannes
*KG*r 606	Do 17/Ju 88	Lannion
Stab/*KG* 27	He 111	Tours
I/*KG* 27	He 111	Tours
II/*KG* 27	He 111	Dinard
III/*KG* 27	He 111	Orleans-Bricy

V *Fliegerkorps* (Villacoublay)

Stab/*KG* 54	Ju 88	Evreux
I/*KG* 54	Ju 88	Evreux
II/*KG* 54	Ju 88	Bretigny
*KG*r 806	Ju 88	Caen
Stab/*KG* 55	He 111	Villacoublay
I/*KG* 55	He 111	Le Bourget/Melun Villaroche
II/*KG* 55	He 111	Chartres
III/*KG* 55	He 111	Villacoublay

Luftflotte 5 (Oslo)

Stab/*KG* 26	He 111	Stavanger
I/*KG* 26	He 111	Aalborg

20 June 1941

Luftflotte 3 (Paris)

IX *Fliegerkorps* (Franc Port)

II/*KG* 2	Do 217	Evreux (non-operational until 11 July 1941)
Stab/*KG* 4	He 111	Soesterburg
I/*KG* 4	He 111	Soesterburg
III/*KG* 4	He 111	Leeuwaarden
I/*KG* 28	He 111	Nantes
Stab/*KG* 30	Ju 88	Eindhoven
I/*KG* 30	Ju 88	Eindhoven
III/*KG* 30	Ju 88	Melun
E/*KG* 30	Ju 88	Bretigny
III/*KG* 26	He 111	Le Bourget
*KG*r 100	He 111	Chartres
IV/*KG* 27	He 111	Avord
3(F)/122	Ju 88	Schiphol

Fliegerführer Atlantik (Lorient)

III/*KG* 40	He 111	Bordeaux
*KG*r 106	Ju 88	Schiphol
*KG*r 606	Ju 88	Lannion

Luftflotte 5 (Oslo)

Stab/*KG* 26	He 111	Stavanger
I/*KG* 26	He 111	Aalborg
II/*KG* 30	Ju 88	Stavanger/Banak

Appendix 3
Known dates, targets & units involved in raids
November 1940-June 1941

All times: German = UK plus 1 hour
Blank entries indicate unit not known

Date	Target	Details
November 1940		
1	Portsmouth	*ZG* 26 (*Jabo*)
	Hucclecote	I/*KG* 51
	Coventry (Cornercraft)	II/*KG* 76
	London	*KG* 1
	Elmdon	II/*KG* 76
	Skegness	II/*KG* 55
	Bristol	II/*KG* 55
	Oxford	II/*KG* 55
	Church Fenton	8/*KG* 30
	Catton	I/*KG* 1
	West Raynham	*KG* 1
	Wattisham	II/*KG* 76, III/*KG* 76
	Waddington	II/*KG* 26
	Great Massingham	II/*KG* 26
	Stradishall	II/*KG* 76, III/*KG* 76
1-2	**London**	*KG* 1 (2000-2050hrs); *KG* 76 (2011-2045hrs); *KG* 77 (2035-0506hrs); I/*LG* 1 (2105-2206hrs); II/*LG* 1 (2134-2150hrs); I/*KG* 27 (2045-2115hrs); I/*KG* 54 (0105-0151hrs); II/*KG* 54 (0004-0045hrs); *KG*r 806 (2219-2255hrs); I/*KG* 55 (2050-2135hrs); II/*KG* 55 (1950-2030hrs); III/*KG* 55 (2206-2259hrs); *Stab*/*KG* 55 (2150-2157hrs)
	Birmingham	I/*LG* 1, I/*KG* 27, III/*KG* 27
	Coventry	*KG*r 100
	Liverpool	*KG*r 606
	Bristol	III/*KG* 27
	Cardiff	*KG*r 606
	Plymouth	*KG*r 606
2	London	I/*KG* 53 (1034-1300hrs)
	Ramsgate	
2-3	London	*KG* 76 (2028-2148hrs); *KG* 26 (2040-2104hrs); II/*LG* 1 (2335-2450hrs); III/*LG* 1 (2310-2335hrs); I/*KG* 27 (2038-2210hrs); II/*KG* 27 (2020-2135hrs); II/*KG* 55 (2015-2055hrs)
3	Crouch End	*KG* 26
	Coventry	*KG* 76
	London	II/*KG* 76, III/*KG* 51, *KG* 3
	Wattisham	II/*KG* 76
	Stradishall	II/*KG* 76
	Banbury	I/*KG* 54
	Daventry	I/*KG* 54
	Rugby	I/*KG* 54
	Weymouth	I/*KG* 54
4	Banbury	I/*KG* 54
	Redditch	II/*KG* 51
	London	II/*KG* 51, I/*KG* 51
	Wattisham	I/*KG* 76

Date	Target	Details

November 1940

4-5	**London**	I/*LG* 1 (0345-0555hrs); III/*LG* 1 (0100-0320hrs); II/*KG* 27 (2012-2115hrs); III/*KG* 27 (2030-0020hrs); I/*KG* 51 (2012-2045hrs); II/*KG* 51 (2212-2231hrs); III/*KG* 51 (2019-2045hrs); I/*KG* 54 (0557-0700hrs); II/*KG* 54 (0630-0720hrs); *KG*r 806 (0501-0515hrs); *KG* 1 (0510-0619hrs); *KG* 76 (1830-2020 and 2348-0018hrs); *KG* 77 (2010-2040 and 0032-0240hrs); *KG* 26 (0025-0553hrs); *KG* 2
5	Catton	III/*KG* 1
	West Raynham/	
	Swanton Morley	III/*KG* 1
	Portland	*ZG* 26 (*Jabo*)
	Humber	4/*KG* 53
	Eastbourne	II/*KG* 51
5-6	**London**	*KG* 1 (19321-2038hrs); II/*KG* 77 (1914-2020hrs); III/*KG* 77 (0707-0751hrs); I/*LG* 1(0105-0338hrs); III/*LG* 1 (0255-0355hrs); I/*KG* 27 (2318-0045hrs); I/*KG* 55 (0520-0600hrs); II/*KG* 55 (0435-0524hrs); III/*KG* 55 (0605-0643hrs); *Stab*/*KG* 55 (0650-0655hrs)
	Brighton	I/*LG* 1
	Eastbourne	I/*KG* 27
	Portland	*KG*r 100, *KG*r 606
	Bournemouth	*KG*r 606
	Exeter	*KG*r 606
	Coventry	*KG*r 100
	Birmingham	*KG*r 100
	Harwich/Ipswich	13° Stormo
6	Hastings	II/*KG* 51, III/*KG* 77
	Southampton	*ZG* 26 (*Jabo*)
	Ramsgate	I/*KG* 53 (0957-1235hrs)
6-7	**London**	I/*LG* 1 (2235-2322hrs); II/*LG* 1 (2310-2340hrs); I/*KG* 27 (2350-0226hrs); II/*KG* 27 (2355-0140hrs); *KG*r 100 (2027-2224hrs); I/*KG* 51 (2350-0110hrs); II/*KG* 51 (2330-0005hrs); III/*KG* 51 (1923-1935hrs); *Stab*/*KG* 55 (2240-2245hrs); I/*KG* 55 (2045-2155hrs); II/*KG* 55 (2005-2055hrs); III/*KG* 55 (2201-2240hrs); I/*KG* 1 (1930-2115hrs); II/*KG* 1 (0612-0715hrs); *KG* 77 (1925-2255hrs); III/*KG* 26 (2000-2140hrs); III/*KG* 27
	Liverpool/Birkenhead	III/*KG* 27
	Birmingham	*KG*r 606
	Coventry	*KG*r 606
	Plymouth	III/*KG* 27
	Southampton	III/*KG* 27
	Bristol	III/*KG* 27
	Brighton	I/*LG* 1
	Bournemouth	I/*KG* 27
	Eastbourne	II/*KG* 51
	Falmouth	III/*KG* 27
	Fowey	III/*KG* 27

Date	Target	Details
November 1940		
7	Railway, Norwich-Bacton	II/*KG* 1
	Wattisham	*KG* 26
7-8	**London**	I/*LG* 1 (2233-0054hrs); II/*KG* 1 (2200-2320hrs); I/*KG* 27 (2030-2210hrs); III/*KG* 27 (2130-2250hrs); I/*KG* 54 (0048-0210hrs); II/*KG* 54 (2340-0018hrs); *KG*r 806 (2128-0405hrs); *Stab*/*KG* 55 (2315hrs); I/*KG* 55 (2105-2210hrs); II/*KG* 55 (2035-2112hrs); III/*KG* 55 (2213-2300hrs); *KG* 76 (1930-0050hrs); *KG* 26 (0005-0455hrs, 2005-2120hrs, 1955-2120hrs)
8	Honington	7/*KG* 1
	Holyhead	*KG*r 806
	Hemswell/Kirton in Lindsey	*KG* 26
8-9	**London**	I/*LG* 1 (1940-2230hrs); III/*LG* 1 (2045-2155hrs); *KG* 76 (1930-2155hrs); *KG* 26 (1950-2109hrs, 2255-0105hrs); I/*KG* 53 (between 0134-0402hrs); *KG*r 126
	Liverpool	*KG*r 100
	Birmingham	*KG*r 100
	Coventry	*KG* 26
	Eastbourne	*KG* 76
9	White Waltham	II/*KG* 54
	London/Hastings	I/*KG* 77
	Birmingham	*KG* 1, I/*KG* 77, III/*KG* 77
	Railway, Torquay-Newton Abbot	I/*KG* 54
	Cropredy	I/*KG* 54
	Harwich	I/*KG* 77
	London	II/*KG* 77, III/*KG* 77, *KG*r 806
	Elmdon	I/*KG* 77
	Portsmouth	*KG*r 806
	Norfolk coast	*KG* 3
9-10	**London**	*KG* 1 (1958-2052hrs 0530-0617hrs); *KG* 77 (1930-2150hrs 0705-0750hrs); I/*LG* 1 (1907-1938hrs); I/*KG* 51 (1950-2010hrs); II/*KG* 51 (2015-2135hrs); III/*KG* 51 (1900-1920hrs); I/*KG* 54 (0609-0710hrs); II/*KG* 54 (0455-0600hrs); *KG* 2
	Hastings	*KG* 77
	Liverpool/Birkenhead	*KG*r 606
	Birmingham	*KG*r 606
	Bournemouth	*KG*r 606
	Pembroke Dock	*KG*r 606
10	West Lulworth	*ZG* 26 (*Jabo*)
	London	I/*KG* 54
10-11	London	II/*KG* 51
	Ramsgate	43° Stormo
11	London	I/*KG* 77, *KG* 77, II/*KG* 54, I/*KG* 53
11-12	South/London	8/*LG* 1

Date	Target	Details
November 1940		
12	London	I/*KG*51, II/*KG*51, III/*KG*51, II/*KG*76
	Bournemouth	III/*KG*55
	Exmouth	III/*KG*55
	Hastings	I/*KG*51
	Land's End	*KG*r 806
	London	I/*KG*1
	Brighton	I/*KG*1
	Worthing	I/*KG*1
	Dover	I/*KG*1
	Horsham	I/*KG*1
12-13	**London**	II/*LG*1 (1954-2035hrs); II/*KG*27 (20005-2130hrs); III/*KG*27 (2020-2130hrs); *KG*r 100 (2150hrs); I/*KG*51 (0140-0217hrs); III/*KG*51 (0207-0250hrs); *Stab*/*KG*55 (2315-2320hrs); I/*KG*55 (0001-0045hrs); II/*KG*55 (2000-2030hrs); III/*KG*55 (2207-2400hrs); *KG*76 (2103-2305hrs); *KG*26 (2058-0340hrs)
	Portsmouth	III/*KG*27
	Liverpool	*KG*r 100
	Coventry	*KG*r 100, III/*KG*26
	Beckton	III/*KG*26
	Birmingham	III/*KG*26
13	Woodford/Gloucester	III/*KG*1
	Newton Heath	III/*KG*1
	London	I/*KG*54, *KG*r 806
	Longbridge/Cheltenham	II/*KG*55
13-14	London	*KG*2
14-15	**Coventry**	I/*LG*1 (0132-0150hrs); II/*LG*1 (0203-0235hrs); III/*LG*1 (0115-0245hrs); I/*KG*27 (0004-0128hrs); II/*KG*27 (0015-0205hrs); III/*KG*27 (0007-0125hrs); *KG*r 100 (2020-2105hrs); *KG*r 606 (2350-0018hrs); I/*KG*51 (0210-0300hrs); II/*KG*51 (0242-0335hrs); III/*KG*51 (0315-0400hrs); I/*KG*54 (0356-0500hrs); II/*KG*54 (0452-0532hrs); *KG*r 806 (0452-0545hrs); *Stab*/*KG*55 (2320-2330hrs); I/*KG*55 (0000-0100hrs); II/*KG*55 (2120-2155hrs); III/*KG*55 (0105-0135hrs); *KG*26 (0000-0342hrs); *KG*76 (0235-0320hrs); *KG*77 (0345-0610hrs); *KG*1 (0117-0335hrs); *KG*2; I/*KG*3; II/*KG*4; II/*KG*53
	Brighton	III/*KG*51
	Eastbourne	I/*KG*1
	Newhaven	I/*KG*1
	Ramsgate	I/*KG*1
	London	I/*KG*26, I/*KG*76
	Peterborough	II/*KG*54
	Isle of Wight	I/*LG*1
	Bournemouth	I/*KG*55
	Portsmouth	I/*KG*27, I/*KG*55
	Weymouth	III/*KG*27
	Portland	II/*KG*51
	Birmingham	
15	Fareham	*ZG*26 (*Jabo*)
	Tyseley/shipping	III/*KG*51

Date	Target	Details

November 1940

15-16	**London**	I/*KG*1 (0547-0736hrs); III/*KG*1 (1917-2045hrs and 0100-0200hrs); II/*KG*76 (2015-2055hrs); *KG* 76 (2345-0036hrs); *KG*77 (1959-2147hrs); *KG*26 (0200-0443hrs); *LG*1 (0141-0320hrs); I/*KG*27 (0020-0148hrs); II/*KG*27 (0010-0210hrs); I/*KG* 51 (0325-0430hrs); II/*KG*51 (0440-0520hrs); III/*KG*51 (0340-0410hrs); *Stab*/*KG*51 (0355hrs); I/*KG*54 (0557-0625hrs); II/*KG*54 (0635-0715hrs); *KG*r 806 (0405-0510hrs); *Stab*/*KG*55 (0050-0055hrs); I/*KG*55 (2348-0010hrs); II/*KG* 55 (2310-2340hrs); III/*KG*55 (0105-0135hrs)
	Portsmouth	I/*KG*27
	Aylesbury	I/*KG*54
	Hastings	*KG*1
	Reigate	II/*KG*26
	NE London	II/*KG*26
	Birmingham	
	Coventry	II/*KG*53
16-17	**London**	*KG*1 (1915-2010hrs and 0705-0728hrs) *KG*77 (1855-2015hrs and 0628-0718hrs)
	Birmingham	II/*KG*53
	Southampton	
17	Newhaven	*ZG*26 (*Jabo*)
17-18	**Southampton**	*LG*1 (2155-2300hrs); I/*KG*27 (2230-0010hrs); III/*KG*27 (2315-2357hrs); I/*KG*54 (0256-0418hrs); II/*KG*54 (0229-0255hrs); *KG*r 806 (0105-0220hrs); I/*KG*55 (0015-0055hrs); II/*KG* 55 (1945-2040hrs); III/*KG*55 (2355-0020hrs); *Stab*/*KG*55 (2325hrs); *KG*26 (0525-0732hrs); *KG* 76 (0640-0825hrs)
	Liverpool/Birkenhead	*KG*r 606
	Becton	III/*KG*26
	Plymouth	*KG*r 606
	Swindon	*LG*1
	Isle of Wight	*KG*27
	Selsey Bill	*KG*54
	Brighton	*KG*76
	Harwich	43° Stormo
18	Langley/Littlehampton	II/*KG*77
	London	*KG*77
18-19	Liverpool	II/*KG*27, *KG*r 100
	Birmingham	I/*KG*1, III/*KG*26
	Coventry	I/*KG*1
	Southampton	I/*KG*54, II/*KG*54, *KG*r 806, II/*KG*27, *KG*r 100
	Bournemouth	II/*KG*27
	London	*KG*2
	Folkestone	
19	Tyseley/shipping off Great Yarmouth	III/*KG*1

Date	Target	Details
November 1940		
19-20	**Birmingham**	*KG* 1 (2245-0017hrs); *KG* 76 (2100-2210hrs); *KG* 77 (2207-0044hrs); *KG* 26 (2021-0030hrs); *LG* 1 (2227-2308hrs); I/*KG* 27 (2102-2302hrs); II/*KG* 27 (2120-2235hrs); III/*KG* 27 (2100-2238hrs); *KGr* 100 (2035-2116hrs); *KGr* 606 (2050-2117hrs); I/*KG* 51 (2230-2330hrs); II/*KG* 51 (2200-2255hrs); III/*KG* 51 (2310-2338hrs); I/*KG* 54 (0025-0105hrs); II/*KG* 54 (0044-0130hrs); *KGr* 806 (2340-0018hrs); *Stab*/*KG* 55 (2123-2125hrs); I/*KG* 55 (2043-2150hrs); II/*KG* 55 (2012-2110hrs); III/*KG* 55 (2134-2211hrs); II/*KG* 30; *KG* 2
	Leicester	I/*LG* 1, I/*KG* 54
	Wolverhampton	I/*LG* 1
	Weymouth	*KGr* 606, *KGr* 806
	Bournemouth	*KGr* 606
	Dartmouth	*KGr* 606
	Northampton	II/*KG* 54
	Harwich	I/*KG* 26
	Ipswich	I/*KG* 26
	Southampton	I/*LG* 1, I/*KG* 27, I/*KG* 55
	London	*LG* 1, II/*KG* 76, *KG* 77, *KG* 26
20-21	**Birmingham**	III/*KG* 27 (2245-0100hrs); *KGr* 100 (2035-2152hrs); *KGr* 606 (2105-2125hrs); II/*KG* 51 (0020hrs); I/*KG* 54 (0208-0352hrs); II/*KG* 54 (0130-0230hrs); *KGr* 806 (0235-0352hrs); I/*KG* 55 (2130-2230hrs); *KG* 1 (0125-0140hrs); III/*KG* 76 (2318hrs); I/*KG* 77 (0045-0150hrs); II & III/*KG* 77 (0240-0318hrs); *KG* 26 (2114-2303hrs 2355-0140hrs); I/*KG* 27 (2350-0106hrs); I/*KG* 51 (2315-0040hrs); III/*KG* 51 (0052-0125hrs) (Castle Bromwich and West Bromwich hit)
	London	*KG* 27, I/*KG* 1, III/*KG* 76, I/*KG* 77, II & III/*KG* 77, *KG* 26, I/*KG* 53 (Heston hit)
	Portland	III/*KG* 27
	Bristol	III/*KG* 27
	Portsmouth	III/*KG* 27, *KGr* 606
	Southampton	*KGr* 806, I/*KG* 55
	Leicester	III/*KG* 27
	Bournemouth	*KGr* 100, *KGr* 806, I/*KG* 55
	Reading	*KGr* 606
	Airfield NW London	*KG* 1
	?	13° Stormo
21	Petersfield	1203hrs
21-22	Birmingham	II/*KG* 26, III/*KG*26
	Coventry	I/*KG* 26
	Bristol	II/*LG* 1, III/*LG* 1
	Southampton	I/*KG* 51, II/*KG* 51, III/*KG* 51
	London	*KG* 2 (Bulphan hit)
	Witney	
22	Eastbourne	
	New Romney	

Date	Target	Details
November 1940		
22-23	**Birmingham**	*KG* 1 (0325-0310hrs); *KG* 76 (2200-2400hrs); *KG* 77 (2012-2330hrs); III/*KG* 26 (2012-2119hrs); I/*LG*1 (0300-0346hrs); II/*LG* 1 (0336-0426hrs); III/*LG* 1 (0255-0427hrs); I/*KG* 27 (0041-0240hrs); II/*KG* 27 (0050-0230hrs); III/*KG* 27 (0051-0220hrs); *KG*r 100 (2014-2055hrs); *KG*r 606 (2132-2200hrs); I/*KG* 51 (0145-0245hrs); II/*KG* 55 (2010-2110hrs); III/*KG* 55 (0045-0120hrs); *Stab*/*KG* 55 (0039hrs and 0230hrs); II/*KG* 51 (Cosford and Elmdon hit)
	London	II/*LG* 1, I/*KG* 54, *KG* 1, *KG* 76, *KG* 77, I/*KG* 53, II/*KG* 53
	Portland	*KG*r 100, *KG*r 606
	Brighton	*KG*r 806, *KG* 76
	Selsey Bill	II/*KG* 54
	Oxford	I/*KG* 55
	Portsmouth	*KG* 1 (Eastney and Eastleigh hit)
	Eastbourne	*KG* 1, *KG* 77
	Swindon	III/*KG* 26
23	Pembroke	Sunderland damaged
	St Athan	
	Grantham	III/*KG* 30
23-24	**Southampton**	I & III/*LG* 1 (2209-2335hrs); I/*KG* 27 (2102-2210hrs); III/*KG* 27 (2020-2232hrs); *KG*r 100 (1950-2045hrs); II/*KG* 51 (2255-2325hrs); I/*KG* 55 (2015-2055hrs); II/*KG* 55 (1920-2012hrs); III/*KG* 55 (2113-2148hrs); *Stab*/*KG* 55 (2110-2135hrs); *KG* 76 (1940-2020hrs); *KG* 26 (2050-2147hrs); *KG*r 606 (2155hrs)
	Bristol	*KG*r 606
	Birkenhead	*KG*r 606
	Portsmouth	*KG* 26 (Eastney and Lee-on-Solent hit)
	London	II/*KG* 30
24	Portland	III/*ZG* 26 (*Jabo*)
24-25	**Bristol**	*LG* 1 (2033-2120hrs); I/*KG* 27 (2105-2200hrs); III/*KG* 27 (2200-2300hrs); *KG*r 100 (1958-2037hrs); *KG*r 606 (2235-2300hrs); I/*KG* 51 (2210-2335hrs); II/*KG* 51 (2239-2320hrs); III/*KG* 51 (2310-2400hrs); I/*KG* 55 (2120-2208hrs); II/*KG* 55 (1930-2015hrs); III/*KG* 55 (2030-2114hrs); *Stab*/*KG* 55 (2015hrs & 2025hrs); *KG* 1 (2148-2300hrs); III/*KG* 26 (1947-2051hrs) (Whitchurch hit)
	Birmingham and Coventry	*KG* 1
	South Coast town	III/*KG* 51
	London	I/*KG* 53, III/*KG* 30
25	Christchurch	*Stab*/*ZG* 26 (*Jabo*)
	Selsey Bill	III/*ZG* 26 (*Jabo*)
25-26	Avonmouth	*KG*r 100 (1945-2011hrs)
26-27	Bristol/Avonmouth	*KG*r 100 (1932-1948hrs); I/*KG* 3
	London	*KG*r 606
	Bristol/Frome	*KG* 26

Date	Target	Details

November 1940

27-28 **Plymouth** *KG* 1 (2030-2310hrs); III/*KG* 26 (2220-2308hrs); *KG* 77 (0155-0310hrs); II & III/*LG* 1 (2333-0132hrs); III/*KG* 27 (1951-2147hrs); II/*KG* 27 (1940-2020hrs); *KG*r 606 (1930-1956hrs); I/*KG* 54 (2223-2330hrs); II/*KG* 54 (2322-0035hrs); *KG*r 806 (2045-2120hrs); *KG* 4, *KG* 53, *KG* 30 (Sunderland N9048 and P9601 of 10 Sqn destroyed)

Ipswich 13° Stormo

London *KG* 2

28-29 **Liverpool/Birkenhead** *LG* 1 (2337-0155hrs); I/*KG* 27 (2235-2345hrs); II/*KG* 27 (2158-2245hrs); III/*KG* 27 (2356-0150hrs); *KG*r 100 (2055-2140hrs); *KG*r 606 (0215-0251hrs); I/*KG* 51 (2340-0150hrs); II/*KG* 51 (0150-0308hrs); III/*KG* 51 (0145-0200hrs); I/*KG* 54 (2327-0050hrs); II/*KG* 54 (2300hrs); *KG*r 806 (2320-0055hrs); *Stab*/*KG* 55 (2135-2145hrs); I/*KG* 55 (2125-2200hrs); II/*KG* 55 (2015-2125hrs); III/*KG* 55 (2150-2240hrs); *KG* 1 (2130-0012hrs); *KG* 76 (2105-2232hrs); *KG* 77 (2140-2330hrs); *KG* 26 (2135-2400hrs); III/*KG* 26 (2112-2155hrs); I/*KG* 53 (Ringway hit)

Glasgow I/*KG* 40

London I/*KG* 54, *KG*r 806, III/*KG* 55, I/*KG* 77, *KG* 26

Bristol II/*LG* 1, III/*KG* 27, *KG*r 100, *KG* 76, *KG* 26

Plymouth II/*LG* 1

Portsmouth II/*KG* 27, III/*KG* 51, *KG* 76

Portland III/*KG* 27

Cardiff *KG*r 606

Bristol I/*KG* 51, *KG* 1, *KG* 76

Southampton II/*KG* 54, *KG*r 806, I/*KG* 55, *KG* 77

Bournemouth II/*LG* 1

Exmouth III/*KG* 27

Brighton I/*KG* 51, II/*KG* 54, III/*KG* 55, *KG* 26

Chichester III/*KG* 51

Toke *KG*r 806

Aldershot I/*KG* 55

Reading II/*KG* 76

Leeds (airfield) II/*KG* 55

Aberdovey (airfield) II/*KG* 55

Fauld

Kidbrook

29 Yarmouth/Harwich/ Ipswich/Lowestoft 13° Stormo

Date	Target	Details
November 1940		
29-30	**London**	*KG* 1 (1955-2225hrs); *KG* 76 (2000-2056hrs); *KG* 77 (1955-2354hrs); I & II/*KG* 26 (2045-0055hrs); III/*KG* 26 (1940-2045hrs); *LG* 1 (2020-2202hrs); I/*KG* 27 (2045-2345hrs); II/*KG* 27 (2207-2245hrs); III/*KG* 27 (2312-0030hrs); *KG*r 100 (2000-2049hrs); *KG*r 606 (0015-0045hrs); *Stab*/*KG* 55 (2115-2222hrs); I/*KG* 55 (2002-2055hrs); II/*KG* 55 (1920-2025hrs); III/*KG* 55 (2054-2147hrs); I/*KG* 51 (2042-2308hrs); II/*KG* 51 (2344-2400hrs); III/*KG* 51 (0012-0035hrs); I/*KG* 54 (0008-0040hrs); II/*KG* 54 (0050-0120hrs); *KG*r 806 (0107-0140hrs); I/*KG* 53
	Birmingham	*KG*r 606
	Liverpool	*KG*r 606, *KG* 2
	Plymouth	*KG*r 606
	Brighton	III/*KG* 55
	Eastbourne	*KG* 76
	Hastings	*KG* 77
	North Weald	*KG*r 606
30	Yeovil/Weymouth	I/*KG* 55
30-1 December		
	Southampton	I/*LG* 1 (1955-2100hrs); III/*LG* 1 (1958-2117hrs); II/*KG* 27 (2115-2147hrs); III/*KG* 27 (2200-2310hrs); *KG*r 100 (1955-2010hrs); I/*KG* 51 (0105-0155hrs); II/*KG* 51 (0016-0055hrs); III/*KG* 51 (0024-0026hrs); *Stab*/*KG* 55 (2300-2312hrs); I/*KG* 55 (2356-0043hrs); II/*KG* 55 (1918-2000hrs); III/*KG* 55 (2325-0050hrs); *KG* 77 (2010-2208hrs); *KG* 26 (1955-2145hrs); III/*KG* 26 (1920-2020hrs)
	London	I/*KG* 51, III/*KG* 51
	Pembroke	*KG*r 100
December 1940		
1	Kenley	
1-2	**Southampton**	I/*LG* 1 (2039-2116hrs); II/*LG* 1 (1937-2037hrs); I/*KG* 27 (2125-2232hrs); III/*KG* 27 (2200-2247hrs); *KG*r 100 (1927-2004hrs); I/*KG* 51 (2255-0008hrs); II/*KG* 51 (0017-0100hrs); I/*KG* 55 (2300-2325hrs); II/*KG* 55 (1920-2002hrs); III/*KG* 55 (2315-2355hrs); II/*KG* 76 (2030-2100hrs); II & III/*KG* 77 (2004-2115hrs); III/*KG* 26 (1915-2050hrs) (Lee-on-Solent hit)
	London	I/*KG* 51
	Liverpool/Birkenhead	III/*KG* 27
	Birmingham	III/*KG* 27
	Brighton	III/*KG* 51
	Derby	
	Nottingham	

Date	Target	Details
December 1940		
2-3	**Bristol**	*KG* 1 (1928-2022hrs); *KG* 77 (2043-2151hrs); II/*LG* 1 (2000-2035hrs); III/*LG* 1 (1948-2040hrs); I/*KG* 27 (2140-2245hrs); III/*KG* 27 (2120-2152hrs); *KG*r 100 (1937-2006hrs); *KG*r 606 (2255-2315hrs); I/*KG* 54 (2250-2330hrs); II/*KG* 54 (2150-2243hrs); *KG*r 806 (2223-2304hrs); I/*KG* 55 (2128-2208hrs); II/*KG* 55 (1930-2055hrs)
	Southampton	*KG*r 606, *KG*r 806, *KG* 77
	Brighton	II/*KG* 55
3	Bristol	III/*KG* 55
	Longbridge/Witney	II/*KG* 55
	Longbridge/Coventry airfield/airfield near Portsmouth (Ford/ Lee-on-Solent)/Cheltenham Abingdon	II/*KG* 55
3-4	**Birmingham**	I/*KG* 1 (1925-2024hrs); III/*KG* 26 (1926-2028hrs); II/*LG* 1 (2010-2042hrs); III/*LG* 1 (1945-2045hrs); I/*KG* 27 (2212-2300hrs); II/*KG* 27 (2120-2140hrs); *KG*r 100 (1948-2020hrs); I/*KG* 55 (2150-2230hrs); II/*KG* 55 (2000-2030hrs)
	London	I/*KG* 1, III/*LG* 1, I/*KG* 55, *KG* 2
	Southampton	II/*LG* 1, II/*KG* 27, III/*KG* 26
	Bournemouth	III/*LG* 1, II/*KG* 55
	Oxford	II/*KG* 55
	Gloucester	*KG*r 100
4	Dover	
4-5	**Birmingham**	I/*LG* 1 (2023-2242hrs); III/*LG* 1 (2044-2123hrs); I/*KG* 27 (2226-2325hrs); II/*KG* 27 (2125-2400hrs); I/*KG* 51 (1950-2035hrs); II/*KG* 51 (2025-2053hrs); III/*KG* 51 (2105-2303hrs); I/*KG* 54 (2255-2315hrs); II/*KG* 54 (2239-2250hrs); *KG* 1 (2120-2130hrs); *KG* 26 (2025-2120hrs); III/*KG* 26 (1915-2200hrs)
	London	I/*LG* 1, II/*KG* 27, III/*KG* 51, II/*KG* 54, *KG* 26
	Southampton	III/*LG* 1, I/*KG* 27, II/*KG* 27, II/*KG* 51, III/*KG* 51, *KG* 26
	Brighton	I/*KG* 51
	Oxford	II/*KG* 54
	Eastbourne	*KG* 26
	Plymouth	*KG*r 126
5-6	**Portsmouth**	I/*LG* 1 (2045-2103hrs); III/*LG* 1 (2050-2134hrs); II/*KG* 27 (2002-2045hrs); III/*KG* 27 (1938-2025hrs); II/*KG* 51 (2000-2033hrs); III/*KG* 51 (1910-2010hrs); I/*KG* 54 (2034-2046hrs); II/*KG* 54 (2055-2114hrs); II & III/*KG* 77 (1947-2132hrs); I/*KG* 26 (2000-2114hrs); III/*KG* 26 (1935-2125hrs)
	London	I/*KG* 53; II/*KG* 54
	Ipswich	13° Stormo
6-7	**Bristol**	I/*LG* 1 (2100-2110hrs); II/*LG* 1 (2100-2118hrs); II/*KG* 27 (2056-2125hrs); I/*KG* 51 (2245-2345hrs); II/*KG* 51 (2150-2235hrs); I/*KG* 55 (2130-2200hrs); II/*KG* 55 (2020-2110hrs); III/*KG* 55 (2050-2120hrs); *KG* 77 (2020-2210hrs)

Date	Target	Details
December 1940		
	Southampton	II/*KG*27 (Gosport hit)
	London	*KG*77
	Sheerness	II/*LG*1
	Bournemouth	I/*KG*55
	Portland	II/*KG*55
	Brighton	*KG*77
	Salisbury	II/*KG*55
	Airfield 40km SE Bristol	II/*KG*55
8-9	**London**	I/*LG*1 (0025-0053hrs); II/*LG*1 (0100-0130hrs); III/*LG*1 (0025-0135hrs); I/*KG*27 (0255-0425hrs); II/*KG*27 (0200-0310hrs); III/*KG*27 (0125-0257hrs); *KG*r 126 (2305-0015hrs); *KG*r 100 (2337-0007hrs); *KG*r 606 (0340-0415hrs); *KG*1 (2300-0453hrs); *KG* 77 (0005-0305hrs); I/*KG*26 (0008-0300hrs); III/*KG* 26 (2307-0157hrs); I/*KG*51 (0300-0402hrs); II/*KG* 51 (2250-0255hrs); III/*KG*51 (0348-0509hrs); I/*KG* 54 (0650-0755hrs); II/*KG*54 (0550-0605hrs); *KG*r 806 (0435-0540hrs); *Stab*/*KG*55 (0010-0018hrs); I/*KG*55 (2255-2400hrs); II/*KG*55 (1912-2025hrs); III/*KG*55 (0025-0130hrs); I/*KG*53; *KG*r 126
	Brighton	I/*KG*26, *Stab*/*KG*55, II/*KG*55, II/*KG*54
	Windsor	I/*LG*1
	Bognor Regis	I/*KG*27
	Portsmouth	*KG*r 126
10-11	**London**	I/*KG*53
11-12	**Birmingham**	*KG*1 (1950-0045hrs); *KG*77 (0015-0205hrs); I & II/*KG*26 (2200-0121hrs); III/*KG*26 (2050-2250hrs); I/*LG*1 (2300-2355hrs); II/*LG*1 (2300hrs); III/*LG*1 (2250-2315hrs); I/*KG*27 (2120-2225hrs); II/*KG*27 (2047-2135hrs); III/*KG*27 (2205-2333hrs); *KG*r 126 (0010-0135hrs); *KG*r 100 (2030-2130hrs); *KG*r 606 (2045-2130hrs); I/*KG*51 (2225-2310hrs); II/*KG*51 (2138-2320hrs); III/*KG*51 (2249-2337hrs); I/*KG*54 (2350-0041hrs); *KG*r 806 (2336-0045hrs); *Stab*/*KG* 55 (2049-2139hrs); III/*KG*55 (2005-2105hrs); *KG*2; *KG*r 126 (Elmdon hit)
	London	I/*LG*1, *KG*r 806, III/*KG*55, *KG*77, I & II/*KG*26
	Bristol	III/*KG*27, *KG*r 806
	Southampton	I/*KG*77, I & II/*KG*26, I/*LG*1, III/*LG*1, I/*KG*27, III/*KG*27, II/*KG*51, *KG*r 806
	Portsmouth	III/*KG*51, *KG*r 806
	Sheerness	*KG*1, III/*KG*51, *KG*r 806
	Brighton	*KG*77, II/*LG*1, I/*KG*27, II/*KG*27, I/*KG*51, III/*KG*51
	Avonmouth	I/*LG*1
	Bournemouth	II/*LG*1, III/*KG*27
	Swindon	III/*LG*1
	Cheltenham	III/*KG*27
	Salisbury	I/*KG*51
	Aldershot	II/*KG*51
	Hemswell	
	Southrop	
	Great Massingham	

Date	Target	Details
December 1940		
12-13	**Sheffield**	*KG* 1 (2400-0205hrs); *KG* 77 (0017-0100hrs); *KG* 26 (2054-0148hrs); I/*LG* 1 (0250-0314hrs); II/*LG* 1 (0130-0225hrs); III/*LG* 1(0130-0220hrs); I/*KG* 27 (0045-0245hrs); II/*KG* 27 (0033-0042hrs); III/*KG* 27 (0119-0214hrs); *KG*r 126 (2338-0057hrs); *KG*r 100 (2041-2136hrs); *KG*r 606 (2350-0100hrs); I/*KG* 51 (0130-0135hrs); II/*KG* 51 (0144-0245hrs); III/*KG* 51 (0050-0155hrs); I/*KG* 54 (0250-0415hrs); II/*KG* 54 (0040-0450hrs); *KG*r 806 (0245-0400hrs); *Stab*/*KG* 55 (0012-0042hrs); I & III/*KG* 55 (2345-0040hrs); II/*KG* 55 (1940-2108hrs); *KG* 2
	Birmingham	I/*LG* 1, I/*KG* 3
	London	III/*LG* 1, I/*KG* 51, III/*KG* 51, I/*KG* 54, III/*KG* 26
	Coventry	III/*LG* 1
	Southampton	I/*KG* 27, *KG*r 126, *KG*r 100, I/*KG* 26, I/*KG* 51
	Plymouth	*KG*r 606
	Brighton	II/*LG* 1, II/*KG* 51, III/*KG* 51
	Bournemouth	I/*KG* 27, III/*KG* 27, *KG*r 100
	Portsmouth	I/*KG* 54, III/*KG* 26
	Portland	I/*KG* 55
	Ramsgate	II/*KG* 1
13-14	Bristol/Avonmouth	*KG* 27
	Harwich	13° and 43° Stormo
14	Stoke-on-Trent	*KG*r 806
14-15	**London**	*KG* 2
15-16	**Sheffield**	*KG*r 126 (2043-2135hrs); I/*KG* 27 (2100-2203hrs); II/*KG* 27 (2030-2116hrs); III/*KG* 27 (2037-2205hrs); *KG*r 100 (2000-2050hrs); *KG*r 606 (2135-2258hrs); I/*KG* 53; *KG* 2
	Bristol	I/*KG* 27
	Southampton	I/*KG* 27, II/*KG* 27
	Birmingham	III/*KG* 27
	Coventry	III/*KG* 27
	Plymouth	*KG*r 606
	Dover	*KG*r 126
	London	
19-20	**London**	I/*KG* 53, *KG* 2, *KG* 3, *KG* 51 (?)
20-21	**Liverpool/Birkenhead**	I/*KG* 27 (2030-2230hrs); II/*KG* 27 (1955-2055hrs); III/*KG* 27 (2016-2042hrs); *KG*r 100 (1935-2050hrs); *KG*r 606 (2020-2050hrs); I/*KG* 51 (0150hrs); II/*KG* 51 (0255-0303hrs); III/*KG* 51 (2345-0140hrs); *Stab*/*KG* 55 (2250hrs); II/*KG* 55 (1928-2110hrs); I & II/*KG* 77 (2307-0100hrs); III/*KG* 77 (1945-2045hrs); I & II/*KG* 26 (2310-0015hrs); III/*KG* 26 (2335-0115hrs); I/*KG* 53; I/*KG* 28
	London	I/*KG* 51, II/*KG* 55, I & II/*KG* 77
	Southampton	III/*KG* 77, I/*KG* 27
	Bristol	III/*KG* 77
	Carlisle	II/*KG* 27
	South of Liverpool	I/*KG* 51, II/*KG* 55
21	Leicester	5/*KG* 2

Date	Target	Details

December 1940

21-22	**Liverpool/Birkenhead**	*KG*r 100 (1951-2042hrs); I/*LG*1 (2039-2119hrs); II/*LG*1 (2003-2128hrs); III/*LG*1 (1942-2007hrs); I/*KG*27 (2046-2153hrs); II/*KG*27 (2045-2158hrs); III/*KG*27 (2110-2210hrs); *KG*r 606 (2230-2330hrs); I/*KG*51 (2030-2205hrs); II/*KG*51 (2240-2317hrs); III/*KG*51 (2200-2330hrs); I/*KG*54 (2355-0025hrs); II/*KG*54 (2320-2355hrs); *KG*r 806 (2325-0043hrs); *Stab*/*KG*55 (2020-2045hrs); I/*KG*55 (1945-2015hrs); II/*KG*55 (2015-2040hrs); III/*KG*55 (2012-2049hrs); *KG*1 (2020-2135hrs); *KG*77 (2033-2337hrs); *KG*26 (2020-0014hrs); III/*KG*26 (2020-2302hrs); I/*KG*28; *KG*2
	London	I/*KG*1, III/*KG*26, I/*KG*51, I/*KG*54, I/*KG*55
	Southampton	I/*KG*27, *KG*r 100, III/*KG*51, II/*KG*54, II/*KG*55, I/*KG*1, *KG*77, *KG*26
	Portsmouth	II/*KG*27, *KG*1
	Birmingham	I/*KG*51, *KG*26
	Poole	II/*KG*27
	South of Bristol	III/*KG*27
	Exmouth	*KG*r 606
	Eastbourne	I/*KG*51
	Brighton	I/*KG*51, I/*KG*54, *KG*26, III/*KG*26
	Dover	*KG*77
	Bournemouth	I/*KG*54
	South coast	*KG*77
	Harwich	3° & 43° Stormo Ipswich 1750hrs (Shotley hit)
22	Fort William (British Aluminium Works)	0850hrs 1/120 (UXB)
22-23	**Manchester**	*KG*r 100 (1955-2033hrs); I/*LG*1 (2025-2115hrs); I/*KG*27 (2120-2210hrs); II/*KG*27 (2130-2217hrs); III/*KG*27 (2128-2255hrs); *KG*r 606 (2110-2150hrs); I/*KG*51 (2125hrs); II/*KG*51 (2155-2215hrs); III/*KG*51 (2202-2310hrs); I/*KG*54 (2257-2342hrs); II/*KG*54 (2335-0032hrs); *KG*r 806 (0040-0120hrs); *Stab*/*KG*55 (2025-2035hrs); I/*KG*55 (1945-2015hrs); II/*KG*55 (2000-2031hrs); III/*KG*55 (2025-2053hrs); *KG*1 (2045-2200hrs); *KG*26 (2105-0034hrs); *KG*77 (2040-2350hrs); III/*KG*26 (2009-2220hrs)
	London	III/*KG*1, I/*KG*55, *KG*77, *KG*26, III/*KG*26
	Bristol	I/*KG*27, III/*KG*27, *KG*r 100
	Southampton	I/*KG*27, II/*KG*54, *KG*26
	Portsmouth	I/*KG*27, II/*KG*27
	Birmingham	I/*KG*51
	Liverpool	I/*KG*55, I/*KG*28
	Plymouth	*KG*r 606
	Bournemouth	I/*LG*1
	Brighton	III/*KG*51, I/*KG*54
	Selsey Bill	*KG*r 606
	Hullavington	I/*LG*1
	Harwich	43° Stormo
23	Railway, Grantham/ Peterborough	3/123

Date	Target	Details
December 1940		
23-24	**Manchester**	I/*KG*28 (2314-0027hrs); I/*LG*1 (2030-2114hrs); I/*KG*27 (2130-2332hrs); II/*KG*27 (2209-2250hrs); III/*KG*27 (2146-2326hrs); *KG*r 100 (2015-2109hrs); *KG*r 606 (2115-2130hrs); I/*KG*51 (2130-2155hrs); II/*KG*51 (2215-2240hrs); III/*KG*51 (2225-2315hrs); I/*KG*54 90015-0100hrs); II/*KG*54 (2306-0010hrs); *KG*r 806 (2230-0005hrs); *Stab*/*KG*55 (2115hrs); I/*KG*55 (2050-2115hrs); II/*KG*55 (2233-2255hrs); III/*KG*655 (2105-2145hrs); *KG*1 (2028-2225hrs); *KG*77 (2030-2201hrs); I & II/*KG*26 (2052-2217hrs); III/*KG*26 (2033-2150hrs)
	Portsmouth	III/*KG*26, *KG*r 806
	London	II/*KG*51, III/*KG*55, *Stab*/*KG*55, *KG*1, III/*KG*26
	Southampton	I/*KG*27, *KG*r 100, II/*KG*51, I/*KG*26
	Portland	III/*KG*27
	Bournemouth	*KG*r 100
	Bristol	*KG*r 606
	Brighton	I/*KG*51, I/*KG*55
	Derby	III/*KG*51
	Birmingham	III/*KG*55
	Plymouth	I/*KG*28
27-28	**London**	I/*KG*27 (2102-2305hrs); I/*KG*28 (2026-2110hrs); *KG*r 100 (1945-2005hrs); *KG*r 806 (2120-2140hrs); I/*KG*3, I/*KG*28
	Brighton	I/*KG*28
28-29	Liverpool	*KG*r 100 (1937-2027hrs); II/*KG*55 (1950-2015hrs); III/*KG*26 (1941-1953hrs)
	Plymouth	
29	Crewe	
29-30	**London**	III/*KG*27 (2014-2055hrs); I/*KG*28 (1943-2010hrs); *KG*r 100 (1917-1950hrs); *KG*r 606 (1935-1950hrs)I/*KG*51 (1930-2035hrs); II/*KG*51 (1953-2035hrs); III/*KG*51 (2031-2050hrs); I/*KG*54 (2052-2132hrs); II/*KG*54 (2136-2236hrs); *KG*r 806 (2045-2145hrs); *KG*1 (1920-2015hrs); III/*KG*26 (1953-2045hrs); *KG*2
30	Airfields	
January 1941		
1-2	**Liverpool**	*KG*2
	Birmingham	
	Chester	
2-3	**Cardiff**	I/*LG*1 (0023-0054hrs); I/*KG*27 (2317-0031hrs); III/*KG*27 (2320-0028hrs); *KG*r 100 (1943-2018hrs); II/*KG*55 (2044-2050hrs); III/*KG*26 (1957-2034hrs); III/*KG*1 (0421-0501hrs); I/*KG*3; *KG*2
	Salisbury	III/*KG*1
	Portsmouth	III/*KG*26
	Eastbourne	III/*KG*26
	Poole	III/*KG*26
	Liverpool	*KG*2
	Hull	I/*KG*4

Date	Target	Details
January 1941		
3-4	**Bristol**	I/*LG*1 (0025hrs); I/*KG*27 (2250-0008hrs); II/*KG*27 (2255-0030hrs); *KG*r 100 (2020-2040hrs); I/*KG*54 (2140-2335hrs); II/*KG*54 (2204-2245hrs); I/*KG*55 (2114-2121hrs); II/*KG*55 (2005-2043hrs); III/*KG*55 (2045-2110hrs); I/*KG*1 (1935-2110hrs); *KG*77 (1955-2135hrs); I/*KG*26 (2020-2100hrs); III/*KG*26 (2035-2106hrs)
	Weymouth	I/*LG*1, I/*KG*27
	Southampton	II/*KG*55
	Dungeness	I/*KG*1
	Salisbury	*KG*77
	Cardiff	I/*KG*28
4-5	**Avonmouth**	I/*KG*27 (2240-2325hrs); II/*KG*27 (2243-2343hrs); *KG*r 100 (1957-2005hrs); I/*KG*51 (1935-2000hrs); II/*KG*51 (2010-2015hrs); III/*KG*51 (2025hrs); I/*KG*54 (2110-2125hrs); II/*KG*54 (2110-2208hrs); *KG*77 (2320-0105hrs); I/*KG*26 (2328-0120hrs)
	Bournemouth	*KG*2
	Newport (Marshfield)	I/*KG*27, *KG*r 100
	Portishead	I/*KG*27
	Bristol	I/*KG*27
	Cardiff	II/*KG*51, II/*KG*54
	Swansea	I/*KG*28
5	Watton/London Honington	I/*KG*3
5-6	London Darlington	*KG*2
6	Sawbridgeworth Bircham Newton Docking	
7	Coventry (Standard Motors) Railway station between Coventry and Leamington	II/*KG*77
	(Long Itchington)	III/*KG*77
	Ipswich	1550hrs (He 111)
	London	I/*KG*3, I/*KG*53
8	Coventry (Standard Motors) Ipswich	8/*KG*77 (*Lt* Karl Höflinger)
9-10	**Manchester**	I/*LG*1 (2259-2315hrs); I/*KG*27 (2353-0015hrs); II/*KG*27 (0017-0025hrs); *KG*r 100 (2104-2120hrs); I/*KG*54 (0047hrs); II/*KG*54 (2353-0048hrs); I/*KG*55 (2042-2255hrs); II/*KG*55 (2042-2255hrs); III/*KG*55 (2300-2350hrs); *KG*r 806 (2350hrs); *KG*1 (2305-0010hrs); *KG*77 (2305-0105hrs); I/*KG*26 (2310-0030hrs); III/*KG*26 (2112-2150hrs)
	London	I/*KG*3, I/*LG*1, I/*KG*27, II/*KG*27, III/*KG*27, *Stab*/*KG*55, I/*KG*55, II/*KG*55, *KG*r 806, *KG*1, *KG*77, I/*KG*26, III/*KG*26
	Southampton	I/*LG*1, II/*KG*27, II/*KG*54, I/*KG*55, II/*KG*55
	Birmingham	II/*KG*27, I/*KG*26
	Bristol	I/*KG*27, *KG*r 100, II/*KG*54
	Portsmouth	III/*KG*26, II/*KG*27, III/*KG*27, *KG*1, *KG*r 806
	Bournemouth	II/*KG*27, III/*KG*27, *KG*r 100, I/*KG*26

Date	Target	Details
January 1941		
	Portland	*KG*r 100
	Liverpool	III/*KG* 55, *KG* 1, *KG* 77
	Plymouth	I/*KG* 26
	Gravesend	I/*KG* 27
	Avonmouth	I/*KG* 27
	Bridgeport	I/*KG* 27
	Poole	III/*KG* 27
	Eastbourne	I/*KG* 54
	Hastings	*KG* 1
	Dover	*KG* 77
	Southend	I/*KG* 26
	Grantham	
	Bolton	
	Halifax	
	Rochdale	
10-11	**Portsmouth**	I/*KG* 27 (0045-0150hrs); II/*KG* 27 (0037-0105hrs); III/*KG* 27 (0145-0226hrs); *KG*r 606 (0050-0110hrs); I/*KG* 51 (2025-2055hrs); II/*KG* 51 (2055-2125hrs); III/*KG* 51 (2055-2108hrs); I/*KG* 54 (2107-2122hrs); *KG*r 806 (2113-2140hrs); II/*KG* 55 (1952-2045hrs); *KG* 1 (2040-2200hrs); I/*KG* 26 (2100-2146hrs); III/*KG* 26 (1958-2057hrs)
	Bristol	I/*KG* 51
	Brighton	I/*KG* 51
	Falmouth	
11	Bassingbourn	3/123 (*Oblt* Edmund Forster); attacked from 60 feet at 1155hrs; two Wellingtons damaged
11-12	**London**	I/*LG* 1 (2158-2231hrs); I/*KG* 27 (2036-2155hrs); III/*KG* 27 (2030-2137hrs); *KG*r 100 (2005-2045hrs); I/*KG* 51 (2020-2050hrs); II/*KG* 51 (2150-2215hrs); III/*KG* 51 (2155-2230hrs); II/*KG* 54 (2055-2132hrs); *KG*r 806 (2134-2152hrs); I & II/*KG* 55 (1950-2020hrs); *KG* 77 (1925-2146hrs); I/*KG* 26 (2045-2118hrs)
	Pembroke	I/*KG* 28
12-13	**London**	I/*LG* 1 (2030-2110hrs); II/*KG* 27 (2205-2305hrs); *KG*r 100 (2003-2030hrs); *KG*r 606 (2055-2150hrs); I/*KG* 51 (1945-2010hrs); II/*KG* 51 (2145-2205hrs); III/*KG* 51 (2215-2230hrs); I/*KG* 54 (2107-2141hrs); *Stab*/*KG* 55 (2105-2125hrs); I/*KG* 55 (2050-2108hrs); III/*KG* 55 (2005-2120hrs); *KG* 77 (1937-2200hrs); I/*KG* 26 (2032-2135hrs); I/*KG* 53
	Portsmouth	*KG*r 100
	Brighton	I/*LG* 1
	Eastbourne	II/*KG* 27
	Liverpool	
	Cardiff	I/*KG* 28
	Falmouth	I/*KG* 28
13-14	**Plymouth**	I/*KG* 27 (2008-2125hrs); III/*KG* 27 (2000-2115hrs); *KG*r 100 (1943-2007hrs); *KG*r 606 (2128-2150hrs)
	Liverpool	I/*KG* 28
	Swansea	

Date	Target	Details
January 1941		
15	Fort William	
15-16	Derby	II/*KG*3, I/*KG*53
	London	
	Liverpool	
	Northampton	
	Dover	
	Peterborough	
	Stoke	
	Nottingham	
	Sheffield	
16	London	I/*KG*53
16-17	**Avonmouth**	III/*KG*26 (2040-2330hrs); I/*KG*51 (2350hrs); II/*KG* 51 (0055-0144hrs); III/*KG*51 (0041-0114hrs); I/*KG* 54 (0120-0220hrs); II/*KG*54 (0230-0325hrs); *KGr* 806 (0255-0343hrs); I/*KG*55 (2345-0030hrs); I & II/*KG*55 (2048-2115hrs); III/*KG*55 (2255-2400hrs); *Stab*/*KG*55 (2330-0040hrs); I/*LG*1 (0515-0608hrs); I/*KG*27 (0312-0425hrs); II/*KG*27 (0303-0455hrs); III/*KG*27 (0320-0447hrs); *KGr* 100 (0230-2120hrs)
	Southampton	I/*LG*1, I/*KG*27, I/*KG*51, II/*KG*51, *KGr* 806, III/*KG* 55
	Bristol	I/*KG*27, I/*KG*51, II/*KG*54, *KGr* 806, I/*KG*55
	Portsmouth	I/*KG*51
	Plymouth	*KGr* 806, II/*KG*55
	Portland	*Stab*/*KG*55
	Bournemouth	*Stab*/*KG*55, I/*KG*54, III/*KG*51
	Isle of Wight	III/*KG*26
	Pembroke	I/*KG*28
17-18	**Swansea**	I/*KG*26 (2144-2333hrs); III/*KG*26 (2244-2338hrs); III/*KG*27 (2330-0036hrs); *KGr* 100 (2043-2130hrs); *KGr* 606 (2325-2335hrs); II/*KG*51 (0350hrs); III/*KG* 51 (0340-0423hrs); I/*KG*54 (0110-0125hrs); II/*KG* 54 (0210-0240hrs); III/*KG*54/*KGr* 806 (0155-0207hrs); I & II/*KG*55 (2050-2155hrs)
	Southampton	III/*KG*26, I/*KG*54, II/*KG*54, *KGr* 806
	Plymouth	*KGr* 100, *KGr* 606
	Bristol	I/*KG*54, II/*KG*54, III/*KG*54
	Portsmouth	I/*KG*54, *KGr* 806
	Portland	III/*KG*27, II/*KG*51
	Eastbourne	III/*KG*26
	Nottingham	III/*KG*26
	Exmouth	III/*KG*27
	Aldershot	II/*KG*54
	Weymouth (*Warmwell*)	I/*KG*26
	Cardiff	I/*KG*28
	Pembroke	I/*KG*28
18	Saxmundham	9/*KG*53
	Watton	2/*KG*3
	Feltwell	
	Great Massingham	

Date	Target	Details

January 1941

19-20	**Southampton**	*KG* 1 (2030-2153hrs); *KG* 77 (2120-2400hrs); III/*KG* 26 (2045-2215hrs)
	London	*KG* 77, III/*KG* 26, I/*KG* 3
	Becton Gasworks	III/*KG* 26
	Dover	*KG* 77
	Brighton	*KG* 77
	Ipswich	0015hrs
20-21	Andover	
21	Feltwell	
21-22	London	II/*KG* 53
22	Stechford/The Wash	III/*KG* 1
	Stechford	III/*KG* 1
	Southend	I/*KG* 53
25	Great Yarmouth	
25-26	St Eval	I/*KG* 28
26	Shipping	III/*KG* 30
27	Grantham (BMARC)	8/*KG* 30 (*Oblt* Friedrich Rinck), 1430hrs; fifteen killed, twenty-six injured
	Newcastle (Vickers)	II/*KG* 77
28	Stechford/Margate	III/*KG* 1
	Hayes (Fairey Aviation)/	
	Portsmouth	III/*KG* 1
	Honington	
28-29	Cardiff	*KG*r 100
29	Newcastle	III/*KG* 1
29/30	London	
30	Stechford/Humber	III/*KG* 1
	London	
	Grantham (BMARC)	III/*KG* 30
31	London	I/*KG* 53
	Essex	I/*KG* 30
	Bedford	
	Wattisham	III/*KG* 3

February 1941

1	Great Yarmouth (Grout & Son)	1221hrs (intercept by 222 Sqn)
	Honington	
	Mildenhall	
2	Lowestoft/Leiston	I/*KG* 53 (intercepted by 222 Sqn)
3	London	II/*KG* 53; I/*KG* 53 (aborted due to weather)
	Airfields	
3-4	Cardiff	*KG*r 100
4	Lowestoft/Mildenhall	II/*KG* 2 (0930hrs, 257 Sqn), I/*KG* 53, I/*KG* 3
	Grantham (BMARC)	8/*KG* 30 (*Lt* Kurt Dahlmann)
	Watton	I/*KG* 3
4-5	London (Chatham)	I/*KG* 53
	Derby	I/*KG* 53; III/*KG* 26; I/*KG* 3; *KG* 2
	Cardiff	I/*KG* 28
	Grimsby	3/122
5-6	Great Yarmouth	3/122

Date	Target	Details
February 1941		
8-9	Cardiff	*KG*r 100
9	London	II/*KG* 30
	Hull	III/*KG* 30
9-10	Plymouth	
	Birmingham	III/*KG* 1
	Humberside	II/*KG* 30
	Liverpool	*KG*r 100
	Campbeltown	I/*KG* 28
10-11	Ipswich	3/122
12-13	Exmouth	I/*KG* 28
	Liverpool	I/*KG* 28
13-14	London	III/*KG* 26; I/*KG* 53
14-15	**London**	*Stab* & I/*KG* 1 (2220-2310hrs); III/*KG* 26 (2046-2112hrs)
	Hull	II/*KG* 30
15-16	**Liverpool**	III/*KG* 27 (0247hrs); *KG* 1 (0131-0246hrs)
	Langley	III/*KG* 26
	Southampton (Marchwood)	III/*KG* 77
	London	*KG* 1, *KG* 26
	Bournemouth	III/*KG* 77
	Birmingham	III/*KG* 77
	Humberside	I/*KG* 53, II/*KG* 4
	Newcastle	3/122
16-17	London	
17	Wattisham	II/*KG* 76
	Elmdon	II/*KG* 76
	West Raynham	II/*KG* 76
	Watton	II/*KG* 76
	Birmingham	*KG* 77
	Sternford	III/*KG* 1
	Leominster	III/*KG* 1
17-18	**London**	*KG*r 606 (2035-2150hrs); II/*KG* 76 (2114-2215hrs); I & III/*KG* 77 (2220-2400hrs); III/*KG* 26 (2224-2255hrs)
	Hull	II/*KG* 53
18	Ipswich	1632hrs, Do 17
	Watton	II/*KG* 53, 0755hrs
	Thorney Island	1440hrs; two Beauforts damaged
18-19	East Anglia	
	Liverpool	I/*KG* 28
19	Newmarket	
19-20	**Swansea**	I/*KG* 27 (2129-2135hrs); II/*KG* 27 (2125-2215hrs); III/*KG* 27 (2039-2150hrs); *KG*r 100 (2102-2122hrs); *KG*r 606 (2145-2240hrs); *KG* 1 (2225-0007hrs)
	Plymouth	III/*KG* 27, *KG*r 100
	E of Plymouth	III/*KG* 27
	Southampton	*KG* 1, I/*KG* 28
	Brighton	*KG* 1
	Portland	I/*KG* 27
	London	
20	Great Yarmouth	III/*KG* 3

Date	Target	Details
February 1941		
20-21	**Swansea**	I/*KG* 27 (2115-2200hrs); II/*KG* 27 (2100-2140hrs); III/*KG* 27 (2107-2114hrs); *KG*r 100 (2102-2136hrs); *KG* 1 (2250-2350hrs); II/*KG* 76 (2228-2245hrs); I & III/*KG* 77 (2307-0045hrs); III/*KG* 26 (2224-2308hrs)
	Portland	*KG* 27
	Portsmouth	*KG* 1
	Eastbourne	*KG* 1
	Brighton	*KG* 1
	Cardiff	II/*KG* 76
	Bridgewater	II/*KG* 76
	Bristol	*KG* 77
	Southampton	*KG* 77, I/*KG* 28
	London (Chatham)	*KG* 4, II/*KG* 2, III/*KG* 2
21-22	**Swansea**	II/*KG* 27 (2050-2230hrs); II/*KG* 27 (2112-2215hrs); III/*KG* 27 (2110-2205hrs); *KG*r 100 (2128-2202hrs); *KG*r 606 (2211-2235hrs); *KG* 1 (2255-0100hrs); III/*KG* 26 (2247-2349hrs)
	Bournemouth	I/*KG* 27
	Plymouth	III/*KG* 27
	London	II/*KG* 30
	Falmouth	I/*KG* 28
22	Avonmouth	II/*KG* 27 (1404hrs)
22-23	Hull	*KG* 4, *KG* 30
23-24	Midlands (Grantham)	III/*KG* 3, III/*KG* 27
	Hull	I/*KG* 53
	Langley	
	London	
24-25	East Anglia	(I, II, III/*KG* 2)
	Midlands	
	Home Counties	
	Cambridge	
25-26	Ipswich	II/*KG* 3 (2150hrs)
	London	II/*KG* 2 (2125hrs)
	Hull	I/*KG* 53, II/*KG* 53 (II & III/*KG* 2, III/*KG* 53, II/*KG* 30)
26-27	**Cardiff**	I/*KG* 27 (2110-2210hrs); II/*KG* 27 (2135-2157hrs); III/*KG* 27 (2135-2210hrs); *KG*r 100 (2125-2200hrs); *KG* 1 (2105-2138hrs); I/*KG* 77 (2135-2159hrs); III/*KG* 26 (2145-2221hrs)
	Southampton	I/*KG* 27, *KG* 1
	Brighton	*KG* 1
	London	I/*KG* 53; II/*KG* 2; II/*KG* 30
	Scunthorpe	
27	Benson	1330hrs
	Ipswich	He 111 (1635hrs)
	Mildenhall	*KG* 2 (1410hrs)
	Yate	II/*KG* 27 (*Oblt* Hermann Lohmann)
28-1 March		London

Date	Target	Details
March 1941		
1-2	**Cardiff**	III/*KG*27 (2130-2140hrs); III/*KG*1 (2120-2130hrs); III/*KG*77 (2104-2210hrs)
	Southampton	I/*KG*27, II/*KG*27, III/*KG*27, III/*KG*1
	Bristol	II/*KG*27
	Hull	II/*KG*3, I/*KG*4, II/*KG*4
	Airfields	I, III/*KG*2
3-4	**Cardiff**	*KG*r 100 (2105-2131hrs); III/*KG*27 (2215-2230hrs); I/*KG*1 (2307-2400hrs); III/*KG*1 (2319-2358hrs); II/*KG*76 (2315hrs); I/*KG*77 (0005-0150hrs); III/*KG*77 (2310-2400hrs); III/*KG*26 (2301-0008hrs); 2309 and 0018hrs
	Southampton	II/*KG*27, III/*KG*27, I/*KG*1, III/*KG*1, I/*KG*77, III/*KG*26
	Plymouth	III/*KG*27
	Great Yarmouth	
	Brighton	
	Newcastle	II/*KG*3, I/*KG*53
4-5	**Cardiff**	I/*KG*27 (2145-2205hrs); II/*KG*27 (2150-2230hrs); III/*KG*27 (2143-2400hrs); *KG*r 100 (2149-2219hrs); I/*KG*77 (2335-0025hrs); II/*KG*77 (2335-0100hrs); III/*KG*77 (0115-0135hrs); III/*KG*26 (2323-0042hrs); I/*KG*28
	Southampton	II/*KG*27, I/*KG*27, I/*KG*77, III/*KG*26, III/*KG*77
	Hull	
	London	
5-6	Portsmouth	
6	Filton	I/*KG*27 (*Oblt* Paul Hollinde)
6-7	Tyneside	
7	Gorleston	2/*KG*3 0735hrs
	Newark	1 & 6/*KG*4 (*Lt* Günther Rudolph and *Oblt* Ulrich Knauth)
	Yate	II/*KG*27 (*Oblt* Hermann Lohmann)
7-8	East coast	1/*KG*26, 5/*KG*30
8-9	**London**	II/*KG*27 (2220-2300hrs); I/*KG*1 (2124-2215hrs); III/*KG*1 (2110-2132hrs); II/*KG*76 (2140-2245hrs); I/*KG*77 (2208-2258hrs); II/*KG*77 (2110-2140hrs); III/*KG*77 (2123-2212hrs); III/*KG*26 (2115-2310hrs); I/*KG*53
	Newcastle	II/*KG*30
9-10	**London**	II/*KG*27 (2140-2149hrs); III/*KG*27 (2140-2300hrs); *KG*r 100 (2121-2150hrs); I/*KG*1 (2230-0005hrs); III/*KG*1 (2215-0005hrs); II/*KG*76 (2225-0015hrs); I/*KG*77 (2203-2247hrs); II/*KG*77 (2232-2312hrs); III/*KG*77 (2300-2336hrs); III/*KG*26 (2212-2324hrs); *KG*r 806 (0120-0331hrs)
	Portsmouth	II/*KG*27, III/*KG*27, *KG*r 806, I/*KG*1, II/*KG*76, III/*KG*26, III/*KG*1

Date	Target	Details

March 1941

10-11 Portsmouth — I/*KG*27 (2116-2157hrs); II/*KG*27 (2114-2220hrs); III/*KG*27 (210-2214hrs); *KG*r 100 (2105-2140hrs); *KG*r 806 (0100-0345hrs); *Stab*/*KG*55 (0205-0222hrs); III/*KG*55 (0105-0150hrs); I/*KG*1 (0035-0155hrs); III/*KG*1 (0050-0115hrs); II/*KG*76 (0105-0250hrs); III/*KG*76 (2108-2120hrs); I/*KG*77 (0150-0246hrs); II/*KG*77 (0027-0242hrs); III/*KG*77 (0104-0143hrs); III/*KG*26 (2120-2230 and 0049-0224hrs)

11-12 Birmingham — I/*KG*27 (2255-2350hrs); II/*KG*27 (2215-2253hrs); III/*KG*27 (2214-2235hrs); *KG*r 100 (2205-2250hrs); *KG*r 806 (2130-0030hrs); *Stab*/*KG*55 (2305-2725hrs); III/*KG*55 (2225-2355hrs); II/*KG*76 (2155-2358hrs); I/*KG*77 (2323-0047hrs); II/*KG*77 (2248-0002hrs); III/*KG*77 (2400-0033hrs); III/*KG*26 (2200-2330hrs); I/*KG*53

Southampton — I/*KG*27, II/*KG*27, III/*KG*27, *KG*r 100, *KG*r 806, III/*KG*55, II/*KG*76, II/*KG*77, III/*KG*77, III/*KG*26

Portsmouth — III/*KG*27, III/*KG*55, II/*KG*76

Plymouth — *KG*r 100

Bristol — *KG*r 100

Stoke — III/*KG*27

Worthing — III/*KG*55

Manchester

12-13 Liverpool/Birkenhead — I/*KG*27 (2240-2323hrs); II/*KG*27 (2240-2350hrs); *KG*r 100 (2205-2240hrs); I & II/*KG*55 (2242-2310hrs); *KG*r 806 (2205-2340hrs); III/*KG*55 (2222-2310hrs); *Stab*/*KG*55 (2245hrs); I/*KG*1 (2215-2307hrs); III/*KG*1 (2203-2245hrs); II/*KG*76 (2225-2350hrs); III/*KG*26 (2211-2320hrs); I/*KG*53; II/*KG*30

Cardiff — II/*KG*27, *KG*r 100, II/*KG*76

Bournemouth (Winton) — *KG*r 806

Swindon — *KG*r 806

Warrington — *KG*r 806

Portsmouth — III/*KG*55

Southampton — *Stab*/*KG*55

Eastbourne — III/*KG*1

Brighton — III/*KG*1

13 Fort William — 1/120

13-14 Glasgow — I/*KG*27 (2234-2332hrs); II/*KG*27 (2313-2325hrs); *KG*r 100 (2254-2325hrs); I/*KG*54 (2248-2355hrs); II/*KG*55 (2347-0040hrs); I/*KG*1 (2327-0030hrs); III/*KG*1 (2350-0017hrs); III/*KG*1 (0305-0408hrs); II/*KG*76 (0322-0410hrs); *KG*77 (2355-0354hrs); III/*KG*26 (0020-0055hrs); II/*KG*30

Hull — *KG*2

Birkenhead — I/*KG*27, II/*KG*27, *KG*r 100, I/*KG*51, II/*KG*51, III/*KG*54, *Stab*/*KG*55, I/*KG*55, III/*KG*55, II/*KG*76

Southampton — III/*KG*27, II/*KG*51, III/*KG*55, II/*KG*76

Portsmouth — II/*KG*76

Falmouth — III/*KG*27

Brighton — I/*KG*51, III/*KG*55

Cardiff — II/*KG*55

Margate — III/*KG*1

Grantham

Alton

Date	Target	Details
March 1941		
14-15	**Glasgow**	I/*KG*27 (2230-2315 and 2307-2335hrs); II/*KG*27 (2305-2345hrs); *KG*r 100 (2400hrs); I/*KG*51 (2308hrs); II/*KG*51 (2314hrs); III/*KG*51 (2245-2255hrs); *KG*r 806 (2350-0005hrs); I/*KG*55 (2330-0010hrs); II/*KG*55 (2340-0010hrs); I/*KG*1 (2323-0040hrs); III/*KG*1 (2320-0035hrs); II/*KG*76 (2245-2330hrs); *KG*77 (2315-2346hrs); III/*KG*26 (0012-0250hrs); I/*KG*53
	Plymouth	I/*KG*27, I/*KG*51, III/*KG*51, *Stab*/*KG*55, II/*KG*55, III/*KG*55
	Southampton	I/*KG*1, III/*KG*1, I/*KG*77
	Sheffield	III/*KG*27, II/*KG*51, I/*KG*54, *Stab*/*KG*55, I/*KG*55, III/*KG*55, II/*KG*1, III/*KG*1, II/*KG*76, III/*KG*26, *KG*2
	Portsmouth	III/*KG*27, III/*KG*51, II/*KG*27, I/*KG*51, III/*KG*55
	Southampton	I/*KG*51, I/*KG*54, II/*KG*54, III/*KG*55, I/*KG*77, I/*KG*27, II/*KG*27, II/*KG*51, *KG*r 806
	Cardiff	*KG*r 100
	Hull	I/*KG*51
	Stamford	III/*KG*55
	Southend	III/*KG*55
	London	III/*KG*55, III/*KG*1
	Chatham	II/*KG*1
	Derby	II/*KG*75
	Birkenhead	I/*KG*27
	Falmouth	I/*KG*27
	Bournemouth	III/*KG*27
	Bideford	*KG*r 100
	Bristol	II/*KG*55
	Hartlepool	*KG*77
	Leeds	
15-16	**London**	I/*KG*51 (2208-2230hrs); II/*KG*51 (2235-2320hrs); III/*KG*51 (2233-2258hrs); I/*KG*54 (2125-2346hrs); II/*KG*54 (2310-2343hrs); III/*KG*54/*KG*r 806 (2148-0010hrs); *Stab*/*KG*55 (0000hrs); I/*KG*55 (2225-2353hrs); II/*KG*55 (2205-0000hrs); III/*KG*55 (2305-0000hrs); *KG*2
	Southampton	I/*KG*51, II/*KG*55, III/*KG*55
16-17	**Bristol/Avonmouth**	I/*KG*55, III/*KG*55, III/*KG*26, II/*KG*76, II/*KG*51
	Southampton	
	Bournemouth	
	Weymouth	
	Portland	
	Yeovil	
	Portsmouth	
	Whitchurch	
	Avonmouth	I/*KG*51

Date	Target	Details
March 1941		
18-19	**Hull**	I/*KG* 27 (0225-0453hrs); II/*KG* 27 (0242-0400hrs); III/*KG* 27 (0309-0407hrs); *KG*r 100 (0145-0250hrs); I/*KG* 51 (0325-0410hrs); II/*KG* 51 (0307-0400hrs); III/*KG* 51 (0224-0235hrs); II/*KG* 54 (0150-0340hrs); III/*KG* 54 (0225-0250hrs); *KG*r 806 (0200-0305hrs); I/*KG* 55 (0230-0345hrs); II/*KG* 55 (0205-0230hrs); III/*KG* 55 (0225-0345hrs); I/*KG* 1 (0230-0320hrs); II/*KG* 1 (0340-0430hrs); III/*KG* 1 (0240-0320hrs); II/*KG* 76 (0420-0430hrs); I/*KG* 77 (0325-0444hrs); II/*KG* 77 (0259-0348hrs); III/*KG* 77 (0236-0335hrs); III/*KG* 26 (0152-0247hrs); I/*KG* 53; I/*KG* 28; *KG* 2; 3/122; II/*KG* 30
	Southampton	I/*KG* 51, II/*KG* 51, III/*KG* 51, II/*KG* 54, III/*KG* 55, III/*KG* 1, III/*KG* 26, III/*KG* 27
	Harwell	I/*KG* 1
	Langley	I/*KG* 77
	Sheffield	II/*KG* 77, III/*KG* 55
	London	II/*KG* 51, I/*KG* 54, II/*KG* 55, *KG*r 806, I/*KG* 77, II/*KG* 76, III/*KG* 1, III/*KG* 51, II/*KG* 1, I/*KG* 51, II/*KG* 55, *KG*r 100, III/*KG* 27, I/*KG* 27, *Stab*/*KG* 55, III/*KG* 77
	Portsmouth	III/*KG* 77, I/*KG* 1
	Brighton	II/*KG* 76
	Hastings	II/*KG* 76
	Airfield E of London	III/*KG* 55
	Dover	I/*KG* 77
	Bristol	III/*KG* 27
	Scarborough	
19-20	**London**	I/*KG* 27 (2208-2310hrs); II/*KG* 27 (2310-2355hrs); III/*KG* 27 (2155-2308hrs); *KG*r 100 (2140-2208hrs); I/*KG* 51 (2302-2345hrs); II/*KG* 51 (2244-2320hrs); III/*KG* 51 (2215-2250hrs); I/*KG* 54 (2250-2338hrs); II/*KG* 54 (2143-2230hrs); *KG*r 806 (2228-2243hrs); I/*KG* 55 (2227-2250hrs); II/*KG* 55 (2227-2250hrs); III/*KG* 55 (2220-2250hrs); *Stab*/*KG* 55 (2245-2250hrs); I/*KG* 1 (2222-2330hrs); II/*KG* 1 (2145-2314hrs); III/*KG* 1 (2150-2245hrs); II/*KG* 76 (2200-2315hrs); I/*KG* 77 (2200-2255hrs); II/*KG* 77 (2218-2358hrs); III/*KG* 77 (2335-0010hrs); III/*KG* 26 (2205-2335hrs); I/*KG* 53; I/*KG* 28; III/*KG* 4; 3/122; II/*KG* 30
	Southampton	II/*KG* 54
	Ford (Tangmere?)	I/*KG* 1
	Hullavington	
	(Windrush 2355hrs?)	III/*KG* 55
	Whitchurch	*Stab*/*KG* 55

Date	Target	Details
March 1941		
20-21	**Plymouth**	I/*KG*27 (2320-0020hrs); II/*KG*27 (2200-2312hrs); III/*KG*27 (2151-2250hrs); *KG*r 100 (2141-2203hrs); II/*KG*51 (2300-2335hrs); III/*KG*51 (2216-2256hrs); I/*KG*54 (2155-2235hrs); II/*KG*54 (2258-2335hrs); *KG*r 806 (2203-2212hrs); I/*KG*55 (2228-2250hrs); II/*KG*55 (2215-2325hrs); III/*KG*55 (2215-2240hrs); *Stab*/*KG*55 (2248-2300hrs)
	St Eval	III/*KG*27 (2056hrs)
	Cardiff	I/*KG*28
	London	I/*KG*53
21-22	**Plymouth**	I/*KG*27 (2225-2325hrs); II/*KG*27 (2205-2253hrs); *KG*r 100 (2150-2210hrs); I/*KG*51 (2208-2332hrs); II/*KG*51 (2255-2325hrs); III/*KG*51 (2232-2248hrs); I/*KG*55 (2215-2305hrs); II/*KG*55 (2215-2305hrs); III/*KG*55 (2220-2235hrs); *Stab*/*KG*55 (2210-2233hrs); II/*KG*76 (2143-2310hrs); I/*KG*77 (2317-0019hrs); II/*KG*77 (2255-2350hrs); III/*KG*77 (2246-2343hrs); III/*KG*26 (2240-0040hrs)
	Portland	I/*KG*77
	Eastbourne	II/*KG*77
	Portsmouth	II/*KG*77, III/*KG*77
22	Airfields (Leeming)	II/*KG*4
23	Airfields (Manchester)	II/*KG*77
23-24	Rotherham	
26	Overton	
	Totton	
	Airfields	II/*KG*76 (Andover 1220hrs)
	Railways	
27-28	Pembroke	I/*KG*28
29	Nottingham/The Wash	I/*KG*53
29-30	**Bristol**	*KG*r 100 (2205-2257hrs); III/*KG*26 (2238-2308hrs); III/*KG*1 (2210-2245hrs); II/*KG*76 (2215-2240hrs)
	Pembroke	I/*KG*28
30-31	Raum C	I/*KG*53
31-1	Hull	I/*KG*53
	Pembroke	I/*KG*28
	Swansea	
	Portsmouth	
April 1941		
1	Birmingham	III/*KG*1 0945hrs
	Leeming	I/*KG*4 1515hrs
	Hornchurch	1810hrs
	Warmwell	III/*KG*27, 1225hrs by three He 111s; six killed, one missing, twenty injured; Wellington, two Battles, Defiant, two Magisters, Spitfire, Zlin destroyed
1-2	St Eval	III/*KG*27
2	Norwich	
3-4	**Avonmouth**	*KG*r 100 (2222-2305hrs); II/*KG*27 (2230-2400hrs); *KG*r 806 (2302-2356hrs); I/*KG*54 (2210-0025hrs); II/*KG*54 (0008-0035hrs); III/*KG*26 (2240-2334hrs)
	Bristol	*KG*r 100, II/*KG*1, III/*KG*1, II/*KG*76
	Bournemouth	II/*KG*27
	Portsmouth	I/*KG*54, II/*KG*54, *KG*r 806

Date	Target	Details
April 1941		
	Southampton	I/*KG*54, II/*KG*54, III/*KG*1
	Poole	III/*KG*1
	Exeter	Wellington destroyed
4-5	**Avonmouth**	II/*KG*27 (2215-2304hrs); *KG*r 100 (2217-2244hrs); I/*KG*54 (2256-0005hrs); II/*KG*54 (2354-0123hrs); *KG*r 806 (2306-2320hrs); I/*KG*77 (2348-0055hrs); II/*KG*77 (0000-0130hrs); III/*KG*77 (0140-0230hrs); III/*KG*26 (2257-0011hrs)
	Portsmouth	I/*KG*54, II/*KG*54, II/*KG*77, III/*KG*77
	Bristol	I/*KG*77, II/*KG*77
	Southampton	II/*KG*77
	Warmwell	I/*KG*54
	St Eval	
	Hull	
	Pembroke	I/*KG*28
5-6	Exeter	Three Ju 88s; Wellington destroyed, three killed
6	Airfields	9/*KG*55
6-7	Liverpool	I/*KG*28
	Belfast	
	Aberdeen	
7-8	**Greenock**	I/*KG*27 (0140-0208hrs); II/*KG*27 (0010-0110hrs); *KG*r 100 (0026-0032hrs); I/*KG*54 (2325-01532hrs); II/*KG*54 (0010-0130hrs); III/*KG*54/*KG*r 806 (0017-0035hrs); I/*KG*55 (0025-0130hrs); II/*KG*55 (0035-0135hrs); *KG*76 (2315-0040hrs); *KG*77 (0045-0225hrs); III/*KG*26 (0035-0324hrs); I/*KG*28; 3/122; II/*KG*30
	Bristol	*KG*r 100, I/*KG*54, II/*KG*54, III/*KG*54/*KG*r 806, I/*KG*55, II/*KG*55, III/*KG*55, II/*KG*1
	Liverpool	III/*KG*27, I/*KG*54, II/*KG*54, Stab/*KG*55, II/*KG*55, III/*KG*55, III/*KG*54/*KG*r 806, I/*KG*55, II/*KG*1, *KG*77, III/*KG*26
	Southampton	I/*KG*27, III/*KG*27
	Bournemouth	*KG*r 806, II/*KG*27
	Andover	III/*KG*55, 3/*KG*76
	Eastbourne	III/*KG*55
	Brighton	III/*KG*55
	Glasgow	II/*KG*55, II/*KG*1, III/*KG*1, *KG*76
	Gloucester	I/*KG*27
	Harwich	*KG*r 100
	Plymouth	*KG*r 100
	Swansea (Mumbles)	*KG*r 100
	St Austell	*KG*r 100
	Dundee	II/*KG*54
	Minehead	II/*KG*54
	Poole	I/*KG*55
	Newcastle	*KG*76, *KG*77
	Hull	*KG*76, *KG*77
	Great Yarmouth	*KG*77
	Belfast	III/*KG*26
	Portsmouth	III/*KG*26, III/*KG*54
	Portland	III/*KG*26, II/*KG*55
	London	*KG*53?

Date	Target	Details
April 1941		
8-9	**Coventry**	I/*KG*27 (0230-0315hrs); II/*KG*27 (0140-0240hrs); III/*KG*27 (0152-0255hrs); *KG*r 100 (2300-2340hrs); II/*KG*1 (0230-0330hrs); III/*KG*1 (0132-0230hrs); *KG*76 (2235-0355hrs); *KG*77 (0155-0450hrs); III/*KG*26 (2304-2352hrs); I/*KG*54 (0143-0300hrs); II/*KG*54 (0214-0230hrs); *KG*r 806 (0100-0145hrs); *Stab*/*KG*55 (0240-0255hrs); I/*KG*55 (0223-0304hrs); II/*KG*55 (0210-0240hrs); III/*KG*55 (0200-0318hrs)
	Portsmouth (Airspeed)	I/*KG*27, III/*KG*27, *KG*r 100, II/*KG*1, III/*KG*1, I/*KG*54, II/*KG*54, I/*KG*55, III/*KG*55
	Portland	II/*KG*54
	Southampton	II/*KG*54
	Norwich	I/*KG*76
9-10	**Birmingham**	I/*KG*27 (0140-0228hrs); II/*KG*27 (0155-0230hrs); III/*KG*27 (0131-0210hrs); *KG*r 100 (2254-2350hrs); I/*KG*54 (0107-0150hrs); II/*KG*54 (0103-0200hrs); III/*KG*54/*KG*r 806 (0045-0112hrs); I/*KG*55 (0132-0207hrs); II/*KG*55 (0055-0200hrs); III/*KG*55 (0130-0205hrs); *Stab*/*KG*55 (0110-0135hrs); II/*KG*1 (0140-0305hrs); III/*KG*1 (0115-0150hrs); *KG*76 (2245-0240hrs); *KG*77 (2331-0240hrs); III/*KG*26 (2315-0043hrs)
	Tyneside	2324hrs 3/122
	Southampton	II/*KG*27, II/*KG*54, I/*KG*54, II/*KG*5, *KG*r 806, I/*KG*27, III/*KG*27, *KG*r 100, II/*KG*55, III/*KG*55, III/*KG*1
	Great Yarmouth	II/*KG*1, *KG*76, *KG*77, III/*KG*26
	Portsmouth	I/*KG*54, I/*KG*55, II/*KG*55
	Brighton	II/*KG*55
	Bristol	I/*KG*55
	Avonmouth	*KG*r 100
	Plymouth	*KG*r 100
10-11	**Birmingham/Coventry**	(0001-0230hrs); I/*KG*27 (0105-0220hrs); II/*KG*27 (0120-0240hrs); III/*KG*27 (0125-0250hrs); *KG*r 100 (2319-0016hrs); I/*KG*54 (0249-0350hrs); II/*KG*54 (0215-0320hrs); III/*KG*54 (0228-0310hrs); I/*KG*55 (0243-0355hrs); II/*KG*55 (0150-0250hrs); III/*KG*55 (0230-0400hrs); *Stab*/*KG*55 (0315hrs); II/*KG*1 (2340-0245hrs); III/*KG*1 (2300-0126); *KG*76 (2240-0340hrs); *KG*77 (2320-0350hrs); III/*KG*26 (2323-0105hrs); I/*KG*28
	Portsmouth	I/*KG*27, III/*KG*27, I/*KG*54, III/*KG*54, I/*KG*55, II/*KG*55, III/*KG*55, II/*KG*1, III/*KG*1, III/*KG*26
	Great Yarmouth	III/*KG*1, *KG*76, *KG*77
	Eastbourne	III/*KG*27
	Bournemouth	*KG*r 100
	Weymouth	*KG*r 100
	Poole	*KG*r 100
	Southampton	I/*KG*54, II/*KG*55
	Portsmouth	*Stab*/*KG*55
	Airfield east of Birmingham	*KG*76
	London	
	Newcastle	I/*KG*53
	Nottingham	

Date	Target	Details
April 1941		
11-12	**Bristol**	(2210-2300hrs); II/*KG*1 (0245-0330hrs); III/*KG*1 (0220-0240hrs); III/*KG*26 (2314-2350hrs); I/*KG*27 (0215-0335hrs); II/*KG*27 (0245-0330hrs); III/*KG*27 (0225-0315hrs); *KG*r 100 (2310-0131hrs); I/*KG*54 (0130-0241hrs); II/*KG*54 (0120-0230hrs); III/*KG*54 (0106-0210hrs); I/*KG*55 (0242-0400hrs); II/*KG*55 (0240-0325hrs); III/*KG*55 (0221-0245hrs); *Stab*/*KG* 55 (0210hrs)
	Portsmouth	III/*KG*26, I/*KG*28
	Plymouth	*KG*r 100, *KG*r 806
	NW of Bournemouth	I/*KG*27
	Exmouth	*KG*r 100
	Portland	I/*KG*54
	Weymouth	I/*KG*54
	Cardiff	I/*KG*54
	Yeovil	II/*KG*54
12-13	Bristol	
	Cardiff	
	Southampton	
14-15	Barrow	*Stab*/*KG*55, I/*KG*28
	Pembroke	III/*KG*27
	Airfields	9/*KG*55
15-16	**Belfast**	I/*KG*27 (0200-0245hrs); II/*KG*27 (0155-0258hrs); III/*KG*27 (0305-0326hrs); I/*KG*54 (0240-0245hrs); III/*KG*54 (2335-0300hrs); *Stab*/*KG*55 (0135hrs); I/*KG*55 (0127-0217hrs); II/*KG*55 (0137-0220hrs); III/*KG*55 (0115-0325hrs); II/*KG*1 (0313-0350hrs); III/*KG*1 (0245-0445hrs); I & III/*KG*76 (0105-0116hrs); II/*KG*76 (0145-0245hrs); I/*KG*77 (0236-0330hrs); II & III/*KG*77 (0130-0325hrs); I/*KG* 28; I/*KG*53; I/*KG*30; II/*KG*30; I/*KG*53
	Plymouth	II/*KG*54, I/*KG*27, *KG*r 100
	Airfields (Elmdon, Kidlington and High Post)	I/*KG*76
	Portland	I/*KG*27, *KG*r 100, I/*KG*54, III/*KG*54/*KG*r 806, II/*KG* 55, II/*KG*1, I/*KG*76, II & III/*KG*77, III/*KG*1
	Liverpool	III/*KG*54/*KG*r 806, *KG*r 100, I/*KG*27, II/*KG*27, III/*KG*27, *KG*r 100, I/*KG*54, II/*KG*54, *Stab*/*KG*55, I/*KG*55, II/*KG*55, III/*KG*5, II/*KG*1, III/*KG*1, I/*KG* 77, II & III/*KG*77
	Braunton (Chivenor)	III/*KG*27
	Warrington	III/*KG*54, *KG*r 806
	Hucclecote	III/*KG*27
	Portsmouth	*KG*r 100, II/*KG*54, I/*KG*5, III/*KG*1
	Bristol	III/*KG*54/*KG*r 806, III/*KG*26, III/*KG*5, II & III/*KG*77
	Avonmouth	*KG*r 100
	Coventry	*KG*r 100
	Southampton	III/*KG*55
	Hull	III/*KG*1, I & III/*KG*76, I/*KG*77, II/*KG*30
	Manchester	I & III/*KG*76
	Great Yarmouth	III/*KG*76
	Weymouth	II/*KG*76
	Newcastle	3/122

Date	Target	Details
April 1941		
16-17	**London**	I/*KG*27 (2205-2400hrs); II/*KG*27 (2215-0003hrs); III/*KG*27 (2235-2318hrs); *KG*r 100 (2250-2333hrs); I/*KG*54 (2223-0020hrs); II/*KG*54 (2310-2347hrs); III/*KG*54 (2200-2318hrs); *Stab*/*KG*55 (2255-0423hrs); I/*KG*55 (2225-2335hrs); II/*KG*55 (2150-2315hrs); III/*KG*55 (2225-2327hrs); II/*KG*1 (2245-0025hrs); III/*KG*1 (2220-0010hrs); I/*KG*76 (2240-0012hrs); II/*KG*76 (2225-2338hrs); III/*KG*76 (2230-0130hrs); I/*KG*77 (2310-2400hrs); II/*KG*77 (2315-2400hrs); III/*KG*77 (2321-0001hrs); III/*KG*26 (2230-2357hrs); 3/122
	London	I/*KG*27 (0253-0331hrs); II/*KG*27 (0241-0445hrs); *KG*r 100 (0330-0446hrs); I/*KG*54 (0145-0320hrs); II/*KG*54 (0400-0430hrs); III/*KG*54 (0102-0210hrs); I/*KG*55 (0330-0445hrs); II/*KG*55 (0215-0345hrs); III/*KG*55 (0140-0440hrs); II/*KG*1 (0220-0510hrs); III/*KG*1 (0120-0340hrs and 0415-0430hrs); I/*KG*76 (0245-0458hrs); II/*KG*76 (0200-0351hrs); III/*KG*76 (0430-0500hrs); I/*KG*77 (0413-0518hrs); II/*KG*77 (0250-0440hrs); III/*KG*77 (0330-0445hrs); III/*KG*26 (0225-0330hrs); I/*KG*28
	Exeter	III/*KG*27
	Portland	III/*KG*27
	Brighton	I/*KG*55, III/*KG*55, II/*KG*76
17-18	**Portsmouth**	II/*KG*1 (0400-0510hrs); III/*KG*1 (0350-0423hrs); II/*KG*77 (0400-0515hrs); III/*KG*77 (0410-0418hrs); III/*KG*26 (0201-0400hrs); II/*KG*27 (0325-0435hrs); I/*KG*54 (0257-0324hrs); II/*KG*54 (0310-0347hrs); *KG*r 806 (0309-0355hrs); I/*KG*53; II/*KG*53; *KG*4; *KG*3; II/*KG*30
	Portland	II/*KG*54
19-20	**London**	I/*KG*27 (2257-0027hrs); II/*KG*27 (2243-2340hrs); III/*KG*27 (2245-2323hrs); *KG*r 100 (2309-2341hrs); II/*KG*1 (2225-2340hrs); III/*KG*1 (2330-2340hrs); I/*KG*76 (2250-2325hrs); II/*KG*76 (2250-2355hrs); III/*KG*76 (2230-2310hrs); I/*KG*77 (2320-2259hrs); II/*KG*77 (2255-2335hrs); III/*KG*77 (2318-0020hrs); III/*KG*26 (2215-2400hrs); III/*KG*40 (2250-2325hrs); I/*KG*54 (2240-2325hrs); II/*KG*54 (2238-2318hrs); III/*KG*54/*KG*r 806 (2240-2315hrs); *Stab*/*KG*55 (2314-0400hrs); I/*KG*55 (2300-2346hrs); II/*KG*55 (2305-2330hrs); III/*KG*55 (2310-2400hrs)
	London	II/*KG*27 (0130-0430hrs); *KG*r 100 (0215-0447hrs); II/*KG*1 (0153-0405hrs); III/*KG*1 (0102-0135hrs); II/*KG*76 (0150-0355hrs); II/*KG*77 (0115-0412hrs); III/*KG*77 (0237-0415hrs); III/*KG*26 (0250-0420hrs); I/*KG*54 (0208-0245hrs); III/*KG*54/*KG*r 806 (0057-0220hrs); *Stab*/*KG*55 (0224-0233hrs); II/*KG*55 (0202-0305hrs); III/*KG*55 (0222-0345hrs)

Date	Target	Details
April 1941		
	London	I/*KG*27 (0314-0430hrs); III/*KG*27 (0415-0455hrs); *KG*r 100 (0450hrs); III/*KG*1 (0315hrs); I/*KG*76 (0415-0515hrs); I/*KG*77 (0320-0445hrs); II/*KG*77 (0400hrs); III/*KG*40 (0310-0340hrs); II/*KG*54 (0315-0420hrs); III/*KG*54/*KG*r 806 (0305-0429hrs); *Stab*/*KG*55 (0440hrs); I/*KG*55 (0302-0445hrs); III/*KG*55 (0455-0515hrs); I & III/*KG*4
	Portsmouth	II/*KG*54, I/*KG*76
20-21	London	
	Fraserburgh	
21-22	**Plymouth**	II/*KG*1 (0045-0127hrs); III/*KG*1 (0142-0240hrs); *KG*77 (0215-0235hrs); III/*KG*26 (2339-0026hrs); *KG*27 (2245-0010hrs); III/*KG*27 (2246-2330hrs); *KG*r 100 (2239-2255hrs); *Stab*/*KG*55 (2315hrs); I/*KG*55 (2300-2345hrs); II/*KG*55 (2300-2320hrs); III/*KG*55 (2320-2350hrs)
	Portsmouth	II/*KG*1, III/*KG*1
	Salcombe	III/*KG*26
22-23	**Plymouth**	I/*KG*27 (2243-2317hrs); II/*KG*27 (2245-2340hrs); *KG*r 100 (2250-2319hrs); *Stab*/*KG*55 (2324hrs); I/*KG*55 (2310-0005hrs); II/*KG*55 (2330-2355hrs); III/*KG*55 (2300-0020hrs); II/*KG*1 (0125-0200hrs); III/*KG*1 (0105-0155hrs); I/*KG*77 (2339-0258hrs); II/*KG*77 (0110-0150hrs); III/*KG*26 (2335-0050hrs)
23-24	**Plymouth**	I/*KG*27 (0050-0151hrs); III/*KG*27 (0015-0100hrs); *KG*r 100 (2246-2330hrs); I/*KG*54 (0000-0105hrs); II/*KG*54 (0005-0105hrs); III/*KG*54/*KG*r 806 (2339-0020hrs); II/*KG*1 (2306-0002hrs); III/*KG*1 (2305-2336hrs); I/*KG*77 (2342-0013hrs); III/*KG*26 (2335-0050hrs)
	Portsmouth	II/*KG*1
	Boscombe Down and	
	Honington	III/*KG*54
	Warmwell	III/*KG*54
	Land's End	III/*KG*40
25-26	Tyneside	II/*KG*30
26-27	**Liverpool**	III/*KG*1 (0012hrs); III/*KG*1 (2345-0010hrs); *KG*76 (2330-0025hrs); *KG*77 (0005-0050hrs); III/*KG*26 (2355-0153hrs)
	Portsmouth	*KG*76
	Great Yarmouth	II/*KG*1
	Harwich	III/*KG*1
	Southend	*KG*77
	Southampton	III/*KG*26
27-28	Portsmouth	
28-29	**Plymouth**	II/*KG* (2305-2343hrs); III/*KG*1 (2343-0009hrs); III/*KG*26 (2330-0112hrs); *KG*77 (2311-0015hrs); II/*KG*27 (2310-2355hrs); III/*KG*27 (2312-2326hrs and 0238-0310hrs); *KG*r 100 (2301-2316hrs and 0040-0147hrs); *Stab*/*KG*55 (2340-2355hrs and 0035hrs); I/*KG*55 (2315-0015hrs); II/*KG*55 (2340-0017hrs); III/*KG*55 (2330-2400hrs)

Date	Target	Details
April 1941		
	Portsmouth	I/*KG* 55
	St Eval	III/*KG* 55
	St Athan	*KG*r 100, III/*KG* 27
29-30	**Plymouth**	II/*KG* 1 (2315-2348hrs); III/*KG* 1 (2353-0138hrs); *KG* 77 (2315-0010hrs); III/*KG* 26 (2320-0030hrs); I/*KG* 27 (2310-2350hrs); III/*KG* 27 (2313-2320hrs); *KG*r 100 (2254-2315hrs); I/*KG* 54 (0015-0120hrs); II/*KG* 54 (0020-0110hrs); III/*KG* 54 (2340-0115hrs); I/*KG* 4; I/*KG* 28
	Andover	I/*KG* 54
	Norwich	
	Cardiff	3/122
May 1941		
1	Portland	*Stab* II/*KG* 54 (*Oblt* Erich Heinrichs)
1-2	**Liverpool**	*KG*r 100 (0017-0034hrs); I/*KG* 27 (0015-0050hrs); II/*KG* 27 (0025-0108hrs); I/*KG* 54 (2350-0035hrs); II/*KG* 54 (0012-0030hrs); bombs landed at Prestatyn 2326hrs
	Portsmouth	II/*KG* 27
	Bristol	I & II/*KG* 54
	Blackpool (Vickers, Squires Gate)	II/*KG* 54
	Brighton	II/*KG* 54
	Exeter	II/*KG* 54
2-3	**Merseyside**	III/*KG* 76 (2258-0024hrs); III/*KG* 77 (0040-0100hrs); I/*KG* 30; II/*KG* 30
	Portsmouth	II/*KG* 76
	Norwich	III/*KG* 76
	Manchester	
3-4	**Merseyside**	I/*KG* 27 (0020-0115hrs); II/*KG* 27 (0034-0105hrs); III/*KG* 27 (0020-0148hrs); *KG*r 100 (0031-0110hrs); I/*KG* 54 (2350-0045hrs); II/*KG* 54 (0010-0132hrs); III/*KG* 54 (0012-0040hrs); *Stab*/*KG* 55 (0030-0035hrs); I/*KG* 55 (0027-0108hrs); II/*KG* 55 (0030-0150hrs); III/*KG* 55 (0010-0040hrs); II/*KG* 1 (0102-0235hrs); III/*KG* 1 (0037-0058hrs); II/*KG* 77 (0017-0210hrs); I & III/*KG* 77 (0055-0130hrs); III/*KG* 26 (0028-0205hrs); *KG* 76 (2355-0113hrs); I/*KG* 53; I/*KG* 4; 3/122; II/*KG* 30; bombs dropped at Nerquis 2310hrs and Brynford 0150hrs
	Portsmouth	II/*KG* 1, III/*KG* 1, III/*KG* 26, *KG* 76, I/*KG* 27, II/*KG* 27, I/*KG* 54, II/*KG* 54, III/*KG* 54, I/*KG* 55, III/*KG* 55
	Great Yarmouth	II/*KG* 1, II/*KG* 1, *KG* 77
	Hull	II/*KG* 1
	Bristol	I/*KG* 54, II/*KG* 55
	Avonmouth	I/*KG* 54
	Plymouth	II/*KG* 54
	Reading area (*Mount Farm*)	II/*KG* 54
	Weymouth	II/*KG* 55
	Barrow	

Date	Target	Details
May 1941		
4-5	**Belfast**	I/*KG* 27 (0125-0200hrs); II/*KG* 27 (0215-0255hrs); III/*KG* 27 (0113-0308hrs); *KG*r 100 (0113-0155hrs); I/*KG* 54 (0120-0153hrs); II/*KG* 54 (0123-0200hrs); III/*KG* 54 (0117-0205hrs); I/*KG* 55 (2122-2150hrs); II/*KG* 55 (0053-0220hrs); III/*KG* 55 (0105-0145hrs); *Stab*/*KG* 55 (0115-0123hrs); II/*KG* 1 (0120-0245hrs); III/*KG* 1 (0105-0215hrs); *KG* 76 (0100-0210hrs); *KG* 77 (0104-0217hrs); III/*KG* 26 (0148-0207hrs); *KuFlGr* 106
	Liverpool	II/*KG* 27, I/*KG* 54, II/*KG* 54, I/*KG* 55, II/*KG* 55, III/*KG* 55, II/*KG* 1, III/*KG* 1, *KG* 76, *KG* 77, I/*KG* 27, III/*KG* 54
	Portland	II/*KG* 27, I/*KG* 54
	Swansea	III/*KG* 27, III/*KG* 26, II/*KG* 76
	Poole	II/*KG* 27
	Plymouth	II/*KG* 54, I/*KG* 27, *KG*r 100, III/*KG* 26
	Exeter	II/*KG* 54, *Stab*/*KG* 55
	Cardiff	II/*KG* 55, III/*KG* 26
	Weymouth	II/*KG* 55
	Newhaven	III/*KG* 1
	Barrow	*KG* 77, I/*KG* 28, 3/122
	St Merryn	III/*KG* 27
	Woodley	III/*KG* 1
	Great Yarmouth	II/*KG* 1
	Greenock	I/*KG* 55
	Portsmouth	I/*KG* 55, III/*KG* 1
	Witney (Stanton Harcourt)	III/*KG* 55
	Shoreham	III/*KG* 1
5-6	**Liverpool**	I/*KG* 27 (0025hrs); I/*KG* 54 (0122-0145hrs); III/*KG* 55 (0035-0135hrs); *Stab*/*KG* 55 (0145hrs)
	Plymouth	I/*KG* 27, III/*KG* 27, *KG*r 100, I/*KG* 54, III/*KG* 54, III/*KG* 27
	Hull	*KG* 76
	Newcastle	*KG* 76
	Glasgow-Hillington	II/*KG* 55, I/*KG* 4, II/*KG* 53, I/*KG* 28, 3/122
	Braunton	III/*KG* 27
	Exeter	*Stab*/*KG* 55
	Bristol	I/*KG* 27, *Stab*/*KG* 55
	Dumbarton	I/*KG* 55, II/*KG* 55, II/*KG* 54 (?)
	Glasgow	I/*KG* 55
	Pershore	III/*KG* 55, I/*KG* 4
6-7	**Clydeside**	III/*KG* 27, I/*KG* 53, *KG* 4, *KuFlGr* 106, II/*KG* 30, I/*KG* 28
	Liverpool	I/*KG* 27, III/*KG* 54, III/*KG* 55, *Stab*/*KG* 55
	Newcastle	*KG* 1, *KG* 76
	Plymouth	*KG*r 100, III/*KG* 27, I/*KG* 54, III/*KG* 54, III/*KG* 55, I/*KG* 27
	Weymouth	II/*KG* 27, III/*KG* 55

Date	Target	Details

May 1941

7-8 **Liverpool** — I/*KG*27 (0053-0155hrs); II/*KG*27 (0105-0145hrs); III/*KG*27 (0030-0140hrs); *KG*r 100 (0054-0132hrs); *KG*76 (0030-0150hrs); I/*KG*77 (0105-0115hrs); II & III/*KG*77 (0025-0157hrs); I/*KG*54 (0120-0230hrs); II/*KG*54 (0223-0340hrs); III/*KG*54 (0047-0135hrs); I/*KG*55 (0125-0220hrs); II/*KG*55 (0147-0215hrs); III/*KG*55 (0035-0130hrs); *Stab*/*KG*55 (0100-0210hrs); *KG*53; I/*KG*3; I/*KG*4

Plymouth — II/*KG*27, III/*KG*54, III/*KG*55, *KG*r 100, I/*KG*54

Bristol — II/*KG*27, III/*KG*27, *KG*r 100, I/*KG*55, II/*KG*55, III/*KG*55

Hull — *KG*76, II & III/*KG*77; *KG*53, 3/122

Airfield W of Dorchester — I/*KG*54

Exmouth — II/*KG*54

Falmouth — III/*KG*556

Great Yarmouth — *KG*76

Airfield near Lincoln (Coningsby) — *KG*76

Ipswich — I/*KG*77

Manchester —

8-9 **Nottingham** — *KG*1 (0042-0140hrs); *KG*76 (0040-0205hrs); *KG*77 (0115-0143hrs); *KG*1 & *KG*77 (0100-0238hrs); III/*KG*26 (0047-0112hrs); II/*KG*27 (0030-0115hrs)

Derby — I/*KG*27, II/*KG*27, III/*KG*27, *KG*r 100

Sheffield — I/*KG*54, III/*KG*54, II/*KG*55, III/*KG*55, *Stab*/*KG*55, II/*KG*53

Hull — II/*KG*53, *KG*76, *KG*77, III/*KG*27, *KG*r 100, II/*KG*54, III/*KG*54, I/*KG*55, II/*KG*55, III/*KG*55, *Stab*/*KG*55, 3/122

Plymouth — I/*KG*27, I/*KG*54, III/*KG*54, III/*KG*55, II/*KG*27, II/*KG*54

Yeovil (Westlands) — III/*KG*55

Harwich — III/*KG*27

Bournemouth — *KG*r 100

Great Yarmouth — *KG*1, II/*KG*55, *KG*77

Lowestoft — *KG*77

Cambridge (Oakington) — III/*KG*26

Bristol — *KG*r 100

Duxford — *KG*77

Airfield near Derby — *KG*r 100

Hurn — *KG*r 100

9-10 St Eval — III/*KG*27, *KG*r 100

Warmwell — II/*KG*54

Exeter — III/*KG*55

Upper Heyford — II/*KG*1

Birmingham — III/*KG*55

Nottingham — I/*KG*76

Swansea — III/*KG*27

Plymouth — III/*KG*77, III/*KG*54

Dundee — II/*KG*55

Glasgow — II/*KG*55

Bournemouth — I/*KG*54

Christchurch airfield (Airspeed) — II/*KG*54

Holyhead — III/*KG*54

Dartmouth — III/*KG*55

Date	Target	Details
May 1941		
	Coventry	I/*KG* 77
	Grimsby	I/*KG* 76
	Portsmouth	II/*KG* 1
	Barrow	
	Corby	
10-11	**London (1)**	*KG* 1 (0030-0215hrs); *KG* 76 (0100-0300hrs); II & III/*KG* 77 (0043-0140hrs and 0005-0030hrs); I/*KG* 77 (0005-0110hrs); III/*KG* 26 (0037-0120hrs); I/*KG* 27 (0037-0120hrs); II/*KG* 27 (0047-0150hrs); III/*KG* 27 (0105-0126hrs); *KG*r 100 (2354-0006hrs); I/*KG* 54 (2315-0015hrs); II/*KG* 54 (2343-0012hrs); III/*KG* 54 (0025-0105hrs); I/*KG* 55 (0035-0122hrs); II/*KG* 55 (0035-0105hrs); III/*KG* 55 (0015-0200hrs); *Stab*/*KG* 55 (0040-0320hrs); I/*KG* 53; I/*KG* 28
	Southend	*KG* 77
	Eastbourne	III/*KG* 26, I/*KG* 54
	London (2)	III/*KG* 1 (0250-0320hrs); II/*KG* 77 (0300-0340hrs); I/*KG* 54 (0144-0404hrs); II/*KG* 54 (0501-0524hrs); III/*KG* 54 (0225-0330hrs); III/*KG* 55 (0250-0350hrs); *Stab*/*KG* 55 (0325hrs); 3/122
	Shoreham	II/*KG* 54
	Birmingham	9/*KG* 55
11-12	Sutton Bridge	II/*KG* 1
	Bicester	III/*KG* 55
	Watton	II/*KG* 1
	St Athan	I/*KG* 27, II/*KG* 27
	St Eval	III/*KG* 27
	Exeter	*KG*r 100
	Pembroke Dock	I/*KG* 27, I/*KG* 28
	Cardiff	I/*KG* 27
	Braunton (Chivenor)	I/*KG* 27
	Dartmouth	I/*KG* 27
	Plymouth	II/*KG* 27
	Hull	
	Christchurch	
	Dover	I/*KG* 54
	Middlesbrough	
12-13	Falmouth	II/*KG* 27, *KG*r 806
	Plymouth	II/*KG* 27, *KG*r 806
	Pembroke Dock	II/*KG* 27
	Shoreham	III/*KG* 1
	Great Yarmouth	II/*KG* 77
	Hull	II/*KG* 76
	Exmouth	II/*KG* 55
	Exmouth	*KG*r 806
13-14	Plymouth	I/*KG* 27, III/*KG* 54
	Falmouth	I/*KG* 27
	Cardiff	I/*KG* 27
	Weymouth	III/*KG* 54
14-15	Weymouth	I/*KG* 54
	Plymouth	I/*KG* 54
	Portland	I/*KG* 54
	Falmouth	II/*KG* 55
	Teignmouth	II/*KG* 55

Date	Target	Details
May 1941		
15-16	Yeovil	*KG*r 100
	Southampton	II/*KG* 27
	St Eval (Portreath)	1/406
	Plymouth	*KG*r 100
	Newcastle	
	Middlesbrough	
	Scarborough	
	Great Yarmouth	
	Barrow in Furness	
16-17	**Birmingham (Nuneaton)**	*KG*r 100 (0047-0052hrs); II/*KG* 55 (0015-0145hrs); III/*KG* 55 (0045-0135hrs); *Stab*/*KG* 55 (0050-0150hrs); *KG* 1 (0108-0151hrs); *KG* 76 (0107-0320hrs); *KG* 26 (0050-0155hrs); 3/122
	St Eval	I/*KG* 27
	Southampton	*KG*r 100, II/*KG* 55, *KG* 76
	Plymouth	II/*KG* 55
	Brighton	II/*KG* 55
	Great Yarmouth	*KG* 1
17-18	Southend	I/*KG* 77
18-19	Falmouth	II/*KG* 55
	Torquay	II/*KG* 55
19-20	Portreath	II/*KG* 27
	Chelmsford	III/*KG* 26
	Plymouth	II/*KG* 27
	Torquay	II/*KG* 54
	Exmouth	II/*KG* 54
	Portsmouth	II/*KG* 54
	Hastings	III/*KG* 1
	Ipswich	III/*KG* 1
	Great Yarmouth	II/*KG* 27
20-21	Portreath	*KG*r 100
	St Eval	III/*KG* 55
	Chelmsford	III/*KG* 26
	Mullion	II/*KG* 54
	Airfield north of Salisbury	III/*KG* 55
	Plymouth	II/*KG* 54
	Falmouth	II/*KG* 54
	Pembroke Dock	II/*KG* 54
	Swansea	II/*KG* 54
	Exeter	II/*KG* 54
	Lowestoft	III/*KG* 1
	Great Yarmouth	II/*KG* 77
22-23	Yeovil	II/*KG* 27
23-24	Theale	III/*KG* 76
	Boscombe Down	II/*KG* 54
	Harwell	II/*KG* 54
	Bicester	II/*KG* 54
	Andover	II/*KG* 54
	Falmouth	I/*KG* 28
24-25	Chatham	I/*KG* 3
	Yeovil	II/*KG* 54
	Newark	III/*KG* 4
	Great Yarmouth	
	Lowestoft	

Date	Target	Details
May 1941		
26-27	Cowes	
	(*J. Samuel & White Co*)	III/*KG*26, III/*KG*1
	Chelmsford	III/*KG*26
	Harwich	III/*KG*1
	Dover	III/*KG*1
	Hunstanton	III/*KG*1
27-28	**Plymouth**	I/*KG*27 (0032-0145hrs); III/*KG*27 (0105-0225hrs)
	Falmouth	III/*KG*27, III/*KG*55
	Exmouth	III/*KG*55
	Weymouth	III/*KG*55
	Torquay	III/*KG*55
	Penzance	II/*KG*55
	Treen	II/*KG*55
	Eastbourne	III/*KG*1
	Chatham	I/210
	Southend	I/210
	Chelmsford	III/*KG*26
	Cowes	III/*KG*26
	Southampton	III/*KG*76 (possibly previous night)
28-29	Merseyside	III/*KG*27
	Folkestone	
	Worth	
	Petham	
	Herne Bay	
	Port William	
29-30	Portland	I/*KG*54
	Trevose Head	*KG*r 806
	Plymouth	*KG*r 806
	Torquay	*KG*r 806
	Fowey	*KG*r 806
	St Ives	*KG*r 806
30-31	Bristol	
	Merseyside	
	Newport	
	Dublin	
31-1 June		
	Merseyside	II/*KG*27, III/*KG*27, *KG*r 806?; bombs dropped at Nannerch 0130hrs, Lower Dyserth 0225hrs, Caerwys 0233hrs, Babell 0240hrs, Connah's Quay 0255hrs, Bagillt 0325hrs
June 1941		
1-2	**Manchester**	I/*KG*55 (0145-0240hrs); *KG*r 806 (0125-0205hrs); I/*KG*54 (0056-0110hrs); I/*KG*27 (0122-0220hrs); III/*KG*27 (0130-0157hrs); II/*KG*53 (0145hrs); I/*KG*28 (0145-0330hrs); III/*KG*26 (0130-0200hrs); II/*KG*1
	Bristol (diversion)	*KG*r 606 (0220-0235hrs)
	Brighton	I/*KG*54
	Plymouth	II/*KG*55
	Liverpool	II/*KG*53
	Penzance	I/*KG*28
	Falmouth	I/*KG*28

Date	Target	Details
June 1941		
4-5	**Birmingham**	I/*KG*53 (0110-0132hrs); I/*KG*27 (0150hrs); II/*KG*27 (0130-0210hrs); *KuFlGr*106 (0120-0148); 3(F)/122 (0155-0200hrs); I/*KG*30 (0114-0200hrs); I/*KG*4 (0138-0235hrs); III/*KG*4 (0210-0243hrs); I/*KG*28
	Chatham	IV/*KG*3, I/*KG*53, I/*KG*3
	Gravesend	I/*KG*3
	Great Yarmouth	*KuFlGr*106, I/*KG*30, III/*KG*4
	Portsmouth	III/*KG*26
	Bristol (Filton, Colerne and Hucclecote)	III/*KG*27
	Bedford	I/*KG*53
	Harwich	I/*KG*53
	Bury St Edmunds	3/122
	Cottesmore	III/*KG*4
6-7	Eastbourne	I/*KG*76
	Southampton	III/*KG*26
	Salisbury	III/*KG*26
7-8	Loch Ewe	II/*KG*30
10-11	Pembroke Dock	*KGr*100
11-12	**Birmingham**	III/*KG*4 (0135-0312hrs); III/*KG*26, I/*KG*30 (0200-0230hrs); I/*KG*28
	Great Yarmouth	I & III/*KG*4
	Kings Lynn	III/*KG*4
	Grimsby	III/*KG*4
	Sutton Bridge	III/*KG*4
	Harwich	I/*KG*4
	Chatham	I/*KG*4
	Birmingham area	I/*KG*4
13-14	**London (Chatham)**	*KGr*100, I/*KG*28, I/*KG*4
14-15	**Filton**	*KGr*100 (0058-0141hrs)
	Great Yarmouth	I/*KG*30
	Margate	I/*KG*30
16-17	Gloucester (Hucclecote)	*KGr*100
17-18	Humber	I/*KG*30
21-22	**Southampton**	*KGr*100 (0141-0153hrs); III/*KG*26 (0135-0210hrs); I/*KG*4 (0241-0331hrs); I/*KG*28 (0200-0225hrs); III/*KG*4 (0311-0426hrs); I/*KG*30 (0200-0232hrs)
	Chatham	I/*KG*30

Appendix 4
Luftflotte 3 Detailed Report No 1
15 November 1940: Major Attack on Coventry

Flieger Korps I

KG 26   28 He 111 between 0000-0342hrs with 3 x SC1800, 8 x SC1000, 7 x SC500, 65 x SC250, 2 x Flam 250, 196 xD50, 1,72 x1E1. New intense fire and many explosions.

KG 76   7 Ju 88 and 13 Do 17 between 0235-0320hrs with 5 x SC500, 5 x Flam 500, 2 x Flam 250, 296 x SD50, 1,44 x B1E1. Intense explosions, burning halls and factories.

KG 77   25 Ju 88 between 0345-0610 with 81 x SC250, 186 x SD50, 1,512 x B1E1. Fires.

KG 1   17 He 111 and 7 Ju 88 between 0117-0335hrs with 1 x SC1000, 7 x SC500, 49 x SC250, 24 x SD50, 2,176 x B1E1. All of Coventry a sea of flame.

Flieger Korps II

I/LG 1   12 Ju 88 between 0132-0150hrs, SW part of the city (Standard Motor Comp and Coventry Radiator & Press Work Co Ltd) with 36 x SC250, 120 x SC50. Hits on city and factories with flames.

II/LG 1   12 Ju 88 between 0203-0235hrs, west part of the city with 1 x SC500, 12 x SC250, 12 x LZZ250. Hits on factories.

III/LG 1   8 Ju 88 between 0115-0245hrs, west part of the city with 5 x SC500, 14 x SC250, 50 x SC50. Many large fires in the city and west of city seen.

I/KG 27   20 He 111 between 0004-0128hrs, SW part of the city with 1 x SC500, 20 x SC250, 375 x SC50. Bombed in target area. At 0008hrs a large explosion with a high tongue of flame and many other explosions and fires.

II/KG 27   14 He 111 between 0015-0205hrs, Alvis Lt, aero engines, with 14 x SC250, 224 x SC50. Bombs in the north part of city. Explosion and four large fires observed.

III/KG 27   13 He 111 between 0007-0125hrs, with 12 x SC250, 200 x SC50. Fire starting at the beginning of the attack. Fires and explosions observed.

KGr 100   13 He 111 between 2020-2105hrs, east part of the city centre with 48 x SC 50, 5112 B1E1, 5112 B1E1Z. Mass of bombs in target centre. Eight large and numerous small fires observed.

KGr 606   5 Do 17 against Cornercraft Ltd and 4 Do 17 against Hill Street gas holder between 2350-0018hrs with 90 x SC50 and 540 B1E1. Because a lot of smoke had developed the effect could not be observed in detail. In all probability it can be assumed that the attacked targets had been destroyed with a lasting effect.

Flieger Korps V

I/*KG* 51   16 Ju 88 between 0210 and 0300hrs with 15 x SC500, 3 x LZZ500, 17 x SC250, 14 x Flam 250, 10 x SC50, 360 x B1E1. NW part of city (The British Piston Ring Co foundry). Large fires observed.

II/*KG* 51   10 Ju 88 between 0242-0335hrs with 3 x SC1000, 10 x SC500, 4 x SC250, 1368 E1B1. NW part of city a sea of flame.

III/*KG* 51   10 Ju 88 between 0314-0400hrs with 3 x SC1000, 4 x SC500, 6 x SC250, 5 x LZZ 250, 3 x Flam, 2 x Flam 250, 10 x SC50 with Jericho, 360 x B1E1.

I/*KG* 54   11 Ju 88 between 0356-0500hrs with 2 x SC500, 22 x SC250, 90 x SC50 (50 with Jericho). Large new fire.

II/*KG* 54   7 Ju 88 between 0452-0545 with 8 x SC500, 8 x LZZ500, 8 x SC250, 8 x Flam 250. Bombed target, strong fires in city.

KGr 806   12 Ju 88 between 0452-0545 with 8 x SC500, 8 x LZZ500, 8 x SC250, 8 x Flam 250. Bombed target, city centre a sea of flame.

Stab/*KG* 55   2 He 111 between 2320-2330 with 40 x SC50, 432 x B1E1. Hit NW part of city. Target covered with smoke.

I/*KG* 55   13 He 111 between 0000-0100hrs with 11 x SC1000, 2 x SC500, 156 x SD50, 1872 x B1E1. Strong explosions and many large fires observed. A gas holder flew into the air.

II/*KG* 55   16 He 111 between 2120-2155hrs with 5 x SC1800, 11 x SC1400, 5 x SC500, 32 x SC50, 32 x SD50, 2,412 x B1E1. Attack on Maintenance Unit C. 15 large and 30 small fires.

III/*KG* 55   9 He 111 between 0105-0135hrs with 144 x SD50, 3,888 x B1E1. Centre of gravity of the attack on Daimler Co. Intense fires.

Appendix 5
Luftwaffe target photographs and maps

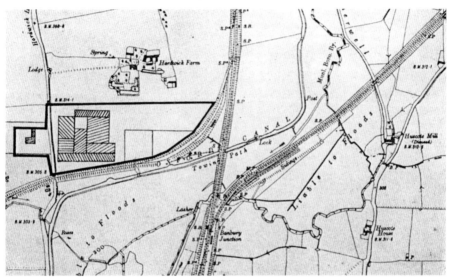

Aluminium rolling & pressworks, Banbury (Target 7119).

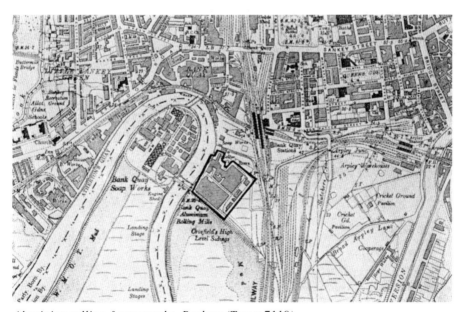

Aluminium rolling & pressworks, Banbury (Target 7119).

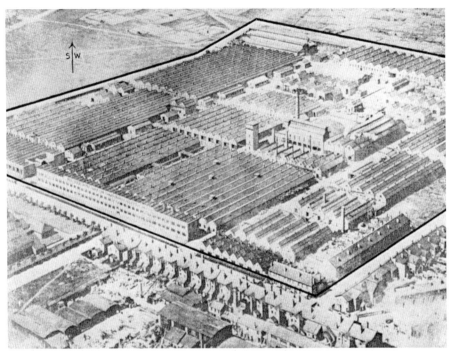

Rolls Royce Works, Derby (Target 7319).

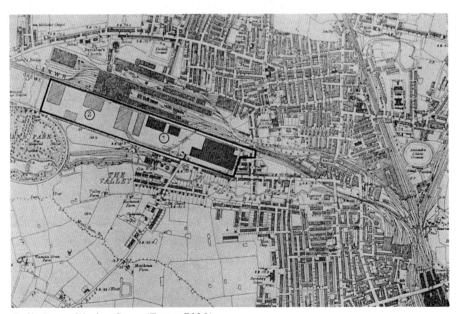

Rolls Royce Works, Crewe (Target 7320).

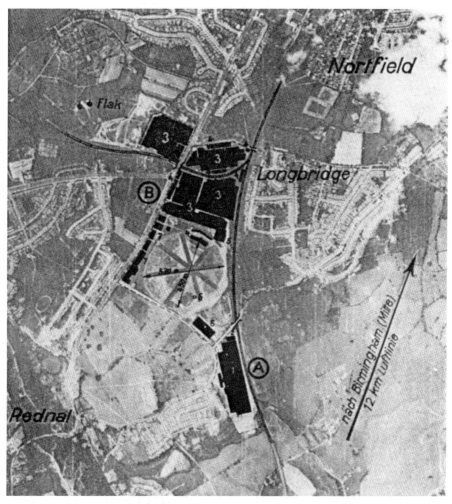

Austin Motors, Birmingham, Longbridge (Targets 7348 & 7448).

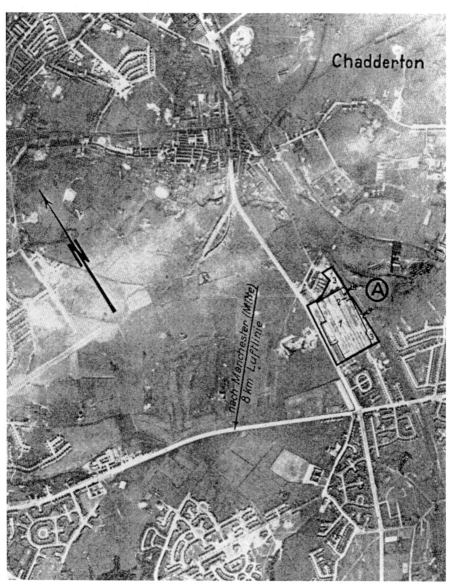

AV Roe, Manchester, Chadderton (Target 7431).

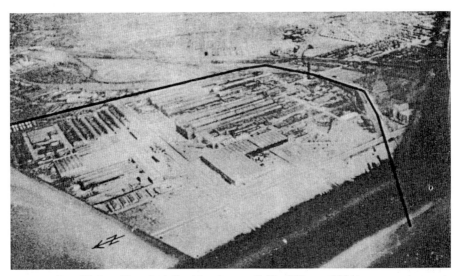

Metropolitan Vickers Electrical Co, Manchester, Salford (Target 7381).

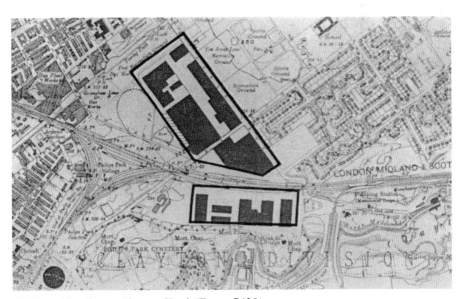

A V Roe, Manchester, Newton Heath (Target 7429).

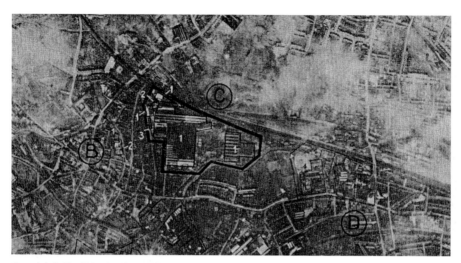

Rootes & Co, Birmingham, West Bromwich (Target 7418).

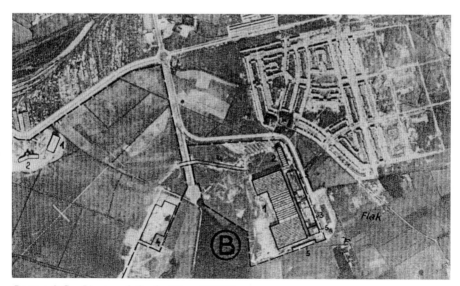

Rootes & Co, Liverpool, Speke (Target 7425).

Morris, Birmingham, Castle Bromwich (Target 7461).

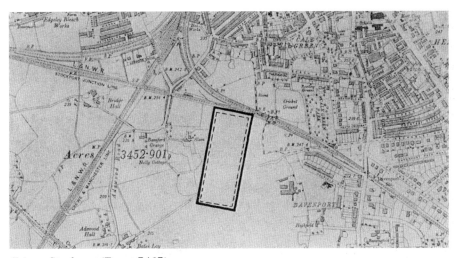

Fairey, Stockport (Target 7467).

Bibliography

Balke, Ulf (1997), *Der Luftkrieg in Europa 1939-1941* (Bechtermünz Verlag, Augsburg)

Brütting, Georg (1977), *Das Waren die Deutschen Kampfflieger Asse 1939-1945* (Motor Buch Verlag, Stuttgart)

Dierich, Wolfgang (1975), *Kampfgeschwader 55 Grief* (Motor Buch Verlag, Stuttgart)

Foreman, John (1988), *Battle of Britain – The Forgotten Months* (Air Research Publications, Walton on Thames)

Foreman, John (2003), *RAF Fighter Command Victory Claims of World War Two – Part One 1939-1940* (Red Kite, Walton on Thames)

Foreman, John (2005,) *RAF Fighter Command Victory Claims of World War Two – Part Two 1941-30 June 1943* (Red Kite, Walton on Thames)

Foreman, John (1994), *1941 Part 1-The Battle of Britain to the Blitz* (Air Research Publications, Walton on Thames)

Foreman, John (1994,) *1941 Part 2 – The Blitz to the Non-Stop Offensive* (Air Research Publications, Walton on Thames

Goss, Chris (2000), *The Luftwaffe Bombers' Battle of Britain* (Crecy Publishing, Manchester)

Norman, Bill (2002), *Broken Eagles 2 – Luftwaffe Losses over Northumberland & Durham* (Leo Cooper, Barnsley)

Price, Alfred (2000), *Blitz on Britain 1939-45* (Sutton Publishing, Stroud)

Ramsey, Winston G (1988), *The Blitz Then and Now – Volume 2 September 1940-May 1941* (Battle of Britain Prints International Ltd, London)

Scherzer, Veit (1992), *Die Träger Des Deutschen Kreuzes in Gold der Luftwaffe 1941-1945* (Scherzer's Militair Verlag, Bayreuth)

Wakefield, Kenneth (1992), *The First Pathfinders* (Crecy Books)

Wynn, Kenneth G (1989), *Men of the Battle of Britain* (Gliddon Books, Norwich)

Index

People Allied/British

People German

Places Europe

Places UK